Grocery Revolution

The New Focus on the Consumer

Grocery Revolution
The New Focus on the Consumer

Barbara E. Kahn
The Wharton School
University of Pennsylvania

Leigh McAlister
University of Texas at Austin

Joel Steckel, Series Editor
New York University

ADDISON-WESLEY

An imprint of Addison Wesley Longman, Inc.

Reading, Massachusetts • Menlo Park, California • New York • Harlow, England
Don Mills, Ontario • Sydney • Mexico City • Madrid • Amsterdam

Publishing Partner Michael Roche

Editorial Assistant Ruth Barry

Prepress Buyer Caroline Fell

Technical Support Supervisor George Brown

Designer, Cover and Interior Regina Hagen

Project Supervisor Billie L. Porter

Copyeditor/Proofreader Diane Freed

Photo Credits Cover and part and chapter opening photos from Images © 1996 PhotoDisc, Inc.

Library of Congress Catologing-in-Publication Data

Kahn, Barbara E.

  The Grocery Revolution : the new focus on the consumer / Barbara E. Kahn, Leigh McAlister.

    p.   cm.

  Includes bibliographical references.

  ISBN 0-673-99880-0 (pbk.)

  1. Grocery trade –United States.   2. Food industry and trade –United States.   3. Brand name products –United States.   4. Consumers' preferences –United States.   5. Consumers–United States–Attitudes.   I. McAlister, Leigh. II. Title.

HD9321.5.K35   1997

658.8'78–dc21   96-49060

                                                                        CIP

    4 5 6 7 8 9 10-MA-010099

To Bob, Alyssa, and Timmy; and to my mother and the memory of my father.

Barbara E. Kahn

To my husband, Jim Warmack; my mother, Mary McAlister; and the rest of my family: Anne, Bick, Kirk, Nancy, Angela, Christopher, Cameron, Philip, Susan, Mary Cathryn, Daryl, Jo, Bill Roy, Steve, Kathy, Tyler, Lynn, Jim, Alexander, Sarah, Michael, Cheryl, Gregory, and Kaitlyn.

Leigh McAlister

TO THE READER

A common complaint of many beginning marketing students is that they fail to get an appreciation of how the four P's (Product, Price, Promotion, and Place[Distribution]) fit together. The first course is a string of seemingly unrelated facts and concepts that only peripherally refer to consumers, or the environment where producers and consumers live. We hope that this volume will provide an insight to the dynamic changes that are occurring in a variety of businesses, and provide a framework for understanding decisions marketing managers confront every day. This book also examines the issues from other functional areas such as accounting, finance, operations management, and information systems that affect the marketing function.

Grocery Revolution is written in two distinctive parts: Part One presents the industry dynamics and Part Two examines the behavior of consumers. Although this structure may be appropriate for most readers, we do want to emphasize that each part can be read independently without any drawbacks. If this book is being assigned as a case for a course, the reader may want to read Part Two of the book first, to gain an appreciation of consumer behavior, and then read Part One which examines how the industry has reacted to the changes in consumer preferences. As the issues confronting the industry are examined, the reader can contemplate other alternatives to the issues than those adopted by the organizations cited in the book.

Contents

Introduction

WHAT IS THE PURPOSE OF THIS BOOK?

Revolutionary change in the underlying structure of the packaged goods industry makes it imperative that all players—manufacturers, wholesalers, retailers, and allied institutions—refocus their organizations on meeting the needs of end consumers. Those companies that don't change or that change too slowly will be driven out of business.

The purpose of this book is to make sense of the seemingly chaotic changes occurring in the packaged goods industry and to provide a starting point for anyone trying to develop a focus on the consumer by giving a "reader-friendly" overview of what academic researchers have discovered about consumer grocery shopping behavior.

In addition, many of these discoveries about grocery shopping behavior may apply as well to shopping behavior in other contexts. Focusing on the specific helps one to understand the more general. By using the packaged goods industry as an illustration, we hope to provide an appreciation of the entire marketing process for other markets and industries.

FOR WHOM IS THIS BOOK INTENDED?

- Students in Marketing Management classes who would like an overview of the packaged goods industry and more depth in consumer behavior
- Students in Consumer Behavior classes who would like more exposure to the ways that consumer behavior theories play out in the real world
- Students in Management or Strategy classes who would like an in-depth example of the interplay between marketing, sales, finance, distribution,

accounting, human resource management, and retailing
- Students considering a career in the packaged goods industry
- Professionals currently working in the packaged goods industry
- Anyone who invests in the packaged goods industry
- Anyone who shops for groceries

WHAT DOES THIS BOOK COVER?

In Part One of this book we try to bring order to the chaotic signals emanating from the packaged goods industry by first acknowledging that much of the change in this industry is universal. All industries are being rocked by the combined forces of globalization, information technology, and flattened organizational structures. Acknowledging this, we also point out that a significant amount of the turmoil that this industry is suffering has been brought on by the industry itself.

In particular, price-cut promotions grip the industry much the way that drugs grip an addict. The industry's appetite seems unbounded. In 1995, promotion took 75 percent of manufacturers' marketing budgets. One-third of the 25 percent spent on advertising was used to support promotions.[1] Further, like drugs, promotion has serious side effects. Distributors (wholesalers and retailers) take advantage of promotions to "stock up." They might hold the extra inventory for themselves for the future or they might divert that inventory to a distributor in another part of the country where the promotion was not offered. These and related inefficiencies (e.g., product damaged in transit, inconsistencies in invoices requiring manual intervention) probably add 10 percent to the cost of everyone's groceries.

Finally, like an obsession with drugs, this obsession with promotion distracts the industry from survival activities. Manufacturers and retailers have been so busy clashing with one another over promotion-related issues that they have taken their eyes off of the consumer.

Retailers like Wal-Mart kept their eye squarely on that consumer. Rather than hook into the inefficiencies associated with promotional smoke and mirrors, Wal-Mart asks that all "deals" be consolidated into a single, consistent low price that they can pass on to their shoppers. This focus on giving the consumer what s/he wants at the lowest possible price allowed these retailers to capture virtually all of the growth in grocery sales between 1986 and 1991. After little (or even negative) growth for several years, traditional format retailers joined together with manufacturers (who were in jeopardy of becoming captives of the fast growing "power retailers" like Wal-Mart) to try to refocus the industry with a series of initiatives labeled Efficient Consumer Response (ECR).

These initiatives, and related survival strategies, are being played out as we write this book. Procter & Gamble made the first move to drive out promotion inefficiencies with their Value Pricing Strategy. Distributors are using activity-based cost accounting to identify and eliminate inefficiencies in their systems. Quaker Oats, using a model called Economic Value Added, began to hold operating managers responsible for asset utilization. The most progressive retailers are organizing themselves to manage categories as strategic business units and are launching high-quality private label lines. The most progressive manufacturers are organizing their selling organizations around retail and wholesale customers rather than by geography.

All of these changes are, to some extent, designed to refocus the packaged goods distribution system on the consumer shopping in the grocery store. All of the players are on new ground. History is of little use in crafting a winning strategy for the new game. Everyone must begin with first principles. Who is the consumer? What does s/he want and need? How can I fill that need more effectively than my competitor? We believe that it should be easier to answer those questions if one understands basic principles driving consumers when shopping.

Toward that end, in Part Two of this book we review academic research on consumers' grocery shopping behavior. This research review considers how consumers choose among stores, how they decide which categories to buy, how they decide which brand within a category to buy, and how they react to retailers' merchandising, pricing, and promotion strategies.

To understand how consumers choose among stores, we present an overview of store types and look at the factors that drive choice among those store types.

To understand how consumers decide which categories to buy, we contrast planned, unplanned, and impulse purchases, while acknowledging the influence of familiarity with the store, time pressure, and children who may be along on the shopping trip. We also consider the impact of the store layout, in-store interventions by manufacturers (e.g., new products, promotions, and sampling) and in-store interventions by retailers (e.g., color, fragrances, and music).

To understand how a consumer decides which brand to buy, we begin by asking which brands the consumer is likely to consider and what influences the composition of this "consideration set." We then look at the importance of brand name, the ability to extend a brand name to other categories, and the power of co-branding. Against this backdrop, we explore the challenges facing a retailer trying to launch a high-quality private label line. Finally, we consider the ways that consumers gather information about brands and the simplified decision rules that consumers apply to this information when making a choice.

To understand how consumers react to retailers' merchandising strategy, we look at the tools retailers use to allocate shelf space among categories and brands, and then consider the impact of these techniques on consumers' choices and on consumers' perceptions of the variety offered. To understand how consumers react to retailers' pricing strategy, we note first that consumers typically don't know a product's actual price, and then review a number of contextual elements that influence price perceptions. We also consider the determinants of consumers' price sensitivity. To understand how consumers react to retailers' promotion strategy, we consider classes of brands that might be able to promote more effectively, the impact of promotion on brand loyalty, and stockpiling, ending with a review of consumer promotional tools.

We close the book with a summary of key research findings and their likely implications for players in the packaged goods industry.

HOW IS THIS BOOK STRUCTURED?

This book is made of two distinct sections. Part One—Revolution in the Grocery Industry, chapters 1 through 7—looks at the packaged goods industry as a whole: financial markets, mass media, manufacturers, wholesalers, retailers, and, of course, consumers. Part Two—Consumers' Grocery Shopping Behavior, chapters 8 through 11—narrows the focus to consumers in their shopping environment.

For those topics touched on in both parts of the book, the reference in Part One will be more pointed; in Part Two, more general. For example, consider retail store formats. In Part One we consider only traditional format supermarkets and the threat posed to them by alternative formats (clubs, mass merchandisers, discount drug and supercenters). In Part Two we overview all retail formats, categorize formats based on pricing and product selection strategies, and discuss the factors that consumers might consider in choosing among the range of retail format options.

Another difference in the treatment of a topic in each part of the book is that, in Part One, a point of view is developed and evaluative statements are made. In Part Two, we step away from evaluation to unprejudicially report a broad range of research findings. For example, in Part One, price promotions are presented as the root cause of inefficiency in the packaged goods industry. In Part Two, we report that, when promoted, a brand experiences a short-term sales spike. The promoted brand's category may also experience a sales increase. Such an increase is more likely if the promotional price cuts in this category are deep and infrequent.

Similarly, in Part One the explosion in the number of "new" products is characterized as wasteful and is credited with having blurred distinctions among brands, eroding differentiation. In Part Two we report that a manufacturer can disguise a price increase by introducing a new, smaller package size offered at the same price as the original.

One final difference in the two parts of the book is that Part One notes trends in the marketplace and projects them. Part Two, in reporting scientific research, has the potential to identify opportunities before they become apparent in the marketplace. Consider, for example, the emerging, high-quality private label brands. In Part One we note their emergence, document their success in categories once believed invulnerable (e.g., soft drinks, cigarettes, diapers), and project continued, solid growth. In Part Two we report a study that reverses one of the "truths" developed through analysis of scanner data. Historically, it has been the case that a national brand, when promoted, took more market share from a private label than that private label, when promoted, could take from a national brand. We now know that that finding was driven by the large gap in quality between national brands and the old, low-quality private label brands. As the quality of private label brands has become as high as (or even higher than) the quality of national brands, the traditional wisdom has reversed. High-quality private label brands, when promoted, take more market share from national brands than national brands, when promoted, can take from high-quality private label brands.[2]

Endnotes

1.   Tenser, James (1996), "Polls Concur: Spending is Flowing to the Trade,"
     Brand Marketing (June 3), 1, 4.
2.   Bronnenberg, Bart J. and Luc Wathieu, "Asymmetric Promotion Effects
     and Brand Positioning," *Marketing Science* (forthcoming).

Part One

Revolution in the Grocery Industry

Ravages of Change

Change is bringing layoffs, consolidations, and plant and store closings to the packaged goods industry. Retailers are experiencing record losses. Wholesalers are consolidating.

Like all other industries, the packaged goods industry is undergoing an unprecedented amount of change, and much of the change is painful. Jobs are being cut. Factories and stores are being closed. Small companies are being driven out of business or are being absorbed by bigger companies.

The American Management Association, in its seven-year study reporting the percentage of firms planning to downsize in the next twelve months, made concrete the general feeling that "no job is safe." As we see in Figure 1–1, in each of those years 14 to 26 percent of the responding firms planned to downsize. The packaged goods industry has not been exempt from this trend. In the late 1980s, Frito-Lay cut 1,800 administrative and marketing jobs.[1] In 1993, Procter & Gamble cut 13,000 jobs and announced plans to close 20 percent of their manufacturing plants within 3 years.[2] In 1994, Kmart closed 110 stores and cut 6,000 jobs.[3] Between 1989 and 1994, Borden cut 7,000 jobs in three major restructures.[4] Similarly, between 1990 and 1994, Scott Paper Company cut 8,300 jobs in three major restructures.[5] In 1995, Kimberly-Clark acquired Scott and announced plans to cut 60,000 jobs from the combined companies.[6]

The continuing need for change in the supermarket sector of the packaged goods industry is apparent from financial data. The Food Marketing Institute's Annual Financial Review of 132 supermarket companies shows that net profit and return on total assets have been falling steadily since 1990 (see Figure 1–2).[7] To be more specific, consider that in the fiscal year ending February 1993, A&P had a sales decline of $1.1 billion and a net income of −$189.5 million.[8] Or,

Figure 1–1
PERCENTAGE OF FIRMS PLANNING TO DOWNSIZE
IN THE NEXT 12 MONTHS

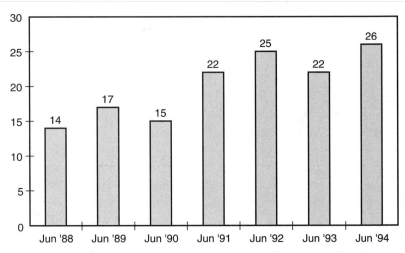

Source: 1994 American Management Association Survey on Downsizing and Assistance to
Displaced Workers

Figure 1–2
SUPERMARKET NET PROFIT AND ROA

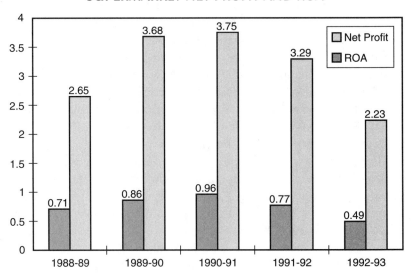

Source: Food Marketing Institute

consider the fact that, in the fall of 1993, Vons, a 345-store grocery chain in southern California, closed seven stores, laid off 250 executives, and cut or froze salaries for other executives.[9]

Change in the wholesale sector of the packaged goods industry is most obviously manifested through consolidation. In 1975 the 10 leading wholesalers covered 9 percent of industry sales. By 1992, the 10 leading wholesalers covered 14 percent of industry sales.[10] In a dramatic continuation of this trend, Oklahoma City-based Fleming acquired Oklahoma City-based Scrivner in the summer of 1994. Going into that summer, the largest three wholesalers in the United States were Minnesota-based Supervalue, Fleming, and Scrivner, in that order. The acquisition of Scrivner made Fleming the largest wholesaler in the United States and the second largest customer for many manufacturers. Industry experts expect Supervalue to respond by swallowing one of the other attractive wholesale acquisition candidates (Super Foods, Richfood, Nash-Finch, Roundy's, Spartan) and further concentrate this sector of the packaged goods industry.[11]

These wrenching changes for manufacturers, retailers, and wholesalers seem chaotic and unpredictable to many industry observers. It is our objective to help make sense of these seemingly incoherent changes and explore the implications of the structure we propose.

We begin by considering those forces driving change across all industries, and then narrow our focus to forces specific to the packaged goods industry. We next explore the industry structure that is likely to emerge as these forces play out. Finally, in Part Two, we explore the academic understanding of consumer shopping behavior from the perspective of managers who will be operating in this newly reconfigured world.

Endnotes

1. McFarlan, Warren F. (1994), "Organizational Transformation," *Proceedings of the Food Marketing Institute's Midwinter Executive Conference*, January 16–19, 1994, 55.

2. Strauss, Gary (1993), "Company Makes Big Cuts to Stay Fit," *USA Today* (July 16).

3. "Kmart to Close 110 Stores, Cutting 6,000 Jobs" (1994), *Austin American Statesman* (September 9), D1–D2.

4. Schifrin, Matthew (1994), "Last Legs?" *Forbes* (September 12), 150–4, 158 and Lesly, Elizabeth (1994), "The Carving of Elsie, Slice by Slice," *Business Week* (January 17), 29.

5. Wells, Melanie and David Henry (1995), "Kimberly-Clark Deal Seeks to Unseat P&G," *USA Today* (July 18).

6. Kimberly-Clark to Sell Some Parts of Scott" (1995), *Supermarket News* (December 25), 39.

7. "Supermarket Profits Slip" (1994), *Food Distribution Magazine*, Vol. 35, Number 1, (January), 11.

8. Garry, Michael (1994), "A&P Strikes Back: Tough Times for A&P," *Progressive Grocer* (February), 32–4.

9. "Vons Cuts Prices" (1994), *Progressive Grocer* (March), 12.

10. Shore, Andrew and Margaret Lenahan (1993), *Cosmetic and Household Products: When the Sun Comes Up Tomorrow, You Had Better Be Running*, Paine Webber (October 11).

11. Mathews, Ryan (1994), "Street Smart," *Progressive Grocer* (August), 56–7.

The Broader Revolution

A part of the change occurring in the packaged goods industry is being driven by forces common to all industries. Communication and transportation lower barriers between countries, causing global competition to grow. The spread of information technology eliminates the need for middle managers. As layers of hierarchy are removed, organizations must become more flexible and responsive.

In the opening of his article titled "Welcome to the Revolution," Thomas Stewart (1993, p. 66) says:

> Let us not use the word cheaply. Revolution, says Webster's, is "a sudden, radical, or complete change . . . a basic reorientation." To anyone in the world of business, that sounds about right. We all sense that the changes surrounding us are not mere trends but the workings of large, unruly forces: the globalization of markets; the spread of information technology and computer networks; the dismantling of hierarchy, the structure that has essentially organized work since the mid-19th century.

These forces, driving change throughout the economy, are also potent in the packaged goods industry. In this chapter we illustrate the relevance of Stewart's three forces for the packaged goods industry.

GLOBALIZATION OF MARKETS

As communication and transportation lower barriers between countries, the set of potential competitors for any given market increases. It is no longer sufficient to be the best option in a particular region. According to Jack Welch, CEO of General Electric:[1]

> You've got to be on the cutting edge of change. You can't simply maintain the status quo, because somebody's always coming from another country with another product, or consumer tastes change, or the cost structure does, or

there's a technology breakthrough. If you're not fast and adaptable, you're vulnerable. This is true for every segment of every business in every country in the world.

To see that competition in the U.S. packaged goods industry is global, one only need consider the fact that the Swiss Company Nestle (the world's biggest branded food company) owns Carnation, Stouffer's, Perrier, Hills Brothers, and Dryers Ice Cream.[2] Joining Nestle in the battle for U.S. ice cream sales is the Dutch company Unilever, who bought Breyer's Ice Cream from Kraft Foods in 1994.[3] Cadbury Schweppes, a British company, bought "third place in the lucrative U.S. soft drink business"[4] when they bought Dr. Pepper/Seven-Up in 1995.

In addition, many U.S. supermarket chains have foreign ownership. The Dutch company Ahold owns a collection of East Coast supermarket chains: Finast, Edwards, Bi-Lo, Tops, and Giant. Great Britain's Sainsbury owns New England-based Shaws. Germany's Tengelmann owns 53 percent of A&P. Belgium's Delhaize owns 35 percent of Food Lion. And Red Food, a chain of 55 supermarkets in Tennessee and Georgia, was sold in 1994 by the French company Promodes to the Dutch company Ahold.[5]

Similarly, note that Fleming became the largest wholesaler in the U.S. by buying Scrivner from Haniel, a German company.[6] Makro, a Dutch company, runs eight wholesale clubs in Thailand, seven in Taiwan, two in Malaysia, and will be opening in Korea and China in 1995.[7]

It is also the case that U.S.-based players in the packaged goods industry participate in other markets. Among S&P 500 companies, 40 percent of all profits came from foreign operations in 1987. By 1992, that proportion had grown to 45 percent.[8] Procter & Gamble now has more than 50 percent, Colgate has 65 to 75 percent, and Gillette has more than 70 percent of their sales from outside the United States.[9] IGA has stores in Singapore, Malaysia, Indonesia, China, Japan, Australia, Korea, and Papua New Guinea.[10] By 1995 Wal-Mart had stores in Argentina, Brazil, Canada, Indonesia, Mexico, and Puerto Rico, with plans to open 30 to 35 more stores in those countries in 1996.[11]

SPREAD OF INFORMATION TECHNOLOGY AND COMPUTER NETWORKS

As long ago as 1958 business observers were predicting that computers would eliminate the need for middle managers.[12] Fredrick Kovac, vice president for planning at Goodyear says:[13]

It used to be, if you wanted information, you had to go up, over, and down through the organization. Now you just tap in. Everybody can know as much about the company as the chairman of the board. That's what broke down the hierarchy.

To see how this phenomenon has played out in one packaged goods company, consider the case of Frito Lay, presented by Warren McFarlan at the Food Marketing Institute's 1994 Midwinter Executive Conference.[14]

In the 1970s, Frito Lay achieved double-digit growth by moving from being a regional player to becoming a national player. In 1982, they began a move toward micromarketing for growth. In 1986, they put a central computing facility in Dallas, Texas to track every bag of chips delivered every day to every store. By midnight each night, all data for the day before was in. From midnight to 5 a.m. specific stocking instructions were generated and distributed through a cascaded network consisting of 161 regional minicomputers and 10,000 hand-held computers. Off line, analysts in the Dallas office would study the data. Organizational structure did not change at this point, but they did reduce stales and reconfigure routes, eliminating 500 trucks.

In the late 1980s, Frito Lay added IRI infoscan scanner data and a satellite-based, wide-area network. They were able to transport data down to 21 regional offices. Local area networks in the regional offices made the data available to analysts using PCs. Ninety percent of what the market analysts had been doing in the central Dallas office was driven out to the regions. Consequently, Frito Lay took 1,800 jobs out of their administration and marketing staff.

Reflecting on this case study, McFarlan drew two important conclusions:[15]

First, this is not something that you do and then it's done. This is a story where the roots of analysis began in 1978, and it is playing out in the technologies of 1994.

Secondly, it has profoundly changed the nature of work and how it is organized inside that firm, in the end making it dramatically more cost competitive. The 1800 workers are gone—we have seen that right across the country. The best numbers we have, two and a half million jobs were taken out between 1989 and 1992 by the new technologies, jobs that will never come back again. They are gone.

But this efficiency is only the first-order effect of technology. Stewart (1993) points out interesting second-order effects: sales, marketing, and distribution have been transformed. Given the huge amount of information a company can have about its market, quick response to changing circumstances becomes more important than careful planning. In subsequent chapters we will look more closely at the changes that this drives in the roles played by sales, marketing, and distribution in the packaged goods industry.

DISMANTLING THE HIERARCHY[16]

To understand more clearly why the existing organizational structures are inappropriate in today's world, it is useful to trace those structures back to their roots. Hammer and Champy (1993), in their book *Reengineering the Corporation*, suggest that it all began in 1776 with the publication of *The Wealth of Nations* by Adam Smith. In that book Smith laid out the principle of division of labor and, with that, touched off the industrial revolution.

The development, in the 1820s, of a system of railways in the United States gave rise to the next major step in business management technology. In order to avoid head-on collisions on single-track lines that carried trains in both directions, formal operating procedures were needed. Bureaucracy was born.

In the 20th century, auto pioneers moved management technology ahead again. Ford broke down car assembly into a series of uncomplicated tasks. Sloan, at General Motors, developed smaller, decentralized divisions and the division of professional labor (marketing specialists, financial specialists, etc.) needed to manage the sprawling organizations.

Between the end of World War II and the 1960s, McNamara at Ford, Geneen at ITT, and Jones at GE made innovations that brought us to the corporations we know today. They built structures in which senior managers decide which businesses to be in, how much capital should be allocated to each business, and what return should be expected from each business. "Large staffs of corporate controllers, planners, and auditors act as executives eyes and ears ferreting out data about divisional performance, and intervening to adjust the plans and activities of operating managers."[17]

The resulting system was well suited to the period of heavy and growing demand that characterized the U.S. market following the Depression and World War II. But in today's world of flat demand and global competition, these structures only serve to increase costs and isolate top management from their customers.

*   *   *   *

The conclusions reached by Stewart (1993) in his article "Welcome to the Revolution," by McFarlan (1994) in his case study of Frito Lay, and by Hammer and Champy (1993) in their book *Reengineering the Corporation* are very similar: Organizations must become more flexible and responsive, and the process of becoming flexible and responsive will require painful change.

In what follows we look more closely at the packaged goods industry. Digging beneath the mega-forces of globalization, information technology, and hierarchy dismantling, we will find that this industry is beset by demographic and socioeconomic shifts and by the emergence of new competitors playing by new rules. We will elaborate on the ways in which packaged goods organizations must become more flexible, and specify more precisely to whom these organizations must become more responsive.

Endnotes

1. "A Master Class in Radical Change" (1993), *Fortune* (December 13), 82–90.

2. Rapoport, Carla (1994), "Nestle's Brand Building Machine," *Fortune* (September 19), 147–56, and Dworin, Diana (1994), "Cold Warriors," *Austin American Statesman* (September 4), E1.

3. Dworin, Diana (1994), "Cold Warriors," *Austin American Statesman* (September 4), E1.

4. "Cadbury to Buy out Dr Pepper/Seven-Up" (1995), *Austin American Statesman*, (January 23), A8.

5. Husson, Mark and Erika Gritman Long (1994), *Private Label: Corner-stone of the New Supermarket Brand Architecture*, JP Morgan Securities, Inc., Equity Research, New York (January 31), 9, and "Ahold Buying Red Food" (1994), *Progressive Grocer* (April), 12.

6. Mathews, Ryan (1994), "Street Smart," *Progressive Grocer* (August), 56–7.

7. Rapoport, Carla (1994), "Nestle's Brand Building Machine," *Fortune* (September 19), 147–156.

8. Shore, Andrew and Margaret Lenahan (1993), *Cosmetic and Household Products: When the Sun Comes Up Tomorrow, You Had Better Be Running*, Paine Webber (October 11), 20.

9. Radice, Carol (1996), "A View from the Street," *Progressive Grocer* (May), 24.

10. Raphel, Murray and Niel Raphel (1966), "What the 'I' in IGA Stands For," *Progressive Grocer* (June), 22.

11. Herndon, Neil (1994), "Wal-Mart Goes to Hong Kong, Looks at China," *Marketing News* (November 21), 2, and "Wal-Mart's 99-Quarter Earnings Growth Streak Ending" (1996), *Investor's Business Daily* (January 18).

12. Leavitt, Harold J. and Thomas L. Whisler (1958), "Management in the 1980's," *Harvard Business Review* (November–December), 41–48.

13. Quote taken from Thomas A. Stewart (1993), "Welcome to the Revolution," *Fortune* (December 13), 72.

14. McFarlan, Warren F. (1994), "Organizational Transformation," *Proceedings of the Food Marketing Institute's Midwinter Executive Conference, January 16–19*, 1994, 52–58.

15. McFarlan, Warren F. (1994), "Organizational Transformation," *Proceedings of the Food Marketing Institute's Midwinter Executive Conference, January 16–19*, 1994, 55.

16. This section draws heavily from Michael Hammer and James Champy (1993), *Reengineering the Corporation*, New York: HarperCollins.

17. Hammer, Michael and James Champy (1993), *Reengineering the Corporation*, New York: HarperCollins, 15.

3

Evolution of the Packaged Goods Industry

Before the price *freeze of 1974, the packaged goods distribution system in the United States was very efficient. However, after the price freeze, manufacturers took their list prices up well beyond the levels needed to restore conventional levels of profitability to protect themselves from future potential price freezes. Manufacturers then took advantage of these unusually high margins to "rent" market share with occasional deep price cuts. Distributors (wholesalers and retailers) exploited these temporary price reductions by forward buying and diverting. The extra handling caused by forward buying and diverting caused increased levels of product damage. The elaborate contracts devised to control forward buying and diverting caused frequent invoice disputes.*

According to Ronald Curhan (1982, p. 92), the U.S. packaged goods industry was very efficient up through the 1960s:

> *The name of the game was "throughput"; "in-and-out." Success was measured by how quickly a [retailer] could turn its inventory. Money was made on the selling of goods, not on buying.*
>
> *In an expanding economy, warehouse space constraints often were very real. New stores to serve and new items to stock preempted the use of storage facilities for speculative purposes. The occasional purchasing splurge was to protect oneself in anticipation of a strike or shortage; to insure cost and supply, as was the case with annual crop products such as canned corn or catsup; or, on rare occasions, to take a position on an important item such as imported Italian tomatoes in order to be able to promote them several months hence when they could be an important promotional draw. But these events were exceptions to the rule. Company treasurers scrutinized off-premises storage charges with a keen eye, and buyers knew better than to be caught in an over-bought position. The operating principle remained "in-and-out."*

Figure 3–1a
MANUFACTURERS GIVE OCCASIONAL DEEP DISCOUNTS

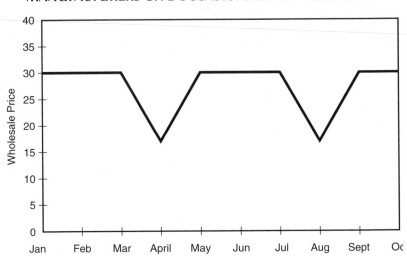

DEEP CUT PROMOTIONAL PRICES

This focus on moving products through the distribution system quickly and efficiently was lost after the price freeze of 1974. During that freeze, manufacturers' costs continued to rise, driving their profit margins ever lower. When the freeze was lifted, manufacturers resolved to never be caught in such a situation again. They protected themselves by establishing new list prices well above the level needed to restore conventional profitability. If another price freeze occurred, they could comfortably accommodate inevitable cost increases without squeezing profits.

Given the unusually high profit margin provided by the new, high list prices, manufacturers decided to "rent" market share with occasional deep price cuts. According to Curhan (1982), typical promotional price cuts before the price freeze ranged from 50¢ per case to $2 per case. By 1982, those price cuts had grown to $12 to $14 per case, and today could be $20 to $40 per case.

The repercussions of the promotional price cuts are wide ranging and severe. Figure 3–1a shows the pattern of prices a manufacturer might have offered a retailer after the price freeze. The graph suggests that the list price was $30 a case and that the manufacturer offered a promotional price of $17 per case in April and again in August.

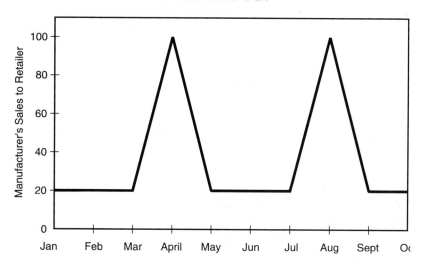

Figure 3–1b
**RETAILERS TAKE ADVANTAGE OF DISCOUNTS
TO "FORWARD BUY"**

FORWARD BUYING

How would you expect a rational retailer to respond to these pricing changes? Assuming that consumer demand for the product was constant across time, would you expect the retailer to continue to focus on "in-and-out," buying the same number of cases each month regardless of price? Absolutely not. As shown in Figure 3–1b, retailers took advantage of the deep price cuts to stock up, or "forward buy" as the practice is called in the industry. As a consequence, retailers reduced their orders during months when prices were high, using product from their forward-buy inventory to meet consumers' demand.

The resulting pattern of spiked retailer demand causes many problems. For the manufacturer, production is inefficient. Plants run overtime during periods of peak demand, and expensive capital equipment sits idle when demand is down. Similarly, transportation and warehouse space are used sub-optimally. For the retailer, warehouse space must be acquired, inventory must be financed and insured, and product freshness is compromised.

Given the inefficiencies caused by this pricing practice, and given the fact that it now seems unlikely that another price freeze will be imposed, one might think that this "high–low" promotional pricing and its attendant spiky demand would simply fade away. Unfortunately that is not the case.

THE PRISONER'S DILEMMA

Figure 3–2 depicts a set of incentives (called "The Prisoner's Dilemma" by game theorists) that can be used to demonstrate the addictive nature of high–low promotional pricing. In this model, much of the market complexity is assumed away. We have only two manufacturers and no wholesalers or retailers. Each manufacturer has only two possible strategies: to offer list price (i.e., not promote) or to offer a promotional price cut (i.e., promote). Boxes in the first column correspond to payoffs associated with Manufacturer 1 selecting the "offer list price" strategy; boxes in the second column, with Manufacturer 1 selecting the "offer promotional price cut" strategy. Similarly, boxes in the first row correspond to Manufacturer 2 selecting the "offer list price" strategy; in the second row, the "offer promotional price cut" strategy. The upper triangle in a box reports the payoff to Manufacturer 1; the lower triangle, the payoff to Manufacturer 2.

Given this, we see that if neither Manufacturer 1 nor Manufacturer 2 promotes, each makes $100,000. However, promotion is very powerful. If Manufacturer 2 promotes while Manufacturer 1 refrains, Manufacturer 2 makes $150,000 and Manufacturer 1 makes only $25,000. Unfortunately, promotion works just as well for all players. Should Manufacturer 2 refrain from promoting in the next period while Manufacturer 1 promotes, then Manufacturer 1 gets the $150,000 and Manufacturer 2 gets only $25,000. In the long run, both Manufacturers find themselves promoting. They make only $80,000 each and dream of the days that they made $100,000 each. But they can't get there. The temptation to promote is too powerful.

Worse yet, the temptation to escalate the amount of the promotional offer is also very powerful. Although this contingency is not accommodated in the simple two-strategy model of Figure 3–2, it is a very real fact of life. As pointed out earlier, the pre-price freeze promotional price cut of 50¢ a case escalated to $12 a case by 1982, and has continued to rise to $20 or more per case today.

The implications of this for a manufacturer's marketing mix are significant. Figure 3–3 shows that in the '80s, trade promotion expenditures grew dramatically while advertising expenditures flattened. If we believe that advertising provides long-term brand building while

Figure 3–2
THE PRISONER'S DILEMMA

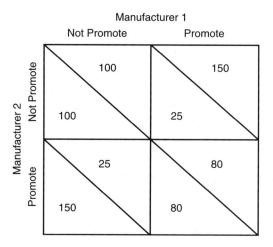

Figure 3–3
TRADE PROMOTION AND ADVERTISING SPENDING

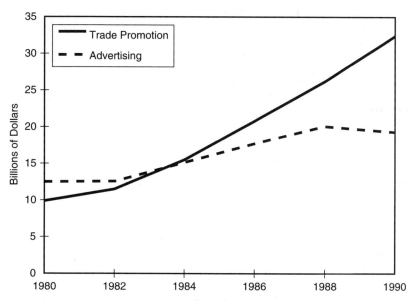

Source: Data from a presentation by Jim Bernhardt at the University of Texas at Austin on February 23, 1994, and Information Resources, Inc. (Chicago).

promotion gives only a short-term sales boost, these spending trends are disturbing. The addictive power of promotion is such that manufacturers must devote ever larger proportions of their marketing budgets to this "short-term fix" and ever smaller proportions to the long-term health of their brands.

This "addictive power" of promotion derives from more than just the horizontal competition among manufacturers that is illustrated by the Prisoner's Dilemma in Figure 3–2. Through time, the packaged goods distribution system has adapted to manufacturers' high–low promotional pricing schemes. As early as 1982, according to Curhan (1982), the system was completely entrenched.

> As one astute industry friend has noted, we now have a whole generation of newer [retail] buyers who have known no way of life other than high list prices and deep-cut deals. Collectively, the benefits realized from forward buying are now a "normal" part of gross margin. Additionally, many firms have added extensive warehouse facilities. The logistical infrastructure is in place to enable wholesalers and retailers physically to handle the inventories which result from deal-driven buying.[1]

This combination of pressure from competitors through the Prisoner's Dilemma and pressure from the distribution system are powerfully compelling to manufacturers. According to the 1994 *Fortune* article titled "Behind the Tumult at P&G":

> At one point, 17% of all [Procter & Gamble] products on average were being sold on deal—and in some categories 100%. "You've lost control," [then CEO Edwin Artzt] says. "And you don't even know what it's costing you."[2]

DIVERTING

In addition to simply stocking up when the price is low to carry them through the times when price is high, retailers and wholesalers found other ways to make "inside margin" through these occasional deep price cuts offered by manufacturers. Exploiting the fact that manufacturers tend to offer these deep price cuts in different parts of the country at different points in time, retailers, wholesalers, and others engage in a form of arbitrage, called diverting in the industry.

An agent (retailer, wholesaler, broker, salesperson, or an independent diverting operation) in one part of the country buys the product from the manufacturer at the reduced price and then, essentially, goes into competition with the manufacturer in some other part of the country that has not been offered the deep price cut. If the diverter buys the product at $17 a case in Florida and offers to sell it at $23 a case in Texas, where the manufacturer is trying to sell the product at its list price of $30 a case, it is easy to predict that the manufacturer will experience disappointing sales in Texas, while the agent in Florida will make $6 a case on all of the cases diverted to Texas, and the buyer in Texas will get the product more cheaply than if no diverting had occurred.

It has been estimated that forward buying and diverting have added $75 billion to $100 billion worth of inventory to the U.S. packaged goods distribution system. The cost of financing and storing that inventory works its way into the prices we pay when shopping for groceries.

In addition, these practices wreak havoc with a manufacturer's marketing plan. They pull more dollars into promotion spending and make that spending less effective. They increase the height of the promotional sales peak, exacerbating manufacturing and distribution inefficiencies. Finally, they compromise the manufacturers' ability to market regionally. A product whose price is sharply reduced to meet fierce, local competition in one part of the country ends up in another part of the country where competition is not so fierce.

The practitioners of forward buying and diverting, of course, feel differently about these practices. According to a 1993 Andersen Consulting study of the Wholesale Food Distribution system, these and related practices make up more than half of a wholesaler's operating revenue.[3] It is easy to see why distributors might be reluctant to give up such practices.

Manufacturers have tried to control forward buying and diverting by allocating a fixed amount of product to each customer. This solution has several problems. First, it is impossible for the manufacturer to know the percentage of the customer's historical purchase quantity that was used to service sales in that customer's outlets. Setting the allocation at the level of the most recent purchase quantity guarantees that at least the amount of forward buying and diverting that has gone on in the past will continue. Setting the allocation at a level below the most recent purchase quantity flies in the face of salespeople's' incentives to grow sales. And, with many of the large retail and wholesale customers, it is very difficult to enforce an allocation.

These customers simply ignore the attempted allocation and order the quantity that they desire. Many manufacturers feel that they have no option but to honor the customer's request.

Manufacturers have also considered legal action. Sales contracts often contain language designed to stop forward buying and diverting. However, similar to their reluctance to enforce allocations, many manufacturers are reluctant to bring legal action against their customers. After all, without the retail and wholesale customers, the manufacturer cannot make sales to consumers.

It seems that the only way to stop forward buying and diverting is for the manufacturers to stop offering deep price cuts. But as we saw in the Prisoner's Dilemma, promotion is a very difficult addiction to kick. Should one manufacturer unilaterally decide to curtail promotional price cuts, that manufacturer's competitors could make dramatic gains in the marketplace. In addition, with the distribution system so dependent on the promotional dollars, a manufacturer curtailing promotional price cuts would risk even more severe losses through distributor retaliation.

As we will see in the following chapters, it takes the emergence of a powerful new distribution competitor, a part of whose competitive advantage is that it is *not* dependent on forward buy and diverting income, to provide an opportunity for the industry to withdraw from this escalating promotional addiction.

DAMAGES[4]

Another facet of the growing acrimony in the manufacturer–distributor relationship is the growing percentage of product that is damaged in distribution and therefore returned to the manufacturer for full reimbursement. It has been estimated that damaged product accounts for $2.5 billion each year.[5] In addition, John Gensler, vice president of purchasing for Seaway Food Town, Inc. in Maumee, Ohio, and co-chairman of the Joint Industry Task Force on Unsalables (JITFU) estimates that:[6]

> *Grocery industry unsalables represent $1.4 billion in wasted time—in product we didn't need to manufacture, order, or transport, handle, sort, or stock, merchandise, return, or discard.*

Not only are these costs big, they are growing. In 1989, the cost to packaged goods manufacturers of damaged goods was .62 percent of sales. By 1994, that quantity had grown to .89 percent of sales, a 43 percent increase.

There is no clear understanding of exactly who is responsible for these growing costs. Distributors blame manufacturers: transportation accidents, package design flaws, failed new products. Manufacturers blame distributors: damage at warehouse, damage at the store, damage in-between (and there's lots of "in-between" with diverting).

It is clear that forward buying and diverting have some impact on this problem. The average supermarket product is moved, touched, or otherwise handled 33 times. In a wholesale club store, a class of trade that does not practice forward buying and diverting, the number of touches is 3 or 4.[7]

But package design flaws also contribute to damages.

> "Packaging damage often starts with ignorance of the distribution system at critical points in the design/marketing process," recalls Rich Poling, manager, sales policies for Procter & Gamble (Cincinnati): "We were experiencing an excessive amount of damage to our deodorant boxes—the cases are opened at the warehouse, and individual units shipped in totes to the stores." Inevitably, the jostling these loose items suffered inside the totes meant that many packages were dog-eared, crushed or otherwise damaged on arrival. The solution: P&G simply eliminated the boxes.
>
> At the Dial Corp. (Phoenix), where a rising level of damage had become a growing concern, brand managers initially were reluctant to assume responsibility because they had no information on which to base action. . . . Now, 17 reason codes describe exactly what kind of damage a product has incurred.[8]

DEACTIONS

Through the years, elaborate promotional pricing schemes and contracts designed to enforce those schemes have grown up. Retailers and wholesalers are bombarded with thousands of such contracts a week. In addition to the problems of forward buying, diverting, and damaged product just mentioned, these complicated, ever-changing pricing schemes have led to many billing and payment errors.

Some industry observers believe that nearly 75 percent of all invoices have some error. When you consider the fact that resolving each disputed invoice can cost the manufacturer and distributor $50 each, the magnitude of the problem becomes clear.

To illustrate, consider that, until recently, Procter & Gamble went to market as five separate businesses: a soap company, a food company, two health and beauty aid companies, and a paper company. Each product line required a separate invoice. P&G had four or more pricing formulas in each category, driving more than 55 price changes per day on approximately 80 brands. One out of every three invoices required some sort of manual intervention, yielding 27,000 interventions per month.[9]

While such detailed information is not available for other companies, it is safe to assume that their problems are as bad as P&G's, or worse. To summarize this chapter on evolution in the packaged goods industry, we turn again to the article "Behind the Tumult at P&G"[10]:

> . . . [T]his promotional tail-chasing sent costs spiraling. The company was making 55 daily price changes on some 80 brands, necessitating rework on every third order. Ordering usually peaked at the end of a quarter (gotta make those numbers), sending factories into paroxysms of overtime followed by periods of under utilization. The phenomenon is known as the bullwhip effect. P&G plants ran at 55% to 60% of rated efficiency on average, with huge variations in output.
>
> The paper trail became bumper-to-bumper, and retailers disputed more and more invoices as inaccurate billing increased in the morass.

Endnotes

1. Curhan, Ronald C. (1982), "Deals, Time for a Reshuffle?" *Progressive Grocer* (January), 92.

2. Saporito, Bill (1994), "Behind the Tumult at P&G," *Fortune* (March 7), 76.

3. The 1993 Andersen Consulting report, *Wholesale Food Distribution Today and Tomorrow*, actually says, on p. 5, that "Service fees, markups, and freight charges collected from retail customers make up less than half of a typical wholesaler's 'operating revenue.'" The other major sources of revenue listed are forward buying and diverting. Slotting fees and support service fees, other revenue sources, are suggested to be break-even.

4. Much of the material in this section was taken from Carol Fensholt (1994), "Unsalables, Does an Information Gap Do the Real Damage?" *Supermarket Business* (August), 25–33.

5. Mathews, Ryan (1994), "Is the Damage Done?" *Progressive Grocer* (June), 35.

6. Fensholt, Carol (1994), "Unsalables, Does an Information Gap Do the Real Damage?" *Supermarket Business* (August), 25.

7. Fensholt, Carol (1994), "Unsalables, Does an Information Gap Do the Real Damage?" *Supermarket Business* (August), 25–33.

8. Fensholt, Carol (1994), "Unsalables, Does an Information Gap Do the Real Damage?" *Supermarket Business* (August), 34.

9. "P&G Plans to Restructure Its Logistics and Pricing" (1994), *Supermarket News* (June 27), 1, 49.

10. Saporito, Bill (1994), "Behind the Tumult at P&G," *Fortune* (March 7), 76.

Erosion of the Infrastructure Supporting Traditional Packaged Goods Marketing[1]

In addition to the destructive trading practices described in Chapter 3, packaged goods manufacturers are also plagued with a changing consumer, a changing media environment, a changing competitive environment, and changing retail and wholesale customers. Consumers are increasingly time starved, sociologically diverse, and jaded to marketing messages. The advertising media grow more expensive even as they fragment and become less effective. Over-proliferation of "new" products has blurred product distinctions and eroded brand equity. Finally, wholesale and retail customers are consolidating and investing in technology.

Central to the brand management system is the notion that one's goal is to move consumers through a four-step progression:

1. Achieve *awareness* through advertising.
2. Stimulate product *trial* through the benefits promised by the product, advertising, and promotion.
3. Stimulate *repeat purchase* through product performance, promotion, and advertising.
4. Build *brand loyalty* through product performance and advertising.

The economic boom following World War II provided a perfect setting in which to achieve these goals. Personal income and birth rates were growing. Suburbs emerged and were filled, by day, with young mothers fascinated by their televisions, and eager to buy the multitude of new products coming on the market.

However, demographic and socioeconomic changes since that time have made it increasingly difficult to follow this traditional route to success. In this chapter, we will consider changes in the consumer, changes in the media environment, changes in the competitive environment, and changes in the retail and wholesale customers through

Figure 4–1
NUMBER OF WORKING WOMEN AND WORKING MOTHERS
(IN MILLIONS)

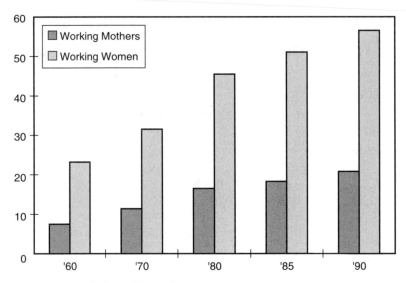

Source: U.S. Bureau of Labor Statistics, Bulletin 2307.

which the product is sold. Taken together, we will see that these changes, too, contribute to the overpowering pressure on the packaged goods industry for radical change.

THE CHANGING CONSUMER

Between 1960 and 1990 the number of working women in the United States more than doubled. In that same time period, the number of working mothers nearly tripled. (See Figure 4–1). If the schedule on the next page represents a typical mother's day, we see that there is no time for watching advertisements on television.

The population of consumers is also becoming more diverse and older, as shown in Table 4–1. Between 1980 and 1990 the population as a whole grew only 10 percent, while the population aged 60 and over grew 17 percent and the minority population grew 34 percent. Among the minorities, the Asian population grew 108 percent and the Hispanic population, 53 percent. This growing diversity makes it more difficult to reach a mass audience with a single message.

A TYPICAL WORKING MOTHER'S DAY

6:00–7:00	Wakes/personal care/dresses for work
7:00–8:00	Dresses/cooks and feeds family/gets kids ready for school
8:00–9:00	Kids to school, day care/commute to work
9:00–5:00	Work
5:00–7:00	Commute/pick up kids/shop/after-school activities
7:00–8:30	Cooks, serves and cleans up dinner (or eat out)
8:30–10:00	Available for 'life' (or additional sleep)
10:00–10:30	Straighten up home/prepare tomorrow's lunch and wardrobe for kids
10:30–11:00	Personal care
11:00–?	Sleep

Additional Mother Activities to "Fit In"

Shopping for self (personal and fashion)
Shopping for children's needs
Shopping for home (grocery and decor)
Shopping for gifts, husband, etc.
General housework
Physical activity/personal sports
Work brought home
Work related to fiscal running of household
Time with friends and relatives
Social/cultural activities/personal entertainment

Source: A presentation by Jim Bernhardt at The University of Texas at Austin on February 23, 1994. Used with permission.

Table 4–2 shows the change in average household income, inflation adjusted to 1970 dollars. As can be seen, real income has been essentially flat since 1970. Consumers are now more interested in value: they want higher quality and lower price. Consumers are less interested in traditional signs of success like "new," and "improved," and "latest fashion." Finally, the consumer has learned the marketing game, and has become cynical about advertising claims.[2]

Table 4.1

GROUP	POPULATION IN 1980 (IN MILLIONS)	POPULATION IN 1990 (IN MILLIONS)	% CHANGE IN POPULATION
Black	26.5	30.0	+13
Hispanic	14.6	22.4	+ 53
Asian	3.5	7.3	+108
Total Minority	44.6	59.7	+ 34
Total Population	227.1	249.9	+ 10
Aged 60 +	35.7	41.8	+ 17

Source: A presentation by Jim Bernhardt at The University of Texas at Austin on February 23, 1994 and the U.S. Government. Used with permission of Jim Bernhardt.

Table 4–2

YEAR	AVERAGE HOUSEHOLD INCOME IN IN 1970 DOLLARS	CHANGE RELATIVE TO 1970
1970	$29,421	—
1980	$28,091	-4.5 %
1985	$28,688	-2.5 %
1990	$29,943	+1.8 %

Source: A presentation by Jim Bernhardt at The University of Texas at Austin on February 23, 1994 and the U.S. Government. Used with permission of Jim Bernhardt.

In sum, it is going to be difficult to build brand awareness among working mothers through TV advertising. They have little time, and they have become cynical about advertising messages. And, because the population is so diverse, it will be difficult, if not impossible, to achieve broad appeal with any one message or any one product.

THE CHANGING MEDIA ENVIRONMENT

Between 1980 and 1990, the consumer price index rose 59 percent. The costs of all advertising media have grown more rapidly. As can be seen in Table 4–3, the cost of network television increased 132 percent; spot television, 102 percent; and so forth.[3] As noted in Chapter 3,

Table 4–3

MEDIA	PRICE INDEXED TO 1980	1990 PRICE RELATIVE TO 1980
Consumer Price Index	100	159
Network TV	100	232
Spot TV	100	202
Magazines	100	196
Network Radio	100	172
Spot Radio	100	166
Newspapers	100	216

Source: A presentation by Jim Bernhardt at The University of Texas at Austin on February 23, 1994, McCann-Ericson, and the U.S. Government. Used with permission of Jim Bernhardt.

dollars spent on advertising have been essentially flat over this period of time. Because advertising space had become more expensive and since advertising dollars haven't changed, it is reasonable to assume that the advertising exposure for national brands has decreased.

Not only have the advertising media become more expensive, but they have also become less effective. In the early 1950s and 1960s, there were, essentially, only three options for television viewing: ABC, NBC, and CBS. As can be seen in Figure 4–2, this situation has changed. By 1980, the average number of channels received by a household had grown to 10; by 1994, to 40. Consistent with this, we see, in Figure 4–3, that cable television penetration has grown from 20 percent of all U.S. households in 1980 to 64 percent in 1995. The result of cable and channel proliferation is a steady decline in television viewing shares for the three networks. Figure 4–4 shows that the network's share of primetime viewers has fallen to 62 percent; their share of daytime viewers has fallen to 50 percent; and their share of late night viewers has fallen to 46 percent.

As bleak as these numbers seem, the outlook for television advertising has been made even bleaker by two electronic innovations. The first, VCRs, were in only 2 percent of all U.S. households in 1980. By 1995, they had made their way into 79 percent of all households. (See Figure 4–5.) These devices allow viewers to use their televisions to watch movies (that include no ads), or to record television programming, including ads, for viewing at a later time. Unfortunately for the advertisers, viewers frequently fast-forward through advertisements in order to see the programming uninterrupted by commercial breaks.

Figure 4–2
AVERAGE NUMBER OF TELEVISION CHANNELS
RECEIVED PER HOUSEHOLD

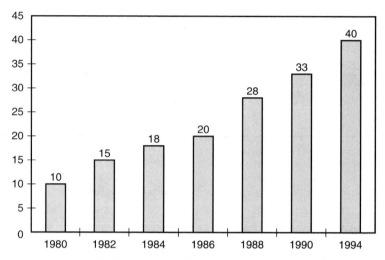

Source: A presentation by Jim Bernhardt at The University of Texas at Austin on February 23, 1994 and Nielsen Media Research. Used by permission of Jim Bernhardt and Nielsen Media Research.

Figure 4–3
CABLE TV HOUSEHOLD PENETRATION

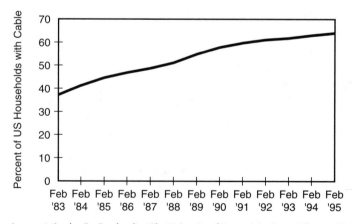

Source: A presentation by Jim Bernhardt at The University of Texas at Austin on February 23, 1994 and Nielsen Media Research. Used by permission of Jim Bernhardt and Nielsen Media Research.

Figure 4–4
NETWORK TELEVISION VIEWING SHARES (BY PERCENTAGE)

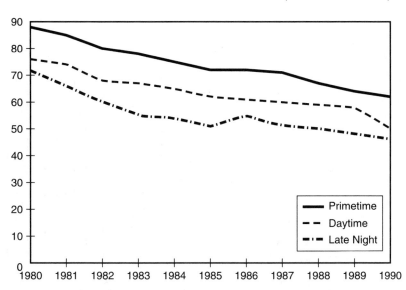

Source: A presentation by Jim Bernhardt at The University of Texas at Austin on February 23, 1994 and Nielsen Media Research. Used by permission of Jim Bernhardt and Nielsen Media Research.

Penetration of the second electronic innovation, remote control devices, was not even measured before 1985. At that time, remote control devices could be found in 30 percent of U.S. households. By 1995, that penetration had grown to 91 percent. (See Figure 4–6.) With these devices, the TV viewer can effortlessly avoid all advertising. When an ad comes on the air, the channel is changed.

Magazines and radio stations also proliferated between 1980 and 1990. Magazine titles[4] grew 47 percent, from 1,450 to 2,135. Radio stations[5] grew 20 percent, from 7,871 to 9,470.

Thus, we see that the cost of advertising media has grown faster than the rate of inflation, but its effectiveness has fallen as television channels, magazines, and radio stations proliferate, and as consumers take control of their exposure to ads with VCRs and remote control devices. Given this, it has become increasingly, and perhaps prohibitively, expensive to advertise, and therefore increasingly difficult, or impossible, to build brand awareness and build brand loyalty.

Figure 4–5
VCR HOUSEHOLD PENETRATION (BY PERCENTAGE)

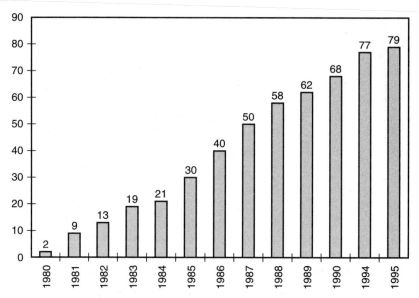

Source: A presentation by Jim Bernhardt at The University of Texas at Austin on February 23, 1994 and Nielsen Media Research. Used by permission of Jim Bernhardt and Nielsen Media Research.

Figure 4–6
PERCENTAGE OF HOUSEHOLDS WITH
REMOTE CONTROL DEVICES

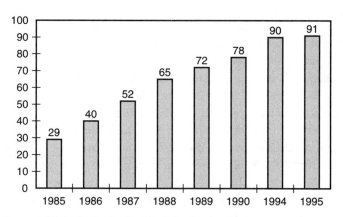

Source: A presentation by Jim Bernhardt at The University of Texas at Austin on February 23, 1994 and Nielsen Media Research. Used by permission of Jim Bernhardt and Nielsen Media Research.

Table 4–4

YEAR	TRULY NEW PRODUCTS	LINE EXTENSIONS	TOTAL NUMBER OF ITEMS LAUNCHED
1990	5,907	9,972	15,879
1991	5,144	10,257	15,401
1992	5,035	10,851	15,886
1993	4.410	12,953	17,363

Source: Marketing Intelligence Service, Productscan.

THE CHANGING COMPETITIVE ENVIRONMENT

An enormous number of "never before offered" items are brought to market each year. However, most of those items aren't really new products. Many are simple line extensions: a new size, color, or flavor of some product already being sold. In fact, as can be seen in Table 4–4, while the total number of items launched each year is increasing, the number of truly new products is declining.[6]

According to a *Supermarket Business* article on Marketing Intelligence Service Ltd., Naples, New York:[7]

> . . . [R]esearch shows that consumers are not fooled by "New!" and "Improved!" starbursts. AcuPoll's 100 panelists rate fewer than 30% of the 630 items studied as being truly new.
>
> "If anything, that's overstating it," [Marketing Intelligence Service Ltd.'s MIS president Richard] Lawrence says, noting that the 630 AcuPoll items were the pick of 1993's new product crop. They were selected "judgmentally," he says, because they seemed to "offer something significant to the consumer."
>
> The glut of me-too items "ultimately imposes a cost on everyone," Lawrence notes. "They divide the existing pie into smaller—and less profitable—pieces without making the pie any bigger."

Another result of this overwhelming product proliferation is that the distinctions between brands have become blurred. In virtually every product category there are many excellent quality, essentially indistinguishable alternatives.

Figure 4–7a
U.S. TREND IN COUPON DISTRIBUTION
(IN BILLIONS OF COUPONS)

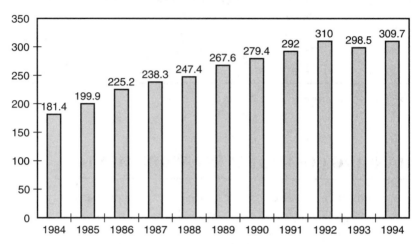

Source: "1995 Coupon Trends & Consumer Usage Patterns: The Leading Edge Collection," *NCH Promotional Services*, Lincolnshire, IL (1995), p. 7. Used with permission.

This situation of product parity is made worse by manufacturers' growing use of coupons. In 1994 more than 300 billion coupons, with an average face value of 63¢, were distributed in the United States (See Figures 4–7a and 4–7b.) This ever-increasing number of coupons offering ever-increasing price reductions provides consumers with an irresistible temptation to try different product alternatives. The lack of true differentiation among brands becomes obvious through trial, and brand loyalty is eroded.

THE CHANGING RETAIL AND WHOLESALE CUSTOMER

A significant amount of consolidation has occurred in the retail and wholesale trade. This consolidation has left manufacturers with very powerful customers. Table 4–5 reports the degree of concentration faced by one U.S. manufacturer in four different "classes of trade":

If packaged goods competition was national in scope, Table 4–5 would suggest that manufacturers were at a disadvantage relative to their retail and wholesale competitors. But the situation is actually worse. Grocery competition is regional. If we look at grocery retail consolidation in the top 10 markets in the United States, we see that, on average, the top five accounts handle 68 percent of the business.[8]

Figure 4–7b
U.S. TREND IN AVERAGE FACE VALUE REDEEMED (IN CENTS)

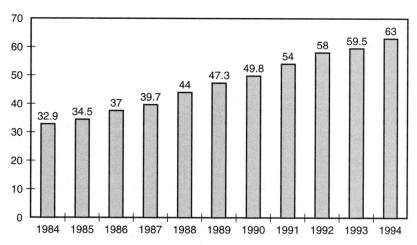

Source: *Worldwide Coupon Distributions and Redemption Trends,* Volume XXVII (1993), p. 16, and *1995 Coupon and Consumer Usage Patterns: The Leading Edge Collection* (1995), p. 27, NCH Promotional Services, Lincolnshire, IL. Used with permission.

Table 4–5

CLASS OF TRADE	PERCENT OF BUSINESS ACCOUNTED FOR BY THE TOP 5 ACCOUNTS IN THIS CLASS OF TRADE
Food	30 %
Drug	45 %
Warehouse Club	87 %
Mass Merchandiser	80 %

Across all classes of trade, manufacturers are facing significant trading partners.

These significant trading partners are becoming technologically sophisticated. Figure 4–8 shows the rate at which electronic scanners have been adopted by grocery chains. With scanners, the information advantage, once held by manufacturers with nationally syndicated data, moves to the retailer. A manufacturer can suggest that a retail customer buy a certain quantity of some product because the product is selling well in the United States, or in the Dallas market. But the category manager at HEB (a grocery chain in South Texas) *knows*

Figure 4–8
PERCENTAGE OF GROCERY WITH SCANNERS

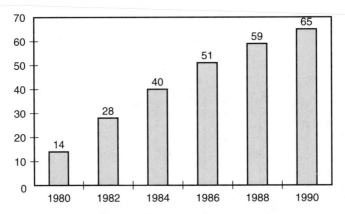

Source: A presentation by Jim Bernhardt at The University of Texas at Austin on February 23, 1994 and Nielsen Media Research. Used by permission of Jim Bernhardt and Nielsen Media Research.

(through analysis of HEB's own scanner data) whether the product is selling well at HEB stores. The retailer can use this information to strike more attractive deals with manufacturers.

In addition, retailers and wholesalers are developing much more sophisticated management systems, which will be discussed in subsequent chapters. What is important to note here is that a manufacturer's retail and wholesale customers are becoming bigger and more sophisticated every day. As these customers become progressively harder to say "no" to, the spending trends noted in Figure 3–3 are likely to continue. Ever larger proportions of the marketing budget are likely to be pulled into promotional spending with retail and wholesale customers. Ever smaller proportions of the marketing budget will be available for advertising.

Endnotes

1. Virtually everything in this chapter is drawn from a presentation at The University of Texas at Austin on February 23, 1994, titled "The Decline of Consumer Package Goods Marketing As We Know It . . . and Its Implications for You," by Jim Bernhardt, VP Marketing, Dow Brands.

2. From a presentation by Jim Bernhardt at The University of Texas at Austin on February 23, 1994, and Yankelovich.

3. It may be that the increase in the real cost of advertising is driven by increased demand. As will be pointed out later, more than 15,000 new products are introduced each year. In addition, completely new categories of advertised products have emerged (e.g., personal computers, Nike).

4. From a presentation by Jim Bernhardt at The University of Texas at Austin on February 23, 1994, and Standard Rate and Data Service.

5. From a presentation by Jim Bernhardt at The University of Texas at Austin on February 23, 1994, and FCC.

6. "Vendors Pushed Record Slew of Not-So-New Items" (1994), *Supermarket Business* (March), 13.

7. "Vendors Pushed Record Slew of Not-So-New Items" (1994), *Supermarket Business* (March), 13.

8. Husson, Mark and Erika Gritman Long (1994), *Private Label: Cornerstone of the New Supermarket Brand Architecture*, JP Morgan Securities Inc., Equity Research, January 31, 1994, New York.

The Market Adjusts

As manufacturers took the prices of national brands ever higher despite falling raw material costs, successful, high-quality private label brands emerged. In a move that lowered the opportunity for private label while also driving out distribution inefficiencies, Procter & Gamble moved away from high–low promotional pricing in 1991. Retailers and wholesalers, initially resistant to Procter & Gamble's "value pricing," became more open to the idea after an industry-commissioned study showed that traditional format retailers' sales were declining because alternative format retailers were leveraging a 26 percent cost advantage to capture the best consumers and the sales in the most profitable categories. Other manufacturers became interested in helping traditional format retailers regain competitiveness as the behemoth "power retailers" became dictatorial.

THE RISE OF PRIVATE LABEL

As we pointed out earlier, during the 1980s consumers were growing harder to reach and more diverse, advertising media were becoming more expensive and less effective, brands were becoming less distinctive, and retail and wholesale customers were consolidating and growing in sophistication. Despite these facts, packaged goods manufacturers were able to increase their profits steadily. In the decade between 1981 and 1991, for example, H. J. Heinz's operating margin went from 11.4 to 18.5 percent, Ralston Purina's from 9.4 to 15.7 percent, Sara Lee's from 7.4 to 10.4 percent, Clorox's from 11.2 to 18 percent.[1]

According to *Forbes*[2], profit increases in the 1980s were attributable to the fact that the cost of raw materials went up much more slowly than did the prices of national brands.

> *Consumers . . . didn't bolt even as prices of some of their favorite soaps and cereals went up 5% or 8% a year. And so profits went up much faster than that. Heinz's earnings*

climbed at an average 13% annual rate [between 1981 and 1991], Clorox's at 15%.[3]

This growing gap between the cost of raw materials and the price of national brands created an opportunity for private label brands. Nowhere was that opportunity more completely exploited than in the cigarette category. Discount brands grew from 11 percent market share in 1988 to over 40 percent in 1993.[4] By early 1993, Marlboros were selling at $2 a pack while discount cigarettes sold at 69¢ a pack.[5] Fearing irreparable damage to brand loyalty, Philip Morris cut the price of Marlboros and other premium cigarettes by 40 percent on April 2, 1993, "Marlboro Friday." The value of Philip Morris's stock fell $13.4 billion.[6] Investors took the Marlboro price cut as a signal that the days of unending price increases for packaged goods products were over. RJR, Procter & Gamble, Coca-Cola, PepsiCo, Quaker Oats, Gillette, and other top brand manufacturers were also hit, bringing total loss of market value to $47.5 billion.[7]

By 1993, even those categories historically dominated by national brands opened up to private label. Sales of private label soft drinks increased 15 percent; private label cold cereal, 27 percent; private label diapers, 18 percent; private label cookies, 27 percent; and private label cigarettes, 56 percent.[8]

With national cereal brands selling at $5 a box and private label selling at $3.50 a box,[9] it is not surprising that cold cereal private label market share grew from 5.4 percent to 9.7 percent between 1990 and 1995.[10] To stop the growth of private label, Post (a unit of Philip Morris Company's Kraft Foods division) cut cereal prices 20 percent in the spring of 1996. Two months later, Kellogg responded with a 19 percent price cut, followed quickly by General Mills and Quaker Oats.[11] "In mid-June, St. Louis-based Ralcorp Holdings, Inc., which makes both branded and private label cereals, predicted that the price cuts by the Big Four could take more than $1 billion in sales from the industry."[12] Unable to sustain such losses, Ralcorp sold its cereal and snack mix lines to General Mills for $570 million.[13]

It has been argued that private label growth in the United States is only a reflection of the recession of the early '90s. As shown in Figure 5–1, between 1971 and estimated 1993, changes in disposable income do seem to closely track changes in private label market share.

However, if we look globally, we see a very different picture. In many European countries, private label grew steadily in the 1980s. Table 5–1 shows that even during the economically successful years

Figure 5–1
REAL PERSONAL DISPOSABLE INCOME
VERSUS OWN LABEL MARKET PENETRATION

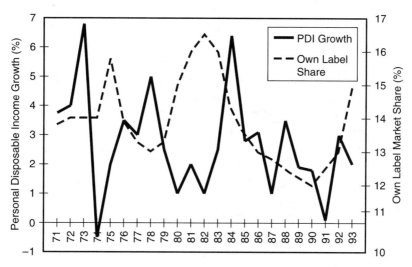

Source: Husson and Long "Private Label: Cornerstone of the New Supermarket Brand Architecture,"
J.P. Morgan Economic Research, New York (January 31, 1994), p. 4, and A. C. Neilsen and the U.S.
Department of Commerce. Used with permission of J. P. Morgan Securities Inc. and A. C. Neilson.

Table 5–1

COUNTRY	PRIVATE-LABEL PENETRATION OF GROCERY SALES	
	1982	1992
France	10%	22%
Germany	13	24
Netherlands	N/A	26
United Kingdom	23	36

Source: Husson and Long, *Private Label: Cornerstone of the New Supermarket Brand Architecture,*"
J. P. Morgan Economic Research, New York (January 31, 1994), p. 5. Used with permission from
J. P. Morgan Securities Inc.

under Mrs. Thatcher, private label penetration increased in the United Kingdom.

Dave Nichol, the man who built the "President's Choice" line of private label products for Canadian grocer Loblaws, contends that private label market share has been artificially depressed in the

United States for several reasons.[14] Television advertising, allowed in the United States but not in the United Kingdom, gave national brand manufacturers an opportunity to build brand loyalty in the United States. Given the leverage of this loyalty, national manufacturers could refuse to participate with retailers in private label manufacturing. Further, Nichol contends, the glut of trade promotion dollars offered by manufacturers kept retailers tactically focused. Combining these forces with the extremely low retail margins in the United States left retailers producing "cheap and nasty" private label products.[15]

Those days are over, though, according to Nichol. He cites a Point of Purchase Institute survey that documents the decline of brand loyalty. This survey indicates that in the 1960s, 80 percent of consumers went into supermarkets for specific brands. Today, over 66 percent of all purchase decisions are made at the point of purchase. He further points out that 25 percent of U.S. supermarkets are owned by foreigners who built their businesses in countries with strong, high quality private label brands. In addition, he points to the tremendous opportunity created in the United States by the national brands' insatiable appetites for price increases.

Nichol's final point is that private label is no longer "cheap and nasty." He contends that his own line of "President's Choice" private label products, now sold by many U.S. retailers, is superior to national brands. His contention is confirmed by a 1996 Gallup study in which 86 percent of the shoppers polled said that "private label products are equal or superior to national brands."[16] Given that national brand manufacturers like Nestle, Campbell, Kraft, and Hershey are beginning to produce private label products,[17] it is not surprising that the quality of private label is increasing.

According to Robert Wehling, Procter & Gamble's senior vice president of advertising:[18]

> *Dave [Nichol] has sent a real wake up call to a lot of brands. . . . If brands don't deliver the best possible value, you bet consumers will revolt—and they should. But that's nothing new. Consumers have* always *demanded superior value and their expectations have always been on the rise. . . .*
>
> *I think that much of the debate about the future of brands has overlooked this point. When I see headlines like "Brands versus Private Labels: Fighting to Win" in the Har-*

vard Business Review, *or "Is Brand Equity at Risk?" in*
Chief Executive *magazine, I get concerned that we're con-*
vincing ourselves the future is an either/or proposition; ei-
ther brands will win or private labels will win, but not
both.

That's not going to happen. There will be brands on both
sides that deliver superior value to consumers—and they're
the ones who'll win.

Consistent with Wehling's conjecture, private label sales in the
United States grew another 3.5 percent in 1995 to $31.2 billion.[19]
"Among the fastest growing private label products were weight
loss/protein supplements, rice and popcorn cakes, sugar substitutes,
and Mexican sauces."[20] The fact that private label is growing most
rapidly in technologically less sophisticated product categories is not
surprising. A McKinsey study of private label in Europe suggests that
private label penetration is highest for those categories in which
(1) there is little product innovation and (2) the price difference between private label and national brands is high.[21]

PROCTER AND GAMBLE'S VALUE PRICING

Faced with the horrible mess to which the U.S. packaged goods industry had evolved, Procter & Gamble took the daring first step away
from the quagmire of promotion spending in November 1991. For a
part of their product line,[22] they dramatically lowered list prices and
dramatically reduced promotional price cuts.[23] The objective was to
establish the true value of a product to retailers and wholesalers and
then to charge that "value price" every day. Given this fairly stable
price from the manufacturer, wholesalers and retailers could smooth
out their purchases through the year, eliminating costs associated
with holding excess inventory.

In moving from "high–low" pricing as depicted in Figure 5–2a to
"value pricing" as depicted in Figure 5–2b, the "value price" was set
so that, accounting for the efficiency savings, the retailer's cost of
goods sold would be no more under value pricing than cost of
goods sold (including inventory expenses) had been under high–low
pricing.

For example, suppose that under the high–low scheme depicted in
Figures 3–1a and 3–1b a retailer or wholesaler was buying 80 percent

Figure 5–2a
"HIGH–LOW" PRICING

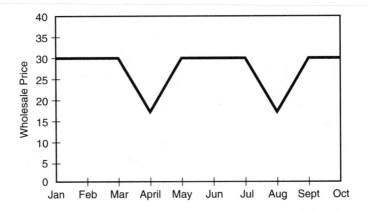

Figure 5–2b
"VALUE" PRICING

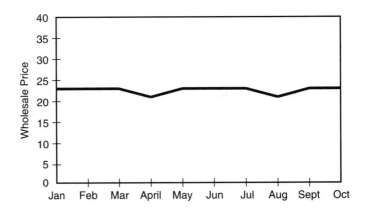

of the product at the promoted price of $17 a case, and 20 percent of the product at the list price of $30 a case. Over the course of a year, this retailer or wholesaler was paying the manufacturer, on average, about $20 a case. In addition, because of inventory buildups associated with deep price cut promotions, the retailer or wholesaler was incurring, on average, an additional $3 a case for inventory handling, storage, and financing. A "value price" of $23 a case every day should be the financial equivalent of the average high–low price of $20 a case plus the attendant average of $3 a case for inventory expenses.

One might expect that such a move on half of P&G's product line—bringing down the wholesale price of products like Jif, Cascade, and Pampers as much as 25 percent[24]—would please the retailers and wholesalers. But, of course, one would be wrong.

This much needed step toward rationality was not well received. Calling P&G a "dictator," the chairman of Stop & Shop said his huge chain would do "everything in its power" to derail P&G's plan.[25] Safeway delisted some P&G products.[26] An A&P spokesman said, "We feel [that value pricing] is not in the best interests of retailers and consumers."[27]

Human beings do not like to change. A move from "high–low" to "value pricing" by a major manufacturer requires that systems and procedures be changed. Probably more significant, this move to "value pricing" eliminated the incentive to forward buy and divert. As noted earlier, these inefficient practices had become institutionalized in retailers and wholesalers, and are thought to be the source of more than 50 percent of wholesalers' operating income.

Interestingly, retailers and wholesalers were initially reluctant to attribute their opposition to "value pricing" to the loss of forward buy and diverting income. Early attacks accused Procter & Gamble of trying to control retailers' pricing strategies. By giving no wholesale price cuts, they argued, P&G was forcing retailers to give no retail price cuts.

This is incorrect for several reasons. First, manufacturers are legally restrained from setting retail prices. Second, as we pointed out earlier, big retailers and wholesalers are quite powerful in their dealings with manufacturers. Manufacturers are no more likely to be able to influence retail price than they are to influence forward buying and diverting through contractual covenants.

Value pricing made Procter & Gamble vulnerable not only to their customers, but also to their competitors. The following quote from a *Progressive Grocer* article suggests that, perhaps, these competitors enjoyed the fact that Procter & Gamble was experiencing difficulties with retailers and wholesalers.

> *One competing supplier says, "I'm just sitting around watching P&G get the shit kicked out of them. They will get hurt on promotions and shelf space. Nobody will drop Tide or Charmin, but they won't promote them either."*[28]

However, in the long run, the competitors did not intensify their promotional efforts as might have been expected based on the Prisoner's Dilemma. *The Economist* points out:[29]

> *[A] threat to P&G's strategy is that big rivals such as [Kraft Foods], Colgate-Palmolive and Unilever will try to take advantage of the ire of many supermarket chains to steal shelf space by boosting their own promotional budgets. To the surprise of many in retailing, this has not yet happened. Privately, managers at some competing firms are rooting for P&G.*

After Procter & Gamble absorbed the initial violently negative reaction to this move away from inefficient practices associated with deep-cut promotional deals, other manufacturers followed. By July of 1992, Kraft Foods was experimenting with alternative pricing options, though they were quick to deny a *New York Times* suggestion that they were following P&G into value pricing.[30] Colgate and Lever cautiously followed P&G's list prices down.[31]

By April of 1993, value pricing was well entrenched. As reported in *Supermarket News*:[32]

> *"There was a big furor initially and just as quickly it died out," said Bill Vitulli, a spokesman for A&P, Montvale, N.J., whose company at one time said it planned to review its P&G product line with an eye on delisting some items.*
>
> *"Today, Procter has clearly established its position. They are committed to this strategy and they are not going to be moved," said Jeffrey Hill, president of Meridian Consulting, Westport, Conn. "But they are also committed to retail partnerships, so a lot of the ruffled feathers are beginning to be smoothed out."*
>
> *The impact on the marketplace, meanwhile, has been profound. From interviews with manufacturers, retailers and analysts, it's clear that the supermarket landscape today is considerably different than it was even six months ago.*

Though they were initially battered by industry response to their new pricing strategy, by 1993, P&G had more than recovered. According to *Business Week:*[33]

> *The immediate effect was major market-share losses.*
>
> *But Procter also achieved major cost reductions by cutting price promotions. And by smoothing out production*

schedules, the steadier pricing should trim $175 million a year from production costs. Thanks to the savings, operating profits in the quarter ended Mar. 31 [1993] rose 11%, to $760 million on sales that dipped 2%, to $7.4 billion.

. . . As [P&G's then CEO Edwin] Artzt is expected to tell analysts, the price cuts are paying off. The company says volume in the more than 70% of its brands that have switched to the new pricing model is growing faster than in the rest. And Procter claims its share in 21 of 31 U.S. product categories is up from last year, led by double-digit gains in detergent and shampoo. "The worst is over," says Paine Webber Inc. analyst Andrew Shore.

WAKE-UP CALL FOR THE SUPERMARKET INDUSTRY

In the mid to late 1980s, the supermarket industry achieved growth rates that exceeded inflation (as measured by the Consumer Price Index). However, in 1990, as shown in Figure 5–3, that situation changed. The Consumer Price Index had grown 5.4 percent while supermarket sales increased only 5.1 percent. Alarmed by this fact, the Food Marketing Institute (a retailer and wholesaler trade association) hired consultants to study the question of why supermarket sales growth was slowing.

Those consultants' report, *Alternative Store Formats: Competing in the Nineties,* had a major impact on the packaged goods industry. The report showed that the lion's share of grocery sales increase between 1981 and 1986 had gone to warehouse club stores (see Figure 5–4). Up until this report, "traditional format" grocery retailers (chains like Kroger, Safeway, and A&P) had not considered themselves as being in competition with "alternative format" retailers (warehouse clubs like SAMs and Price Club, mass merchandisers like Wal-Mart and Kmart, discount drug chains like Drug Emporium and Phar-Mor). The report details the extent to which these traditional format retailers did, in fact, compete with the alternative formats. Now we will focus on what was, when the report was published, the biggest threat among these alternative formats, warehouse clubs.

Theoretically, these club stores were designed to serve as a wholesaler for small businesses in their area. As such, the clubs charge an annual membership fee (around $25), they carry a limited assortment of products in a no-frills environment, and they try to offer significantly lower prices than traditional format retailers. The consultants

Figure 5–3
CHANGE IN GROCERY SALES VERSUS CHANGE IN CPI

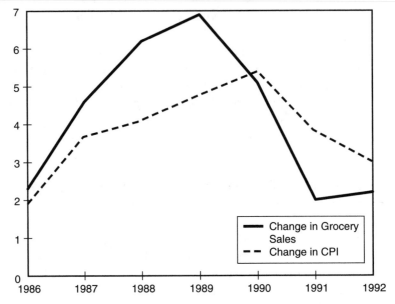

Source: Shore and Lenahan (1993), *Cosmetic and Household Products: When the Sun Comes Up To-morrow, You Had Better Be Running*, Paine Webber (October 11).

found, however, that only 65 percent of the club's customers were businesses. And, of the purchases made by the business members, only 35 to 40 percent were for business uses. Therefore, 60 to 65 percent of all purchases made at clubs were actually for personal use, and many of the products purchased (food, health and beauty aids, etc.) are also sold in traditional format outlets.

Heavy users of club stores, they found, were more likely to be in the 25 to 49 age group, to be married, and to have multiple children—the most important shoppers to traditional format retailers.

For one analysis, the consultants asked consumers where they shop (supermarket, club, and/or mass merchandiser) for various product categories. Table 5–2 summarizes some of the results of that analysis. The top segment of the table lists product categories for which supermarkets are still the dominant source. We see that 90 percent of consumers shop for fresh fruit and vegetables at supermarkets, while only 4% shop for fresh fruit and vegetables at clubs, and only 3 percent at mass merchandisers.[34] The middle segment of

Figure 5–4
GROCERY SALES DOLLARS
(IN BILLIONS OF DOLLARS)

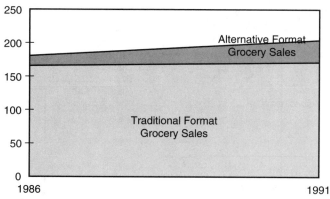

Source: Data from "Alternative Store Formats: Competing in the Nineties," *Food Marketing Institute,* Report #9-511, Washington, D.C. (January 1992), p. 5, and *Supermarket Business,* September 1994, p. 36.

Table 5–2

CATEGORY	SUPERMARKET	CLUB	MASS MERCHANDISER
Fresh fruit and vegetables	90	4	3
Dairy	90	10	2
Cereal	86	16	6
Meat	85	13	3
Frozen prepared foods	84	19	2
Canned goods	83	23	6
Bakery	81	10	4
Coffee	75	16	12
Soft drinks	74	17	18
Snacks	73	19	26
Pet food and supplies	54	18	25
Laundry and household cleaners	51	29	35
Paper products	49	33	41
Health and beauty aids	35	14	31

Source: Adapted from "Alternative Store Formats: Competing in the Nineties," *Food Marketing Institute,* Report #9-511, Washington, D.C. (January 1992), pp. 45-47. Used with permission.

Figure 5–5
TRADITIONAL GROCERY COST STRUCTURE
VERSUS CLUB COST STRUCTURE

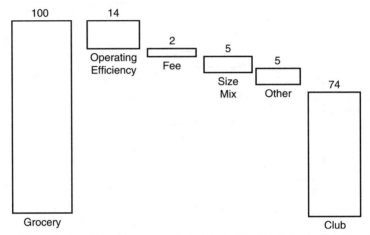

Source: "Alternative Store Formats: Competing in the Nineties," *Food Marketing Institute,* Report #9-511, Washington D.C. (January 1992), p. 116. Used with permission.

the table lists product categories for which supermarkets are under attack by alternative formats, and the bottom segment of the table lists product categories in which supermarkets are no longer the dominant source.

The clubs were able to offer their very low prices, the report discovered, because of a 26 percent cost advantage. If the cost to a traditional format retailer of selling a particular item is 1 dollar, the cost to a club of selling that same item is 74¢. As shown in Figure 5–5, 14¢ of that 26¢ cost advantage is operating efficiency. Clubs' narrower range of offerings drives 5 to 6 cents of the operating efficiency. The very low service levels in clubs gives them another 3 to 5 cents of operating efficiency advantage. Their lower warehouse and transportation costs account for another 1 to 2 cents; lower administration, 1 to 2 cents; and very low advertising expenditures, less than 1 cent.

The balance of the 26¢ cost advantage comes from membership fees (2¢), size mix (5¢), and other (5¢). The "size mix" differential reflected the fact that manufacturers charge a lower price per unit for larger sized packages. Club stores tend to carry only very large, "club pack" sizes of products while supermarkets carried the entire range of product sizes. Hence, the average per unit cost in supermarkets

Figure 5–6
TRADITIONAL GROCERY FINANCIAL RETURNS VERSUS CLUB FINANCIAL RETURNS

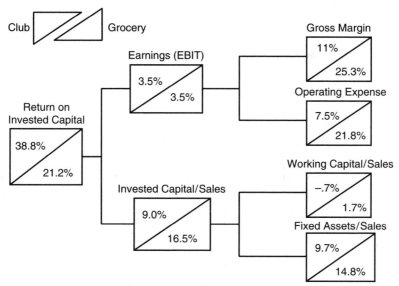

Source: "Alternative Store Formats: Competing in the Nineties," *Food Marketing Institute,* Report # 9–511, Washington D.C. (January 1992), p. 114. Used with permission.

was larger than for clubs. The last 5 cents associated with "other" wasn't specifically identified, but many traditional format retailers believe that this last 5 cent differential resulted because club operators were able to wring extra price concessions out of manufacturers.

These findings had the attention of traditional format retailers. They were losing the most profitable consumers and the most profitable categories to a competitor that had significantly lower operating costs. But the situation was even worse. The consultants showed that although this class of competitors' earnings were roughly equivalent to those of traditional format retailers, their return on investment was nearly double that of traditional format retailers.

Figure 5–6 contrasts the financial returns for club stores (upper triangles) to financial returns for traditional grocery (lower triangles). The 14 percent operating efficiency advantage for clubs presented in Figure 5–5 can be seen in the operating expenses box—grocery's 21.8 percent operating expense level minus club's 7.5 percent operating expense. But clubs pour all of that operating expense advantage into lower prices, as can be seen in the gross margin box. By lowering prices significantly, clubs lower gross margin to 11 percent. Grocery, with their higher prices, post the higher, 25.3 percent gross margin. These two gaps wash out in earnings (gross margin minus operating expense). Both clubs (11% − 7.5% = 3.5%) and grocery (25.3% − 21.8% = 3.5%) have earnings of approximately 3.5 percent.

Clubs are able to generate these earnings with significantly fewer assets than can grocery. The clubs' "no frills" environment requires a smaller investment in fixed assets than does grocery (9.7% of sales for clubs versus 14.8% of sales for grocery).

In addition, clubs actually have a negative need for working capital. That is, they sell their inventory before they have to pay for it. For example, a club might receive $100,000 worth of product on the first day of the month. If it sold all of that product on the second day of the month and put the proceeds in the bank to earn interest until the last day of the month when the manufacturer must be paid, the club would actually make money on the financial transaction with the manufacturer, yielding a negative number for working capital needed.[35] Grocery, with their inefficient forward buy inventories, has a positive 1.7 percent of sales need for working capital.

Combining the working capital and fixed asset needs, we see that clubs invest only 9 percent of sales to generate their 3.5 percent earnings while grocery invests 16.5 percent of sales to generate 3.5 percent earnings. Return on invested capital, then, is 39 percent for clubs and only 21.2 percent for grocery.

The upshot of that 1992 report was that traditional format grocers had to reduce their operating expenses radically and lower prices to become price competitive. Further, these retailers had to reduce their use of fixed assets and working capital. They had to do more with less.

The threat from club stores waned in the mid-1990s. However, a new format, the supercenter (combining a mass merchandiser with a grocery store), continues the pressure for lower prices and better asset utilization. With 250 supercenters, Wal-Mart was the third largest grocery operator in the United States with a 3.16 percent dollar share of the food retail market in 1995.[36] Aggressive growth plans including 110 more supercenters in 1996 prompted Donaldson Lufkin and Jenrette, New York, to predict that Wal-Mart will take 8.67 percent of the food retail market in the year 2000.[37]

Figure 5–7
THE PRODUCTIVITY LOOP

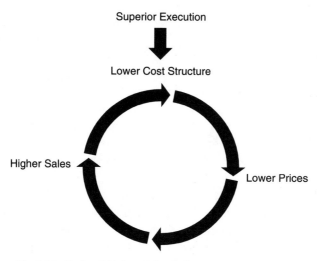

Adapted from Mandel, Jr., Stephen F. "A Competitive Challenge: How Supermarkets Can Get Into the Productivity Loop," *International Trends in Retailing*, Vol. 8, No. 1 (Spring, 1991), p. 40. Used with permission.

WAKE-UP CALL FOR MANUFACTURERS

In trying to help investors understand how to choose winners and losers among retailers' stocks, Stephen Mandel, Jr., formulated "'The Productivity Loop" model pictured in Figure 5–7. He explains his model as follows:[38]

> *In previous periods during retailing history, even the leading chains were generally not able to consistently drive down their operating costs, and, as a result, the differences in cost structure between competitors tended to be modest. The difference in the 1980's has been technology, with scanning, distribution automation, satellite communications, and more sophisticated buying, merchandising, and scheduling systems permitting well-run chains to consistently drive down operating costs.*
>
> *The retailers who have done a superior job executing in these areas, or who have developed formats able to "leap" competition in terms of cost structure, are in what we call*

the "productivity loop." Either through new formats or through the implementation of technology, such as scanning or labor scheduling systems, a retailer is able to gain confidence that it can drive down its operating costs. Armed with this confidence, the retailer then reinvests these cost savings in lower shelf prices, better service levels, or both, in an attempt to drive sales productivity higher. The higher sales productivity in and of itself drives operating costs down further, completing the loop.

To better understand how the productivity loop works, we will look at financial statements for several retailers. There are four important quantities that we will study in these financial statements:

Expense Ratio   *Total expenses/total sales.*
A measure of productivity: the lower the expense ratio, the more productive the retailer.

Gross Margin   *Amount consumer pays retailer minus amount retailer pays manufacturer.*
A measure of retailer's price level: All else held constant, the lower the retailer sets its prices, the lower the gross margin will be.

Operating Margin   *Gross margin − expense ratio.*
A measure of profit from operations.

Same Store Sales Increases   *The amount, on average, by which sales increased in a particular year for stores that were open for the entire year.* (This may be lower than overall sales growth since some sales growth may be accounted for by new stores.)

If the productivity loop is in action for a particular retailer, we should see that retailer's expense ratio getting smaller through time. If, as dictated by the productivity loop, the retailer reinvests the productivity savings in lower prices, then gross margin should also be getting smaller through time. These lower prices should lead to sales increases without compromising operating margins because the price decreases (lower gross margins) have been compensated for by cost reductions (lower expense ratios).

Table 5–3 shows gross margin, expense ratio, operating margin, and same store sales increases for Toys 'R' Us for the years 1985–1989:[39]

Table 5–3   TOYS 'R' US FINANCIALS

	85	86	87	88	89
Gross Margin	32.8	31.8	31.2	30.8	30.8
Expense Ratio	20.7	18.8	18.6	18.4	18.1
Operating Margin	12.1	13.0	12.6	12.4	12.7
Same Store Sales Increases	+2%	+29%	+10%	+11%	+7%

Source: Mandel, Jr., Stephen F., "Implications of Declining Cost Structures in Mass Merchandise Retailing," speech given to Second Annual Seminar for International Investors in Retailing (April 5, 1990), p. 5. Goldman Sachs Investment Research. Used with permission.

We see that Toys 'R' Us is clearly in the productivity loop. Their expense ratio fell from 20.7 to 18.1 and their gross margin also declined from 32.8 to 30.8. Further, these ever lower prices did, indeed, drive significant sales gains each year without compromising operating profits.

When you look at the financial figures for Toys 'R' Us versus their competitors in 1988, shown in Table 5–4, the power of the productivity loop becomes apparent:[40]

Table 5–4   COMPARATIVE FINANCIALS IN 1988

	CHILD WORLD	LIONEL	TOYS 'R' US
Gross Margin	30.4	28.5	30.8
Expense Ratio	25.8	25.9	18.4
Operating Margin	4.5	2.4	12.4
Same Store Sales Increases	.5%	2.4%	11.3%

Source: Mandel, Jr., Stephen F., "Implications of Declining Cost Structures in Mass Merchandise Retailing," speech given to Second Annual Seminar for International Investors in Retailing (April 5, 1990), p. 10. Goldman Sachs Investment Research. Used with permission.

We see that Toys 'R' Us had a significant cost advantage with an expense ratio of 18.4 when competitors were near 26. Comparable gross margin numbers suggest that competitors seem to be trying to match or even beat Toys 'R' Us's prices with disastrous results for their operating margin. Toys 'R' Us, with their healthy 12.4% operating margins, was also enjoying healthy sales gains. It is not surprising that Child World and Lionel were both driven out of business in 1993.[41]

Table 5–5 **POWER RETAILERS**

COMPANY	1994 SALES (IN BILLIONS)
Wal-Mart	$77.8
Kmart	34.1
Target	21.3
Price/Costco	16.1
Home Depot	12.5
Toys 'R' Us	8.7
Dillards	5.5

Source: Data from "State of the Industry" (1995), *Chain Store Age Executive* (August), 3A–7A.

According to Theresa Byrne, editor of *Retail Maxim*, a newsletter reporting on retail and real estate issues, "Most of the initial growth among category killers [like Toys 'R' Us] came at the expense of inefficient, smaller retailers."[42] By 1996, Ms. Byrne points out, "Those days are over. [Category killers'] margins have gotten thinner and thinner."[43] At Toys 'R' Us, net margin in 1996 was only 24 percent of what net margin had been in 1988.[44]

But the effectiveness of the productivity loop is not limited to category killers. A whole class of "power retailers," driven forward by the productivity loop, has emerged. As shown in Table 5–5, these retailers command almost unthinkably high levels of sales each year.

These retailers pose a very real threat to manufacturers. As ever greater proportions of a manufacturer's sales become concentrated in a few distributors, that manufacturer becomes the captive of those distributors. Table 5–6, reflecting the situation in 1991, gives a sense of the degree of concentration that has occurred:

> From the tiniest of private-label suppliers to giant Procter & Gamble Co., manufacturers are overhauling themselves to cope with the demands of retailing's kingmakers. "They're not difficult to deal with," says Lawrence Zalusky, chairman of Health o meter Products Inc., the leading maker of bathroom scales. "It's very simple. They say, 'We want this. Either you do it, or we'll get it from somebody else.'"[45]

Table 5–6

MANUFACTURER	% OF MANUFACTURER'S SALES THROUGH TOP CUSTOMER	% OF MANUFACTURER'S SALES THROUGH TOP 5 CUSTOMERS
Gibson Greetings	13%	35%
Gitano	26	56
Haggar	26.6	—
Hasbro	17	75*
Huffy	—	23**
Mattell	13	—
Mr. Coffee	21	31**
P&G	11.1	—

* Top 10 customers.
** Top 2 customers.
Source: Data from Zachary Schiller and Wendy Zellner (1992), "Clout! More and More, Retail Giants Rule the Marketplace," *Business Week*, (December 21), 69.

This trend toward big, powerful retailers is not limited to the U.S. market. While four of the world's ten largest retailers are U.S.-based (Wal-Mart, Kmart, Sears, Kroger), three are German (Metro Int., Tengelmann, Rewe Zentrale), two are Japanese (Ito-Yokado and Daiei) and one is French (Carrefour).[46]

Endnotes

1. Morgenson, Gretchen (1991), "The Trend is Not their Friend," *Forbes*, (September 16), 115.

2. Morgenson, Gretchen (1991), "The Trend is Not their Friend," *Forbes*, (September 16), 115.

3. Morgenson, Gretchen (1991), "The Trend is Not their Friend," *Forbes*, (September 16), 115.

4. Atlas, Riva (1994), "Food, Drink and Tobacco," *Forbes* (January 3), 152.

5. "Shoot Out at the Check-Out" (1993), *The Economist* (June 5), 69.

6. "Shoot Out at the Check-Out" (1993), *The Economist* (June 5), 69.

7. Sellers, Patricia (1993), "Brands: It's Thrive or Die," *Fortune* (August 23), 52.

8. Saxton, Lisa (1994), "Private Label Gains Ground," *Supermarket News*, (June 13), 45-46.

9. Morgenson, Gretchen (1996), "Denial in Battle Creek," *Forbes* (October 7), 45–46.

10. Morgenson, Gretchen (1996), "Denial in Battle Creek," *Forbes* (October 7), 46.

11. De Santa, Richard (1996), "Grabbing Share with Vise Grips," *Supermarket Business* (September), 20.

12. De Santa, Richard (1996), "Grabbing Share with Vise Grips," *Supermarket Business* (September), 20.

13. De Santa, Richard (1996), "Grabbing Share with Vise Grips," *Supermarket Business* (September), 20.

14. Nichol, Dave (1993), "Hell is Truth Seen too Late," keynote address to The Private Label Manufacturing Conference, Miami, Florida, (March).

15. The early success of private label in Canada, a country that *does* allow television advertising, is often attributed to the high degree of retail concentration in Canada. One chain, Loblaws, controls more than 25% of all grocery sales in Canada. Scale is generally believed to have given Loblaws the leverage needed to develop and distribute a high quality private label line.

16. Morgenson, Gretchen (1996), "Denial in Battle Creek," *Forbes* (October 7), 46.

17. Morris, Kathleen (1993), "No-Name Power," *Financial World* (March 16), 32.

18. "The Future of Brands: Getting Brands In Shape Today to Win the Loyalty of Tomorrow's Consumers," remarks by Robert L. Wehling, senior vice president of advertising, Procter & Gamble, at The Fisher School's Cullman Symposium, Ohio State University, April 25, 1996.

19. "Store-Brand Sales Reported Rising in Supermarkets" (1996), *Supermarket Business* (July), 9.

20. "Store-Brand Sales Reported Rising in Supermarkets" (1996), *Supermarket Business* (July), 9.

21. Glement, Francois and Rafael Mira, "The Brand Leader's Dilemma" (1993), *The McKinsey Quarterly*, No. 2, 3–15.

22. According to Harvard Business School case 9-593-108 (July 25, 1994) titled "P&G and Everyday Low Prices," P&G launched this policy with its Pampers, Folgers, and Pringles brands. Once the marketplace had begun to adapt to the new pricing scheme for these brands, P&G extended the policy to cover their most important brands (e.g., Tide and Crest).

23. P&G did not completely eliminate promotional price cuts; they merely reduced them to a level that would not support forward buying and diverting. In the text we use the more extreme case in which price cuts are eliminated completely. We do this to simplify exposition.

24. "Procter's Gamble" (1992), *The Economist* (July 25), 61.

25. "Procter's Gamble" (1992), *The Economist* (July 25), 62.

26. Weinstein, Steve (1992), "Will Procter's Gamble Work?" *Progressive Grocer* (July), 36.

27. Weinstein, Steve (1992), "Will Procter's Gamble Work?" *Progressive Grocer* (July), 36.

28. Weinstein, Steve (1992), "Will Procter's Gamble Work?" *Progressive Grocer* (July), 36-38.

29. "Procter's Gamble" (1992), *The Economist* (July 25), 62.

30. Weinstein, Steve (1992), "Will Procter's Gamble Work?" *Progressive Grocer* (July), 38.

31. Weinstein, Steve (1992), "Will Procter's Gamble Work?" *Progressive Grocer* (July), 38.

32. Klepacki, Laura (1993), "P&G Commits Its Heavy Guns," *Supermarket News* (April 12), 10.

33. Schiller, Zachary (1993), "Procter & Gamble Hits Back," *Business Week* (July 19), 21.

34. The numbers across a row might add up to more than 100% if consumers shop at more than one type of outlet for the associated product category. This is the case for cereal, for example.

35. We estimate that, with 2% net 10 payment terms, the distributor crosses over to negative working capital needs at 31 inventory turns per year. The more turns beyond 31 per year, the more negative the working capital needs.

36. Emert, Carol (1996), "Wal-Mart Aim: To Increase Food Market Penetration," *Supermarket News*, (June 17).

37. Emert, Carol (1996), "Wal-Mart Aim: To Increase Food Market Penetration," *Supermarket News*, (June 17); and Zwiebach, Elliot (1995), "Super Moves," *Supermarket News* (December 25).

38. Mandel, Jr., Stephen F. (1991), "A Competitive Challenge: How Supermarkets Can Get Into the Productivity Loop," *Andersen Consulting International Trends in Retailing* 8 (1), 39-40.

39. Gross margin for 1989 was listed as 30.9 in this paper. We altered the number to make it consistent with the table.

40. In Mandel (1990), for Toys 'R' Us, expense ratio was listed as 19.9 and operating margin was listed as 12.6. We altered the numbers to make them consistent with those listed in the table and so that they would add up.

41. Walters, Donna K. H. (1993), "Big Guys Rule Toy Industry Playground," *Austin American Statesman* (September 7).

42. Morgenson, Gretchen (1996), "Too Much of a Good Thing?" *Forbes* (June 3), 115.

43. Morgenson, Gretchen (1996), "Too Much of a Good Thing?" *Forbes* (June 3), 115.

44. Morgenson, Gretchen (1996), "Too Much of a Good Thing?" *Forbes* (June 3), 115.

45. Schiller, Zachary and Wendy Zellner (1992), "Clout! More and More, Retail Giants Rule the Marketplace," *Business Week*, (December 21), 67.

46. "Change at the Check-Out" (1995), *The Economist* (March 4), 4.

The Solution: Efficient Consumer Response

*With, essentially, no alternative, manufacturers and tradi-
tional format retailers joined together to pursue a series of initiatives,
collectively called Efficient Consumer Response (ECR), designed to restore traditional format retailers to competitiveness and curb the
growth of alternative format retailers. Among the ECR initiatives are
Efficient Assortment (reconsideration of the broad set of items offered
in each category), Efficient Replenishment (a move toward continuous replenishment), Efficient Promotion (a move away from the inefficiencies associated with high–low pricing), and Efficient New
Product Introductions (an attempt to curb product over-proliferation).*

*To implement these initiatives effectively, it will probably be neces-
sary to move the focus from gross profit margin to a net profit margin
in which all direct and indirect overhead costs are appropriately allocated to products using activity-based cost accounting. To stimulate
more responsible use of assets, reward systems will have to be modi-
fied. Finally, both manufacturers and distributors must completely
overhaul their organizational structures, moving strategic decision-
making authority to those people positioned at the manufacturer/
distributor interface.*

With proverbial guns to their heads, traditional format retailers joined
together with manufacturers in an attempt to survive. If these retailers
were not able to reduce operating costs dramatically and increase asset utilization, the alternative format retailers were going to drive
them out of business. If the traditional format retailers were driven
out of business, then manufacturers would become virtual puppets of
the "power retailers."

Though they had historically been bitter combatants, traditional
format retailers and manufacturers joined together in hiring consultants Kurt Salmon Associates, Inc. to formulate a road map to survival.
In their 1993 report titled *Efficient Consumer Response: Enhancing*

Consumer Value in the Grocery Industry (researched by Kurt Salmon and Associates), the Joint Industry Project on ECR did just that.

Years of acrimonious relationships had left retailers and manufacturers distrustful of one another. A set of "guiding principles" was needed to structure discussion between the trading partners. Those principles outlined in the *Efficient Consumer Response* report can be paraphrased as:

1. *Focus on providing better value to consumers.*
   Rather than myopically pursuing self-interest, the parties were going to have to consider options in which both sides gave a little so that the entire system could be improved.

2. *Move from win/lose to win/win.*
   Given the long and bitter history of the retailer–manufacturer relationship, this principle may have been the most difficult to implement. Fundamental and deeply ingrained attitudes had to be changed.

3. *Develop accurate and timely information.*
   The logical conclusion of this principle is a completely paperless system. Pricing and promotion information, invoices, and shipping notices would be communicated through EDI (electronic data interchange). Payment would be made with EFT (electronic funds transfer).

4. *Maximize value-adding processes.*
   We believe that this seemingly uncontroversial principle is actually an euphemism. The true intent here, we believe, is to move away from forward buying and diverting (non-value-adding processes). The obscurity of the original wording[1] was probably driven by the dependence of many retailers and wholesalers on income from forward buying and diverting.

5. *Develop a common and consistent performance and reward system.*
   Full implementation of the Efficient Consumer Response (ECR) initiatives will require the adoption of activity-based cost accounting and a broadening of responsibility for asset utilization.

Figure 6–1
ECR VERSUS CURRENT GROCERY: FINANCIAL RETURNS

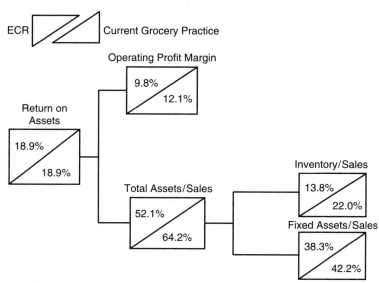

Source: *Efficient Consumer Response—Enhancing Consumer Value in the Grocery Industry,* 1993.
Reprinted with permission of the Food Marketing Institute and the Joint Industry Project on ECR.

Assuming that the trading partners could agree to the guiding principles and implement the suggested initiatives, the potential benefits were estimated to be enormous. The industry could drive out $30 billion of excess costs, eliminate 41 percent of the existing inventory, and cut cycle time (the time between the completion of the manufacturing process and the time of consumer purchase) from 104 days to 61 days.

Another way of looking at the value of the initiatives is to consider their impact on consumer prices. Assuming that all savings are passed through to consumers, the *Efficient Consumer Response* report estimates that grocery prices could be reduced 10.8 percent. Eighty percent of the reduction would come from direct cost savings in the system. Twenty percent of the reduction would come from what they term "financial savings."

These financial savings come because the players in the system agree to accept lower profit levels. The lower profit levels should be acceptable, so the consultants maintain, because total assets employed will be reduced. Hence, profits can be lowered without effecting return on assets.

Table 6–1

ECR INITIATIVE	COST SAVINGS	FINANCIAL SAVINGS	TOTAL SAVINGS
Efficient Assortment	1.3%	.2%	1.5%
Efficient Replenishment	2.8%	1.3%	4.1%
Efficient Promotion	3.5%	.8%	4.3%
Efficient Product Introduction	.9%	—	.9%
Total			10.8%

Source: Adapted from *Efficient Consumer Response–Enhancing Consumer Value in the Grocery Industry,* 1993. Reprinted with permission of the Food Marketing Institute and the Joint Industry Project on ECR.

Figure 6–1 details the consultants' reasoning. Upper triangles represent the financial situation if the ECR initiatives are fully implemented and lower triangles represent the existing financial situation in the grocery supply chain. We see that reductions in fixed assets and inventory lead to a reduction of total assets employed from 64.2 to 52.1 percent. This allows the system to lower operating profit from 12.1 to 9.8 percent while holding return on assets constant at 18.9 percent.

The *Efficient Consumer Response* report prescribes four general initiatives to achieve the savings previously discussed. Table 6-1 breaks out the savings associated with each initiative.

EFFICIENT ASSORTMENT

This initiative suggests that retailers reconsider the set of brands they offer consumers. Studies show that retailers offer too many brands and brand sizes in a category. According to Durk Jager, president and COO of Procter & Gamble:[2]

> *[In 1996, the] average supermarket has about 31,000 SKUs and only about 500—or less than 2%—move a case or more in a week (in an average store). The bottom 7,000 SKUs— almost 23% of the total—move less than one unit in a week.*
>
> *The number of SKUs stocked by the average store is estimated to have increased 20–50% in the past five years.*
>
> *During this same five-year period, the average time a consumer spends per shopping trip has declined 25%—to about 21 minutes per trip. Net, consumers are spending 25% LESS TIME to sort through 20–25% more SKUs.*

Jager illustrates the problem created by this plethora of products with a personal anecdote he recounted in his keynote address to the April 1996 Grocery Products Manufacturers Council.[3]

> I went into a grocery store not so long ago looking for a cold medicine. Now bear in mind, I was sick before I even walked into the store—but what I saw there made my head hurt even more.
>
> The first challenge I had was to find anything in the mountain of products on the shelf. The average grocery store carries 6,000 SKUs in this category—and to make matters worse, there was no sense of organization in shelf presentation.
>
> I stood there, with my head in my hand, trying to figure it out: "Is it organized by brand? Or maybe by color—all the reds in one place and the blues in another? Perhaps it's alphabetical, like a library." I started looking for a card catalog.
>
> Once I finally found the basic sub-category, I was confused by all the types of relief. I found myself saying, "I only have a stuffed up nose now, but it could get worse. Should I get something that also treats sore throat pain? How about the version that also helps with flu and body aches—you never know. Do I need one for the night? Or for day? After all, I plan to be sick all 24 hours!"
>
> There was the dizzying array of pill types; tablets, caplets, coated caplets, liquicaps, gel caps, solid gel caps (is that possible?).
>
> Finally, I had narrowed my list down to a handful of finalists. And then I was faced with pricing: Should I buy 24 tablets for $3.15? 50 caplets for $4.69? 48 gel caps for $5.79? And should I get extra strength, or just buy regular and take twice as many?
>
> I walked out of there thinking, "It's no wonder so many consumers just buy the private label. There's such a good chance they're buying the wrong thing that they might as well minimize the cash outlay."

A number of studies have shown that brands and brand sizes can be reduced without affecting sales or consumers' perceptions of variety.[4] In addition to simplifying the decision process for consumers, a cutback in SKUs in a category allows a retailer to reduce out-of-stocks, cut back on stocking frequency, and lower warehouse costs. *Progressive Grocer* reported a study[5] in which the number of alternatives in the cat box filler category was reduced from 26 to 16. There was no effect on category sales, but logistics savings drove an 87 percent increase in operating profit.

EFFICIENT REPLENISHMENT

This initiative, setting up a continuous replenishment inventory system for the industry, is expected to provide the second largest savings. In the first phase of this initiative, a manufacturer monitors withdrawals from a distributor's warehouse and automatically replenishes the stock when the inventory falls below some critical level. In the second phase, the warehouse will begin to automatically replenish individual stores based on scanned sales data. In the final phase, the two independent replenishment cycles will be melded into one system in which the manufacturer replenishes both stores and warehouse based on scanned store sales data. There are significant technological, data accuracy, and security problems involved in each phase of this process, but implementation of the first phase seems to be well underway.

Consider, for example, Procter & Gamble's history with continuous replenishment.[6] In 1985, P&G tested continuous replenishment with a moderate-sized grocery chain. This trial resulted in inventory reductions, few stockouts, and the elimination of several buyers positions for the retailer. For P&G, the new ordering process was more expensive. In 1986, P&G began a second continuous replenishment test with a large mass merchandiser. In 1988, a third test was begun with another mass merchandiser. In 1990 and 1991, three grocery chains adopted continuous replenishment with P&G; in 1992, 14 more grocery chains adopted. By July 1994, a total of 47 channel customers had adopted continuous replenishment covering 26 percent of P&G's sales volume. P&G projected that 50 percent or more of its U.S. volume would be on continuous replenishment by the end of 1995.

> *Increased retail sales were an important benefit of the [continuous replenishment] program for P&G and its distributors. Sales of P&G products through [continuous replenishment] retailers increased 4% more on average during 1993 than sales through non-[continuous replen-*

ishment] retailers. Although some of this difference could be attributed to faster-growing retailers adopting [continuous replenishment], [P&G Vice President of Customer Services, Ralph] Drayer believed that some of the gain was due to sales gained from competing products due to reduced stockouts, lower retail pricing, and expanded product selection in the store. However, even if only 1% of the 4% sales increase was due to competitive share gains, this represented a huge competitive and economic gain for P&G. One food division manager said he would "gain more market share by expanding [continuous replenishment] than through [product] line extensions."[7]

Retailers have embraced continuous replenishment. By 1996, Kroger had 126 vendor partners in their continuous replenishment program[8] and at HEB, more than 70 percent of grocery replenishment came via continuous replenishment.[9] According to a Deloitte & Touche Consulting Group study titled "Benchmarking for Success," retailers find continuous replenishment beneficial. The study suggests that the retail sector "has attained higher profit margins over the recent five-year period than it has historically. . . . According to the study, this trend indicates that retailers have been able to maintain profits in light of slowing sales growth by focusing on maximizing operating efficiencies and minimizing replenishment and inventory costs."[10]

EFFICIENT PROMOTION

The simplest way to eliminate the many promotion-related problems discussed earlier in this book would be to eliminate promotion completely. However, because many retailers and wholesalers are dependent on forward buy and diverting income, the Efficient Promotion initiative takes a more moderate position. It suggests that the structure of promotional offers be radically simplified, that effort be devoted to eliminating the confusion driving the problem of deductions (discussed earlier in this book), and that retailers and wholesalers be offered a menu of promotion alternatives. As can be seen in Table 6–1, even these half-measures hold the potential for great savings.

Unfortunately, it seems that many manufacturers have been unable or unwilling to take even these half measures. An Anderson Consulting study reports that manufacturers spent $49 billion (11% of sales) on promotions in 1994, up from $15 billion (5% of sales) in 1978.[11]

These high levels of promotional spending by manufacturers result in high levels of promotional purchases by consumers. Information Resources, Inc. (IRI) scan data for the 52-week period ending March 24, 1996 show that one-third of the dollars that consumers spent on the top 20 grocery categories was spent for products on special promotional merchandising.[12]

> *In some categories the percentage of sales riding on the coattails of promotional merchandising is staggering. An example is carbonated beverages, the largest supermarket category that IRI included in the survey, with sales of almost $11 billion. It is also the category that is most affected by promotion. Almost 71% of total supermarket sales of carbonated beverages comes when the products are being promoted.*[13]

Other supermarket categories that IRI points out as being highly influenced by promotion are:[14]

Category	% Dollars Bought on Promotion
Carbonated soft drinks	70%
Suntan products	65
Frozen pizza	51
Canned ham	44
Wine coolers	44
Crackers	43
Cookies	43
Chips and snacks	43
Stuffing mixes	41
Refrigerated juices	41

EFFICIENT PRODUCT INTRODUCTION

This initiative addresses the concern raised earlier in this book about the alarming number of so-called new products launched each year, and the fact that most of these "new" products are little more than line extensions. According to the *Efficient Consumer Response* report:[15]

> *Suppliers' estimates of the excess cost to the grocery system in the product development and introduction process range as high as 4% of net sales. These costs include:*
> - *All development and introduction costs associated with failed products, including products canceled before introduction as well as products withdrawn after launching;*
> - *Excess costs incurred in launching new successful products, principally excess manufacturing, warehousing and distribution costs due to an initial massive inventory buildup needed for introductory deals and special offers (e.g., free goods).*

Consistent with the *Efficient Consumer Response* report, we have testimony from Nabisco and Procter & Gamble.[16]

> *H. John Greeniaus, CEO of new-product star Nabisco, estimates that the company's 77 new products [in 1995] were about 20% too many. More than a quarter of the $428 million pretax restructuring charge it took in June [1996] will be used to eliminate more than 300 of the items it now carries, such as single-serving sizes of Lorna Doones and king-size packages of Nutter Butter cookies.*
>
> *. . . Weeding out the losers doesn't stop with product extensions. To instill greater financial discipline—and measure the results based on the contribution of each business to shareholder return—P&G has tossed out brands that aren't leaders. Since [1995], it has gotten rid of 11 brands from Lestoil household cleaner to Lava soap.*
>
> *. . . Not only is Procter shucking unproductive items and brands, but it is also practicing what [President and COO Durk] Jager calls birth control for new products, by charging managers' budgets when they launch new items. "There is a real push in the company to do fewer, bigger things," one P&G executive says.*

In summary, Manly Molpus, president and CEO of Grocery Manufacturers Association, evaluates the industry's implementation of ECR as ". . . good, solid, steady progress."[17] He goes on to say that ". . . there's no question that almost every company in this industry 'buys in' to ECR. The only question . . . is how long it will take to get there. . . . [T]here is an emphasis . . . on the ways specific dollars are being invested. Instead of being invested in shotgun-style promotions, as they were in the past, they are being invested in the most effective way possible."[18]

The successful implementation of these ECR initiatives is believed to hinge on two further factors: adoption of activity-based cost accounting and the development of category management. Next, we will discuss these and related topics.

ACTIVITY-BASED COST ACCOUNTING[19]

Traditional accounting systems were designed more than 50 years ago to deal with smokestack industries. Because direct labor was such a large proportion of total costs, other "fixed" costs were allocated to products in proportion to the amount of direct labor the product required. Accounting systems today tend to follow this same form. A leading accounting scholar refers to this as the "peanut butter approach to accounting." Under this approach, you spread a "big glob" of "fixed" overhead across products, as a percentage of purchase price, expected sales, or some similar measure. For example, a supermarket with 20 percent operating expense might mark up every product by 20 percent.[20]

Traditional accounting looks at an enterprise as a collection of departments (human resources, purchasing, maintenance, etc.) that make products. Activity-based costing looks at an enterprise as a collection of individuals performing activities (training employees, processing purchase orders, fixing machines, etc.) to satisfy customer demands.[21]

A *Fortune* article points out that:[22]

> *Old-style accounting identifies costs according to the category of expense. The new math tells you that your real costs are what you pay for the different tasks your employees perform. Find that out, and you will manage better.*

They illustrate their perspective with the example at the top of the next page:[23]

It is easy to see in the example that activity-based costing provides much more diagnostic information than does the traditional accounting. It is this sort of information about activities that is needed to appropriately implement ECR.

For example, Spartan, a wholesaler in Grand Rapids, Michigan, used activity-based costing to develop a new freight rate system. They estimated the cost of each of the freight-related activities like yard time, cost per mile to the store, and cost per minute at the store.[24]

Traditional Accounting	
Salaries	$371,917
Fringes	118,069
Supplies	76,745
Fixed Costs	23,614
Total	$590,345
Activity-Based Costing	
Process sales order	$144,846
Source parts	$136,320
Expedite supplier order	$72,143
Expedite internal processing	$49,945
Resolve supplier quality	$47,599
Expedite customer orders	$27,747
Schedule intracompany sales	$17,768
Request engineering change	$16,704
Resolve problems	$16,648
Schedule parts	$15,390
Total	$590,345

They found that it cost them 67¢ per minute to have a truck at a store. When they began charging their retailer customers that rate, the average time for the truck to stay at a store fell from 1 hour and 10 minutes to 38 minutes. The retailers reorganized their back rooms and reduced inventory and labor. These changes drove further cost reductions.

Of course change is never universally well received. "When we first did this we had stores calling us saying, 'This is terrible, we can't do it,'" [Spartan's CEO Patrick] Quinn said, recalling a retailer who was unloading his deliveries by hand.

"We have one customer who took between seven and seven-and-a-half hours to unload a truck," he said. "He didn't have a forklift and wasn't too happy with the new system.

*"But when he called up I told him, 'Put a pencil to it
and, at 67 cents a minute, figure out exactly how long
your payback period is if you buy a forklift.'*

*"The savings for the warehouse have been immense. Dri-
vers' wages during the initial phase of the new policy were
reduced by $195,000."*[25]

The inefficient practices that have grown up in the packaged goods
industry spiraled out of control, in part, because traditional accounting data did not provide the measures needed to identify those practices that give rise to non-value-adding activities. Activity-based
costing provides such measures.

EVA: ECONOMIC VALUE ADDED

Unfortunately, a better understanding of cost alone is not sufficient to
untangle the mess into which the packaged goods industry has
evolved. This industry must also reconsider the way in which assets
are utilized. Think back to Chapter 2, The Broader Revolution. We
saw that responsibility for asset utilization was pulled into the hands
of top management during the post-World War II era of conglomer-
ates. Managers running operating divisions were allocated assets and
charged, simply, with maximizing profits. Inevitably, this led to the
inefficient use of assets.

Evidence of the vulnerability caused by inefficient asset use can be
seen in the advantage gained by warehouse club stores as presented
in Chapter 5, The Market Adjusts. We saw that clubs' bare bones operations allowed them to operate on fixed assets of 9.7 percent of sales
while traditional grocery devoted 14.8 percent of sales to fixed assets.
Even worse for traditional grocery, the clubs' inventory policy allowed
clubs to sell products before they paid for them, giving clubs a negative working capital need (–.7%). Traditional grocery, with huge forward buy inventories, had 1.7 percent of sales tied up in working
capital. As shown in Figure 5–6, the clubs' ability to generate similar
earnings levels with significantly fewer assets made clubs a much
more attractive investment opportunity than traditional grocery.

Driving responsibility for asset utilization back down into the organization is a theme that is beginning to echo throughout the economy. Adopting a model that holds operational managers responsible
for asset utilization (called "EVA: Economic Value Added," or "Con-
trollable Earnings") has been credited with driving Briggs & Stratton's

stock price from the mid-20s to near 80 in a year and a half and with driving Coca-Cola's stock price from $3 to $43 in 12 years.[26] A *Fortune* article describes the impact of this shift at Quaker Oats:[27]

> *Until Quaker adopted the concept in 1991, its businesses had one overriding goal—increasing quarterly earnings. To do it, they guzzled capital. They offered sharp price discounts at the end of each quarter, so plants ran overtime turning out huge shipments of Gatorade, Rice-A-Roni, 100% Natural Cereal, and other products. Managers led the late rush, since their bonuses depended on raising operating profits each quarter.*
>
> *This is the pernicious practice known as trade loading (because it loads up the trade, or retailers, with product), and many consumer products companies are finally admitting it damages long-term returns. An important reason is that it demands so much capital. Pumping up sales requires many warehouses (capital) to hold vast temporary inventories (more capital). But who cared? Quaker operating businesses paid no charge for capital in internal accounting, so they barely noticed. It took EVA to spotlight the problem.*

THE NEW RETAILER STRUCTURE: CATEGORY MANAGEMENT

In order to implement the ECR initiatives, retailers must rethink their organizational structure. The *Efficient Consumer Response* report (1993) contrasted the traditional view of retail buying with the more sophisticated "category management" perspective that they advocate as depicted in Figure 6–2.

Note first that the traditional view is focused on profit margin while the category management view is focused on return on investment (putting responsibility for asset utilization back in the hands of those who run the business.)

Second, the traditional perspective has as its focus the SKU (stock-keeping unit[28]) while category management focuses on the category as a whole. In the traditional perspective, each SKU that is offered to a retailer is evaluated independently. Having made decisions at the SKU level, the retailer might combine a particular vendor's SKUs to evaluate the vendor, or combine SKUs into subcategories to evaluate those entities. Categories are built up in this way.

Figure 6-2
EFFICIENT CONSUMER RESPONSE CONTRAST TRADITIONAL
VIEW VERSUS CATEGORY MANAGEMENT VIEW

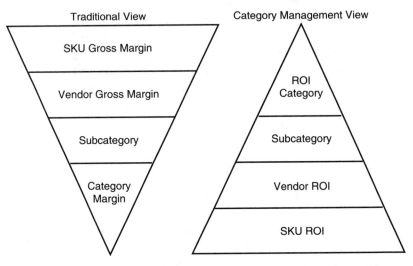

Source: *Efficient Consumer Response–Enhancing Consumer Value in the Grocery Industry,* 1993. Reprinted with permission of the Food Marketing Institute and the Joint Industry Project on ECR.

In the category management perspective, the category is assigned a strategic role to play, and then it is evaluated relative to that role. Individual SKUs that might seem quite attractive when evaluated in a vacuum, might be much less so when viewed in the context of the category as a whole. Recall the example of the cat box filler category mentioned earlier in this chapter. A retailer reduced its cat box filler offering from 26 to 16 SKUs. Category sales were unchanged, but operating profit increased 87 percent because of reduced out-of-stocks, lower warehouse costs, and so forth.

At this point, the science of category management is not very well developed. Harris and McPartland (1993, pp. 5–6) tell us that:

Category management consists of three interrelated elements.

First, it is a philosophy for strategically managing a retailer's or a supplier's business that recognizes categories as strategic business units for the purpose of planning and achieving sales and profit goals. . . .

The second element of the definition of category management is that it is a process through which retailers and suppliers jointly develop strategic category plans. These plans, usually set on an annual basis, set clearly defined strategies and financial performance measures at the category level. . . .

The third element of the definition is that category management is an organizational concept that dictates the integration of responsibility for buying and merchandising decisions. This integration is essential to allow category managers to effectively allocate the assets of product inventory, space and customer traffic.

"The organizational design—in terms of job responsibilities, organizational structures, communication mechanisms and job performance measures—must facilitate this requirement. It is this integrated responsibility for buying and selling in conjunction with a process for strategic category planning that most clearly distinguishes category management from more traditional approaches to managing the buying and merchandising function.

HEB, a grocery chain in South Texas, is widely acknowledged to be the industry leader in the development of category management.[29] Harvey McCoy, vice president of category management for HEB, said that, "Among the benefits . . . [that] HEB has realized [from category management] are a 40 percent reduction in SKUs, double-digit growth and increased profits."[30] Despite these impressive results, HEB has not yet exploited the full potential of category management. Referring to their development of category management, McCoy says, "On a 10-point scale, we're at about 2.5."[31]

According to Chris Hoyt, president of Hoyt & Co., a Stamford, Connecticut-based marketing and consulting firm:

. . .*[C]ategory management is moving at a "painfully slow" pace.*

"Despite all the millions of words put into category management," Hoyt said, "its progress is very slow.

"In its purest sense, category management is wonderful, but the fact is, only 13 or 14 retailers are investing in it," Hoyt said.

Among those retailers that Hoyt made sure to mention and praise, are [HEB], Hannaford Bros., Schnucks, Shaw's and Tops, which is owned by Ahold.

According to Hoyt, HEB deserves high praise for its policy of hiring highly educated and intensely trained employees.

"For category management to succeed," Hoyt said, "we need retailers to think like HEB." [32]

THE NEW MANUFACTURER STRUCTURE: CUSTOMER TEAMS

For manufacturers to be able to work effectively with new, well-educated, strategically focused category managers on the retail side, the manufacturers' organizations must change, too.

The prototype of this new manufacturer structure is the team that Procter & Gamble put together in the late 1980s to work with Wal-Mart. According to Lou Pritchett, who was Procter & Gamble's vice president of sales at that time:

. . . Ever since the 1940's, P&G's strategy had been driven by two strategies: P&G product superiority, and P&G advertising superiority.

Little else mattered. Three generations of Procter managers had grown up in this environment; the concept of top management having anything to do with customers was totally foreign. [33]

In 1987, Pritchett broke that tradition and, on a canoe trip with Sam Walton, laid the groundwork for developing a "customer team."

[P&G] brought in representatives of most of our major departments, including sales, marketing, systems, manufacturing, distribution, and finance, to devise new ways of doing business with their counterparts at Wal-Mart in each specific segment of business. This "partnering" approach proved vastly cost-effective and productive in every way for both Procter & Gamble and Wal-Mart. Initially, we assigned twelve of our people and moved them to live permanently in Bentonville. . . . Eventually, Procter & Gamble would have more than seventy-five executives and employees living in Bentonville. And basically, we invented the whole partnership as we went along and it worked out beautifully." [34]

As Procter & Gamble has gone on to form cross-functional teams to work with other big retail and wholesale customers, other manufacturers have followed. In January of 1995, Kraft Foods announced that it would establish 300 customer business teams. According to Richard Lenny, senior vice president of sales and customer service at Kraft Foods:

> [Kraft Foods'] model calls for headquarters selling and retail execution for each account to come under the supervision of one team manager. . . . Each team leader is supported by as many as five category managers, depending on account size, who participate in the headquarters sales. The team is supported by a retail sales force to execute at store level. . . .
>
> In support of the account teams, the new Kraft Foods field organization will be organized into approximately 20 geographic regions. Those will have decentralized, cross-functional resources to support the account teams. [35]

In June of 1995, General Mills announced that its ". . . current sales and service organization will be streamlined into 10 management centers with responsibility for all regional and local customer-focused teams, and 12 national account teams."[36] According to John McMillan, a securities analyst with Prudential Securities in New York:

> . . . General Mills is following in the footsteps of Procter & Gamble Co., Cincinnati, and Kraft Foods, Northfield, Ill., which are both implementing customer-driven sales forces.
>
> 'The idea is to get closer to the customer and give more customized service.' [37]

According to McKinsey:

> Successful marketers will go well beyond this important first step and convert their sales managers into general managers. They will reward them for customer profitability, make them responsible for leading cross-functional teams dedicated to major customers, and ensure that they are capable of making substantive decisions about how the company will meet its customers' demands. A recent McKinsey survey of developments in consumer products salesforces confirms this trend: leading companies are building alliances with their customers, pushing functions and resources into the field . . . , and managing their salesforces on profitability, not just revenues. [38]

Endnotes

1. From the *Efficient Consumer Response* (1993) report, p. 2, the exact wording is as follows: "Product must flow with a maximization of value-adding processes from the end of production/packing to the consumer's basket so as to ensure the right product is available at the right time."

2. Jager, Durk I., president and COO of Procter & Gamble, "General Session—Opening Remarks," presentation to Joint Industry ECR Conference, Chicago Hilton & Towers, March 21, 1996.

3. Jager, Durk I., president and COO of Procter & Gamble, "Focusing on the Consumer: The Operative Word in Efficient Consumer Response," keynote address, Grocery Products Manufacturers Council, April 10, 1996, Toronto.

4. Willard Bishop Consulting, Ltd. (1993*), Variety or Duplication: A Process to Know Where You Stand*, Food Marketing Institute Report, Washington, DC; Xavier Dreze, Stephen J. Joch, and Mary E. Purk (1994), "Shelf Management and Price Elasticity," University of Chicago Working Paper (January); Susan Broniarczyk, Wayne Hoyer, and Leigh McAlister (1996), "Consumer's Perceptions of the Assortment Offered in a Grocery Category: The Influence of Number of Items and Heuristics," University of Texas Working Paper (October).

5. Krum, Franklin (1994), "Quantum Leap," *Progressive Grocer* (January), 413.

6. Clark, Theodore H. (1995), "Procter & Gamble: Improving Consumer Value Through Process Redesign," Harvard Business School Case 9-195-126, 4–6.

7. Clark, Theodore H. (1995), "Procter & Gamble: Improving Consumer Value Through Process Redesign," Harvard Business School Case 9-195-126, 6.

8. Mathews, Ryan (1996), "Partnerships and Progress," *Progressive Grocer* (June), 31.

9. Garry, Michael (1996), "HEB: The Tech Leader," *Progressive Grocer* (May), 66.

10. "ECR and Partnering Go Hand in Hand" (1996), *Grocery Marketing* (May), 8.

11. Schiller, Zachary, Greg Burns, and Karen Lowry Miller (1996), "Make It Simple," *Business Week* (September 9), 99, 102.

12. Litwak, David (1996), "What Price Sales Glory," *Supermarket Business* (July), 27.

13. Litwak, David (1996), "What Price Sales Glory," *Supermarket Business* (July), 27.

14. Litwak, David (1996), "What Price Sales Glory," *Supermarket Business* (July), 35.

15. *Efficient Consumer Response* (1993) report, 88–9.

16. Schiller, Zachary, Greg Burns, and Karen Lowry Miller (1996), "Make It Simple," *Business Week* (September 9), 99.

17. Mathews, Ryan (1996), "Partnerships and Progress," *Progressive Grocer* (June), 31.

18. Mathews, Ryan (1996), "Partnerships and Progress," *Progressive Grocer* (June), 32.

19. DPP, Direct Product Profitability, is an accounting mechanism popularized in the grocery industry to better allocate direct overhead costs (e.g., costs in the warehouse of receiving, storing, selecting, and loading a product). Activity-based cost accounting goes beyond DPP to also better allocate indirect overhead costs (e.g., costs to process invoices, plan space, manage promotional events).

20. These quotes are attributed to Professor Robert S. Kaplan, Harvard University, in Ryan Mathews (1993), "Relearning the 'ABC' of Business," *Grocery Marketing* (August), 6, 10.

21. Pare, Terence P. (1993), "A New Tool for Managing Costs," *Fortune* (June 14), 124.

22. Pare, Terence P. (1993), "A New Tool for Managing Costs," *Fortune* (June 14), 124.

23. This contrast was drawn from Terence P. Pare (1993), "A New Tool for Managing Costs," *Fortune* (June 14), 124.

24. This anecdote is drawn from Ryan Mathews (1993), "'Rudimentary' ABC Efforts Yield Big Results for Spartan," *Grocery Marketing* (August), 12.

25. Mathews, Ryan (1993), "'Rudimentary' ABC Efforts Yield Big Results for Spartan," *Grocery Marketing* (August), 12.

26. Tully, Shawn (1993), "The Real Key to Creating Wealth," *Fortune* (September 20), 38–50.

27. Tully, Shawn (1993), "The Real Key to Creating Wealth," *Fortune* (September 20), 48.

28. A "stockkeeping unit" is the smallest unit of inventory measurement. Any given brand might account for several stockkeeping units, as each flavor, size, form, etc. of the brand would have its own identification code.

29. "Manufacturers Rate Retailers" (1995), *Supermarket Business* (October).

30. Lowe, Kimberly (1995), "Retailers Offered a Full Plate of Category Management," *Grocery Marketing*, (June), 14–7.

31. Lowe, Kimberly (1995), "Retailers Offered a Full Plate of Category Management," *Grocery Marketing*, (June), 14–7.

32. Lowe, Kimberly (1995), "Rating Progress Through Category Management," *Grocery Marketing*, (May) , 22–5.

33. Pritchett, Lou (1995), *Stop Paddling & Start Rocking the Boat*, HarperBusiness, 25.

34. Pritchett, Lou (1995), *Stop Paddling & Start Rocking the Boat*, HarperBusiness, 31–2.

35. Tenser, James (1995), "Realigned Kraft Planning 300 Dedicated Teams," *Brand Marketing*, (January 16), 1, 4.

36. Turcsik, Richard (1995), "General Mills Shuffle Is Called a Good Move," *Supermarket News*, (June 5), 27–8.

37. Turcsik, Richard (1995), "General Mills Shuffle Is Called a Good Move," *Supermarket News*, (June 5), 27–8

38. George, Michael, Anthony Freeling, and David Court (1994), "Reinventing the Marketing Organization," *The McKinsey Quarterly*, 4, 43–62.

7

The Shape of the Future

The larger forces driving change in all industries (globalization, information technology, and flattening organizational structures), combined with the inefficient practices that have evolved in the packaged goods industry and the fundamental shift in socioeconomic factors that underpin the traditional packaged goods distribution system, dictate radical change. To survive and thrive in this tumultuous industry, it is critical to maintain an unflinching focus on understanding and serving the consumer.

Considering the many and powerful forces at work in the packaged goods industry, it is not surprising that we see downsizing, consolidation, bankruptcies, and complete redefinition of jobs. The larger forces at work in the economy as a whole (globalization of markets, spread of information technology and computer networks, and the dismantling of hierarchy) guarantee fiercely intense competition, powerful customers, and endlessly changing organizational designs.

The pain of becoming flexible enough to deal with these larger forces in the economy is exacerbated by the fact that this industry has developed a collection of badly inefficient practices. The high–low pricing that manufacturers initiated in the 1970s to protect themselves from any possible future price freezes marked the beginning of runaway trade promotion spending. Many retailers and wholesalers now depend on low price periods for speculative purchases (forward buying) and arbitrage (diverting) to maintain profitability.

One result of these practices is an estimated $100 billion dollars worth of excess inventory sitting idle in forward buy warehouses, or worse yet, cruising the American highways as a part of a diverting deal. Further, the increased incidence of handling products brought on by forward buying and diverting probably contributes to the growth in the cost of damaged and unsalable products.

Manufacturers have made the problem even worse by creating ever more complex selling terms and contracts in an attempt to curb forward buying and diverting. The result of these complex arrangements is a system in which one out of every three invoices contains an error that requires expensive manual intervention.

In addition to the burden imposed by these inefficient practices, the fundamental socioeconomic factors that underpin the traditional packaged goods marketing organizational structure have eroded. Television advertising no longer provides an affordable venue to reach and persuade a mass market. The cost of network television advertising has grown faster than inflation, despite the explosion in cable viewing alternatives that has driven network viewing shares down. Consumers are too busy and too cynical to be persuaded by advertising. Consumers are so diverse that there no longer exists a single, "mass," market. Finally, the widespread use of VCRs and remote control devices now allows consumers to avoid any advertising to which they might otherwise be vulnerable.

All of this is happening at a time when lucrative promotional offers drive consumers to switch around among the outpouring of "me-too" brands. Once consumers have tried several brands and realized that there are no real differences between brands, consumer brand loyalty erodes.

The sum of these changes has created "opportunities" in the marketplace. Retailers have leveraged the decline in national brand loyalty to launch high quality, and successful, private label brands. Wal-Mart has exploited the relative inefficiency of traditional format retailers to establish a position in the grocery industry. Traditional format retailers and manufacturers have banded together, through the Efficient Consumer Response initiatives, to hold Wal-Mart at bay.

All players in this industry are changing and will continue to change. As retailers and wholesalers move seriously into category management, they will become less tactically focused on the "deals" offered by manufacturers and more strategically focused on meeting the needs of their shoppers. Their organizations will change as they bring in more analytically sophisticated people who think and act strategically. These talented people will have other, fast-track career options. To hire and retain such people, retailers and wholesalers will have to allow them to move quickly through the hierarchy, even though "it has never been done that way before."

Similar changes are occurring for manufacturers. P&G's president and chief operating officer, Durk Jager, has gone on record[1] as saying that, as unthinkable as it was 10 years ago, P&G's senior executives will now get out in the field on a regular basis to try to understand retail and wholesale customers. Further, he suggests that this is a trend that is sweeping the industry as a whole. As profit responsibility moves toward the customer-focused, multifunctional teams stationed in the field, the people needed for those teams will be different from the people traditionally hired into sales jobs. These analytically sophisticated, strategic thinkers must also be allowed to move quickly through the hierarchy even though "it has never been done that way before."

Many people in the packaged goods industry today will not be there tomorrow. Many firms in the packaged goods industry today will not be there tomorrow. Those people and firms who do survive will be the ones who can retain a focus on serving consumers while freeing themselves from all other prejudices about how business should be done.

To effectively serve consumers, one must understand consumers. In Part Two of this book, we review findings from nearly 200 academic studies focused on consumers' motivation and behavior when shopping. We first consider how consumers decide where to shop and what to buy. We then look at the ways that consumers react to marketing interventions in the shopping environment.

Endnotes

1. Mathews, Ryan (1995), "In the Trenches," *Progressive Grocer,* (March), 30–36.

Part Two

Consumers' Grocery Shopping Behavior

8

How Do Consumers Decide Where to Purchase Groceries?

In this chapter, we begin by defining what a supermarket is. Times have changed greatly from when groceries were purchased from the neighborhood mom-and-pop grocery store. Today, there are eleven different supermarket formats in the United States. Here we describe each of these formats, and include a discussion of the emerging possibilities for supermarket shopping on the Internet.

We then examine the various factors consumers consider when deciding which supermarkets they want to patronize. Although different groups of consumers may rate different factors as important, there are some common trends across all consumers. We also look at consumers' general shopping behavior. How often does the average consumer go supermarket shopping? Are consumers loyal to one supermarket, or do they tend to visit more than one?

Because consumers' loyalties to supermarkets are divided, and because there are usually many different supermarkets in one geographic area, the supermarket business is very competitive. In recent years, supermarkets have made use of aggressive in-store marketing strategies to draw consumers into the stores and to encourage consumers to buy more while they are there.

Finally, not only are supermarkets facing competition from other supermarkets, but they have also been losing customers to other types of retailers, namely, mass merchandisers and, in some cases, category killers (e.g., Toys 'R' Us, Petco). Recently, supermarkets have focused on trying to persuade consumers to purchase non-food products in supermarkets rather than in alternative formats.

TYPES OF SUPERMARKETS

What is a supermarket? The answer used to be simple—the neighborhood grocery store. The Great Atlantic and Pacific Company, or A&P as it is known today, was one of the first supermarket chains, beginning business in New York City in 1859.[1] As A&P has changed over the years, so has the supermarket business in general. Although A&P still operates conventional supermarkets, known as A&P, Super-fresh, Kohl's, Waldbaum, Dominion, or Farmer Jack (the names vary in different regions), the chain has followed the general trend in the supermarket business, and offers different supermarket formats for different types of shopping needs.[2]

Today, there are twelve basic food retailing formats in the United States.[3] As shown in Figure 8–1,[4] consumers' perceptions of super-markets can be classified based on two key dimensions. First, su-permarkets differ depending upon how much variety, or choice, is offered. Variety is defined by how many product categories the store has, how extensive the selection is in each of these categories, and the quality and nature of the choices within the categories (e.g., Are there gourmet or exotic options? Are all the major national brands present?). Second, consumers classify supermarkets based on their pricing strategies, which in turn are based on retailers' gross margins: high margins mean premium pricing, low margins mean economic pricing. In the center of this figure are the tradi-tional format retailers (*conventional supermarkets* and *mom and pop* stores) that are rapidly fading from the scene as the alternative format retailers (e.g., clubs and supercenters) offer better value propositions. The figure provides four basic groupings of the new supermarket formats.

Missing from this map is any recognition of how grocery shopping on the Internet may affect consumers' perceptions of supermarkets. Although still a very small part of overall grocery shopping today, it is possible that sometime in the future, electronic shopping may be-come more prevalent.

Premium Price Supermarkets with Extensive Product Selection

Supermarkets in this quadrant, like A&P's Futurestores, place an em-phasis on service, quality, and expanded categories such as pre-pre-pared dishes, salad bars, and full-service meat and seafood counters. The *superstore* is bigger than the traditional supermarket, and usually has a larger selection of fresh products and non-food items. The *com-bination store* combines a superstore and a drugstore under the same roof with common check-out cash registers. In these stores, the drug-store section represents at least 25 percent of the selling area and at least 15 percent of sales.

Figure 8–1
CONSUMER'S PERCEPTUAL MAP OF SUPERMARKETS

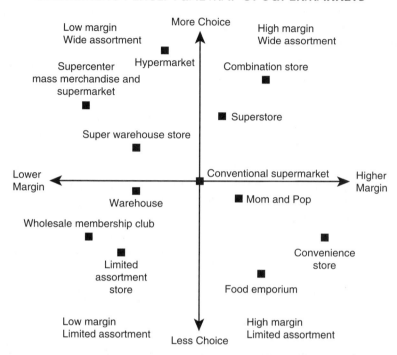

Source: Adapted from "Superstore Formats of the Future," *Progressive Grocer*, Food Marketing Institute, Washington, D.C. (December 1986 and April 1987). Used with permission.

Premium Price Supermarkets with Limited Product Selection

Like A&P's Food Emporium, the *food emporiums* tend to have a wide selection of fresh products in special displays and selected grocery items, but they do not have as wide a selection of non-food items as the superstores. These food emporiums operate as gourmet stores and place a particular emphasis on health-connected products.

There are some stores that have extended the "fresh" image to new heights. For example, H-E-B Marketplace in San Antonio or the Central Market in Austin, both owned by H.E.B. Grocery Co. of San Antonio, Texas, are like indoor farmer's markets. There is a bakery, a butcher, and a café all under one roof. The bakeries make 10,000 doughnuts a day and prepare over 25 different breads. Raw fish and fresh seafood are flown in daily.[5]

Whole Foods Markets in Austin, Texas started as a health food store, and its history is still evident in its merchandising. Quality standards are listed on signs throughout the store, and there are other signs explaining the nutritional value of specific products. Shoppers are encouraged to sample anything they want. The paper products carried are environmentally correct, no dyes, perfumes, phosphates, or chlorine. Similarly, Fresh Fields (originally headquartered in Rockville, Maryland, but in 1996 bought by Whole Foods) carries only foods that are free of preservatives and artificial colors, flavors, and sweeteners. In the produce department of a Fresh Fields supermarket almost every item is labeled with its calories and nutrients, and with information on how to choose and store the produce.[6]

Convenience stores have high prices but limited product assortments. A 1988 study found that although 92 percent of American shoppers do most of their shopping in supermarkets, 35 percent say they do some food shopping in convenience stores.[7] Convenience stores are generally used for fill-in purchases, fast food, and impulse purchases. Historically, the convenience store has had its typical customer, the 18- to 30-year-old blue collar male, but the trend is for a broader appeal. Changes in modern convenience stores include improved parking and lighting, and more competitive pricing. Some convenience stores are also beginning to offer gourmet foods-to-go, video rentals, and banking services.[8]

Economy-Priced Supermarkets with Limited Product Selection

Other supermarkets tend to focus on low price rather than on service. The *warehouse store* is one in which personnel, service, and design costs are reduced by offering bare minimums. Many items are sold only in bulk sizes and product categories are not broadly stocked. Because services tend to be limited in these stores, consumers generally use them for stock-up and routine purchases.

Wholesale clubs, such as the Price Club, also have lower prices and limited services and selection. In these types of stores, consumers have to pay an annual membership fee, generally under $50, to shop. Finally, there are the *limited assortment stores,* such as Aldi in Chicago, that are combinations of convenience and warehouse stores. These stores offer a smaller assortment than regular supermarkets, reduced service, and generally feature lower prices.

Economy-Priced Supermarkets with Wide Product Selection

The last type of supermarkets are those that offer a wide product selection, but still feature lower prices. *Hypermarkets*, which incorporate food and non-food products at discount prices, are popular in Europe but not as popular in the United States. Some experts suggest that they do not work as well in the United States because the American consumer is not used to shopping for food and big ticket items, like furniture or bicycles, in the same store. The American consumer shops for non-food items in malls, department stores, or mass merchandisers—each of which offers more variety in any particular product category than does the hypermarket.[9]

Superwarehouse stores, like A&P's Savacenter, are larger than regular warehouses and may include fresh and pre-prepared foods as well. A&P's Savacenter has a promotional character and a heavy price orientation. They are built in neighborhoods where the competition is primarily discount centers and warehouses.

Supercenters are discount stores, such as Wal-Mart or Kmart, that have added on a supermarket. They offer more choice than combination stores, but less than hypermarkets. They are lower priced than any except the clubs. Unlike clubs though, consumers do not have to buy in bulk. When Wal-Mart converts a mass merchandise store to include a supermarket, their non-foods business generally increases by 30 to 50 percent,[10] thus many consumers are welcoming the opportunity to cross shop.

Supermarket Shopping on the Internet

Food shopping on the Internet is not something that is customarily done by most consumers, but there is evidence that it may become more common. One of the most successful Internet grocery shopping outlets is Chicago-based Peapod (www.peapod.com). This service, initiated in 1989, is an on-line grocery shopping and delivery service. In 1996, Peapod had more than 20,000 subscribers (over 80% of them women and 89% college-educated). These shoppers mostly shop in the evenings and spend an average of 37 minutes on line deciding which groceries to purchase. There is access, just by clicking a mouse, to over 20,000 grocery and drugstore items that are ultimately delivered to the consumer's house. The service currently operates in Chicago, San Francisco, Columbus, and Boston, where Peapod has made arrangements with local supermarkets, such as Jewel/Osco in Chicago or Safeway in San Francisco.

Shopping by computer, or virtual shopping, differs from shopping in an actual physical location. In a virtual supermarket, consumers can shop in a traditional way by traveling down "aisles" and stopping to explore specific product categories. But in a virtual supermarket, consumers can also shop in nontraditional ways. Shoppers can sort items in the store by price, by nutritional content, by brand name, or by what they bought last time. Consumers who have shopped at Peapod say that they are less likely to purchase on impulse, and comparison shopping is easier.

Although Peapod is probably the most well-known Internet service, there are other alternatives. Bethesda, Maryland-based Shoppers Express lets customers order groceries through America On-Line. Grocery clerks in local supermarkets fill the orders and deliver them. Shoppers Express is basically a middleman connecting the computer user to the local grocery store.

Smart Foods Co-op, originally started in 1980 as a MIT student food co-op, is another alternative. Advertising themselves as the "first supermarket on the Internet," they arrange to receive their customers' orders and deliver the groceries to their homes. Unlike Peapod, they specifically advertise their service as low-priced, in keeping with their original co-op image.

Individual supermarkets focusing on premium quality and extensive selection, such as H-E-B in Texas, Piggly Wiggly in Tennessee, or Ramey's Supermarket in Mississippi and Alabama, also have a presence on the Internet. These individual supermarkets have created Web pages where they feature new items, sponsor contents and sweepstakes, provide history and culture of their supermarket, and prepare recipes and entertaining ideas as a service for their customers.

These differences in the physical supermarkets, and the differences in their virtual counterparts on the computer, have evolved because of the need to respond to the heterogeneity in customer demands. As the supermarket business becomes more competitive, there is a greater focus on the different needs of the consumers and more importance is placed on understanding how consumers decide where to shop.

HOW DO CONSUMERS DECIDE WHERE TO SHOP?

Consumer Reports surveyed 10,000 readers about their supermarket shopping habits.[11] They found that the most important factor in choosing a supermarket was location, location, location (where location is defined as closeness to home). After location, then product/brand variety and price were also considered.

These results are consistent across many different studies. Another study found that distance, low prices, quality of products sold, and atmosphere tended to be the chief variables that explained which grocery stores were chosen by consumers.[12] Even studies across countries, such as the United States, Canada, the Netherlands, and the United Kingdom, find that, in general, the chief variables that explain grocery store patronage are location, convenience, low price, fast check-out, friendly courteous service, best weekly specials, and shopping environment.[13]

However, when price gaps between formats become very large, price may begin to drive the "where to shop" decision. As shown earlier in Figure 5–4, the alternative formats that were competing on lower prices absorbed all growth in grocery sales from 1986 to 1991, suggesting that price had been a strong motivating factor.

Importance of Various Factors Differ by Consumer Group

Although there are some key variables that all shoppers consider in choosing stores, the relative importance of the different factors does vary for different groups of consumers.

Demographics make a difference in consumer preferences. Older shoppers rate low price as most important, followed by atmosphere and availability of coupon promotions. Baby boomers tend to value the quality of goods as most important, followed by distance and ease of writing checks.[14] For two-income families, the definition of location of the store needs to include distance from work as well as distance from home,[15] in order to have this variable emerge as important.

International differences mean that culture matters too. Consumers in European markets, such as the United Kingdom and the Netherlands, place less importance on location than do consumers in the United States and Canada, although location is still an important criterion for Europeans. Also, in the United Kingdom, the most important determinant of store choice is low overall prices, while in the Netherlands it is a pleasant shopping environment.[16]

The "Clientele Effect"

The marketing strategies that supermarkets use affect how consumers will choose where to shop. This is known as the "clientele effect."[17] For example, if a supermarket chain features high price reductions in its advertising, more frequent price cuts, and more in-store displays, then more promotion-sensitive customers are drawn into the store. On the other hand, if a supermarket chain is known as a higher price chain, then fewer promotion sensitive consumers are drawn to the store.

These observations were also made in the *Consumer Reports* study. *Consumer Reports* found that loyal shoppers of supermarkets that feature low prices, such as Food Lion, Shop-Rite, Lucky, Meijer, and Pathmark, tend to view price as the critical variable. On the other hand, supermarkets such as Harris-Teeter that cultivate a fresh foods image tend to draw shoppers who believe good produce departments are an important consideration. Publix, whose motto is "where shopping is a pleasure," tends to draw shoppers who think courteous service is a must in a supermarket.

Consumers Shop at More Than One Supermarket

Do consumers tend to shop at only one supermarket? Most evidence says no. Shoppers are aware of differences among supermarkets, even within the same chain and the same format,[18] and they plan their shopping needs around which store they are visiting when.

The average American household makes 2.2 visits to a supermarket per week. Over 80 percent of these households shop less than once a week in their most-preferred store. Approximately 10 percent are very loyal to their favorite store, visiting them on average almost two times per week.[19]

Consumers go shopping for different reasons.[20] Sometimes a consumer goes to the supermarket to make a regular or major shopping trip. These regular shopping trips are made more or less on a weekly basis, generally at the consumer's favorite supermarket, and more money is spent on these trips.[21] At other times, a consumer will run to the store for a quick, fill-in shopping trip. These trips are made more frequently (on average every 2 to 4 days), are more likely to occur at a non-favorite store, and fewer items are purchased on each of these trips.

The nature of the shopping trip also affects the importance consumers place on various factors in a supermarket.[22] For example, if a consumer makes a quick, fill-in purchase, then convenience is most important. If a consumer is on a major shopping trip, purchasing in large quantities to stockpile for the future, then price may be the dominant factor. On the other hand, if the shopping trip serves as the entertainment for the day, then ambiance and atmosphere may be the most important feature. All of this implies that the importance of the different factors in a supermarket vary within each consumer as well as across consumer groups.

With so many different types of supermarkets in a given neighborhood, competition for the shopper becomes intense. The margins in the supermarket business, even in the premium priced stores, tend to be low (with gross margins averaging across all product classes at around 25%).[23] Thus, getting as many customers through the doors, and then getting those customers to buy as much as possible once inside the stores, is the key to profitability.

STRATEGIES TO BRING SHOPPERS INTO THE STORES

When a shopper has a choice among various food retailing outlets, supermarkets have to be creative in order to draw customers into their stores. As mentioned earlier, different customers are attracted to different features. Some shoppers are price oriented, so low-pricing strategies, such as featured pricing on key items, makes sense.

Price-Based Strategies

There are three ways to communicate low prices to a price-oriented consumer:

1. Everyday low pricing (EDLP)
2. High–low pricing
3. Retail promotions

Everyday low pricing. One way to lure price-sensitive customers into a supermarket is to advertise an everyday-low-price strategy (EDLP). Here, these supermarkets have low prices all the time, and therefore generally do not offer many deep-discount promotions. This is the strategy that helped make Wal-Mart the retailing success that it is today. It is the same strategy being used by supermarkets such as H.E.B., Food Lion, Winn-Dixie, Cub Foods, and Omni. The EDLP format is more popular in the southern part of the United States and less popular in the northeastern areas.[24]

The basic advantage of an EDLP-strategy is that it is simple and consistent, and thus it is easier to communicate the emphasis on low prices to consumers. Also, the EDLP format makes it possible for the retailers to lower operating costs. The low-price strategy can be chain-wide, store-wide, or just category-wide. EDLP store prices are on average 9 percent below the prices of high–low stores, and the general discount in EDLP stores is not as steep as the deep discounts in high–low stores.[25]

Because EDLP strategies lower the retailer margin on each unit sold, profitability depends on both lower operating costs and on the increased demand generated as a result of the lower prices. An increase in demand is either generated from convincing current shoppers to buy more or from encouraging new shoppers into the store. It is unlikely that current users will increase drastically the volume they purchase from supermarkets, except perhaps for impulse purchases or in expandable categories, such as cookies or chips. In order for demand to increase among shoppers at other stores, the EDLP store must promote a low-price image, particularly in comparison to the other shopping options. This suggests that an EDLP strategy needs advertising support to promote the low-price image, in addition to lower prices, in order to succeed.[26]

High–low pricing.   The second way to attract consumers who are price sensitive is to advertise price discounts on certain key items, known as a "high-low" pricing strategy. Here, key low-priced items in the store are featured in local newspaper advertising, on store coupons, or on distributed flyers. Other items in the store continue to be priced at their regular, higher (than discount or than EDLP-pricing) price.[27] Predictably, these other products are priced high enough to compensate for the deals offered on the featured items.[28]

Some items are more likely to be featured as low-priced specials than others. Soft drinks and frozen entrees sell more quickly when advertised at a low price than do dish detergents. Consumers don't wash more dishes just because the detergent is on sale, but they may eat more frozen dinners or drink more soda pop if the price is right.[29]

Retailers price this way for several reasons. The first, most obvious reason is to promote store traffic, because low prices on certain attractive products will bring consumers into the store.[30, 31] The second reason stores use high–low pricing is to convey the impression that the store has low prices,[32] while not actually discounting everything in the store. The price image of the store is a function of the number of discounts offered rather than the cumulative savings.[33] The third reason is to influence the sales volumes of different merchandise within the store to achieve greater overall store profitability.[34]

Known as "loss leaders," sometimes products featured at low prices are those that the grocer actually loses money on. The price charged to the consumer is usually at or below the retailer's marginal cost (retailers incur a *loss* when they sell these items). Loss leaders are usually shelved in inconvenient locations, like the back of the store or the lower shelves. The grocer does not want these items to be picked up on impulse by shoppers who are already in the supermarket for other reasons. These items are used to draw shoppers into the store and, hopefully, these shoppers will buy other goods once inside the store. Sometimes high-profit items are incorporated into the loss leader display.

From a retailer's point of view, products that are bought relatively often and with high storage costs should be used as loss leaders, otherwise consumers would ignore the offer or stockpile the loss leaders. Thus the rational choices for loss leaders are perishables or frequently purchased and consumed products that require a lot of storage space.[35] Empirical observation suggests that carbonated drinks, bread, eggs, and flour are often used as loss leaders.[36] It is also common for stores to set quantity restrictions to limit how much a consumer can buy at the featured price.[37]

The success of a store's strategy to promote certain key items, or loss leaders, depends on how well these promotions draw shoppers into the store. The overall profitability depends on whether increased revenue generated by the price discounts is greater than the revenues lost by putting items on discount. For example, every time a consumer pays a sale price for an item rather than the full price, the retailer loses revenue. On the other hand, if a consumer comes into the store to buy an item that has been featured in the store advertising, and while in the store purchases other items at regular price, then sales revenues are being boosted. Empirical profitability studies found that loss leader strategies produced only a small increase in store traffic, but that store traffic had a positive influence on the sales of both promoted and non-promoted products.[38]

"Cherry picking" is a problem that hinders the effectiveness of loss leader pricing. In this case, customers hop from store to store, buying only the loss leader items and not buying the full basket of goods at one store. Obviously, if too many customers cherry pick, loss leader strategies may not be profitable, per se. The store must then determine why it uses loss leader strategies. Some analytical and empirical work suggests that loss leader strategies still make sense, even if some consumers are cherry picking, if these strategies are being used as a defensive tool to prevent the loss of the non-cherry-picking customer base, rather than as an offensive tool to steal consumers away from competition.[39]

To increase the profitability of high–low pricing, retailers who want to encourage the sales of unpromoted items can physically place high-margin, unpromoted items closer to the promoted items. For example, a retailer selling hot dog buns at a featured price, or at even at a loss, can place hot dog meats that are selling at higher margins next to the low-priced buns and achieve satisfactory profits. Examples of other complementary products include fresh produce and salad dressings, meats and gravy, noodles and sauces, and breakfast waffles and syrup.[40]

Empirical testing of this type of strategy was done by studying how the promotion of Duncan Hines cake mixes affected the sales of both Duncan Hines frostings and the store brands of frosting, and how the promotion of the frostings affected the sales of cake mixes. The results were not symmetrical: promoting frostings did not necessarily increase the sale of cake mixes. However, promoting Duncan Hines cake mixes stimulated the sales of both Duncan Hines frostings and store brand frostings. These results suggest that consumers first decide on their cake mix and then pick a frosting, rather than the other way around.[41]

Retail promotions.　Finally, a third way for grocers to attract price-conscious shoppers is to offer general retail-based promotions, rather than featuring discounts on particular key items. One common practice among grocers is to promote general discounts for shopping in the store. For example, many supermarkets offer double coupons, which means the shopper is allowed to deduct double the face value of a coupon when the appropriate products are purchased. In this case, the manufacturer pays the original face value of the coupon and the retailer also pays the face value.

Some supermarkets offer their shoppers the equivalent of a frequent flier card. For example, Kroger in Columbia, South Carolina, offered shoppers a $25 "free food" coupon if they spent $25 or more on each of 13 visits over 17 weeks.[42] Another promotion used by supermarkets to lure shoppers is "Buy one, get one free" promotion.

One study compared the performance of EDLP to high–low pricing. The relative profitability of EDLP versus high–low pricing strategies was evaluated experimentally.[43] Eighty-six stores in the Dominick's chain in Chicago were involved in the test. Stores were assigned randomly to one of three conditions on a category-by-category basis. The three conditions were: (1) *control,* where all everyday non-promotional prices were kept at pre-existing conditions, (2) *EDLP,* where everyday non-promotional prices were decreased by a constant factor ranging from a 6 to 24 percent discount, averaging 10 percent across all categories, and (3) *high–low,* where everyday prices were increased an average of 10 percent. The average price of a complete market basket of goods remained unchanged across all three conditions, however, because for any particular store, prices were raised in some categories and lowered in others. Price promotions occurred in all conditions as they would in a normal business. The average sale price was 15 percent below normal price. In the high–low stores these discounts resulted in a greater percentage of savings as compared to the EDLP stores.

The results showed that although volume increased in the EDLP categories as compared to the high–low categories, profitability was higher for the high–low categories. The net conclusion of the experiment was that the lower prices did not sufficiently increase volume to be profitable.

Some significant limitations to this study must be pointed out, and caution should be taken in overgeneralizing the results. First, the experiment was run for only a limited time (approximately 16 weeks). It is likely that it would take some experience on the part of the consumers to become fully aware of the lower price changes. Second, the EDLP stores were not promoted as EDLP in advertising campaigns. Success of an EDLP strategy clearly depends on consumers noticing the price discounts, or at least noticing the overall drop in their total grocery bill. This awareness would be heightened by advertising.

In another examination of the relative profitability of the two different formats, a detailed financial analysis was conducted over many different retailers.[44] This analysis concluded that both EDLP and high–low formats can be profitable. Each can also be unprofitable. On average they are equally profitable, neither is clearly superior. The analysts conclude that profitability is a function of how well the respective strategy is executed.

Service-Based Strategies

Some consumers are not particularly motivated by price considerations. For these consumers, service-based strategies are likely to be more effective. Service-based strategies focus on providing high-quality products, or interesting assortments of products, to lure consumers into the store. Some stores try to make the trip to the supermarket an adventure, where discoveries of interesting products or new ideas can be found.[45] These supermarkets provide in-store entertainment as the lure.

Festivities are one way for supermarkets to build loyalty from shoppers. Perhaps no supermarket is as famous for its creativity than Stew Leonard's Dairy Store in Norwalk, Connecticut. The store is so famous that tourists come to visit. At Stew Leonard's, the customer is *always* right—in fact, this phrase is engraved in stone at the store's entrance. Among the attractions at Stew Leonard's are the largest in-store bakery in the world, animated robots that play the Stew Leonard theme song, a mechanical mooing cow, a four-foot mechanical hen, free foods to sample, and a parking lot petting zoo. Stew Leonard's has been called the "Disney World of Supermarkets."[46]

Another supermarket that doubles as a tourist spot is The Market Place in Chicago. Local celebrities, sports stars, and key political figures come into this store, earning it the title "Store of the Stars." The produce section at The Market Place offers an assortment of over 400 items, including tamarillos, pepenios, edible flowers, fresh herbs, and exotic mushrooms. Not only is the assortment creative, the method of merchandising is as well; funny faces are sometimes drawn on the melon halves, earning a chuckle from the local shoppers.[47]

The local Piggly Wiggly, in Columbia, South Carolina, once featured a seafood festival and served free seafood gumbo, clams, and crabs to attract shoppers to their store.[48] In other markets, elegance and acute attention to customer service has been used to appeal to shoppers. In Edina, Minnesota, Byerly's supermarket creates an elegant ambiance, including restaurants, carpeting, and chandeliers to appeal to shoppers. Vincent's Market in Birmingham, Alabama brought in an executive chef to help with the prepared foods. In West Point Markets in Akron, Ohio, there is fine art on the walls, in-store philharmonic concerts, and formal black-tie dinners for charity.[49]

Another way a supermarket can build loyalty from shoppers is by emphasizing its links to the community. For example, Wegman's of Rochester sponsors a scholarship program for inner city high school students.[50] In other areas, supermarkets collaborate with other local businesses to provide benefits for their loyal customers. For example, Vons in California has arrangements for discounts with Disneyland; Bashas in Arizona offers to their loyal customers discount programs with local bowling alleys, museums, and zoos.[51]

In the Dallas area, the supermarket Carnival features certain products that are particularly in demand in the African-American and Hispanic neighborhoods surrounding the store. After surveying the market, Carnival learned that the key categories of interest to these consumers are the meat and produce departments, so it expanded its produce department and added more variety. Store managers watched which items were selling and increased the selection of them; for example, the tortilla category went from two or three brands to eight brands. The produce sections include large tubs filled with bulk pinto beans, and hanging strands of chili peppers and garlic. In the meat department, whole chickens are put on ice in the meat service department—something no other store has been doing.[52]

STORE IMAGE

Once a supermarket has decided on the strategy or positioning that it will use to bring shoppers into the store, it is important that this strategy is consistently executed in all merchandising decisions. The store image, or general impression of the store, is a very important aspect of a supermarket's positioning. Some marketing consulting studies indicate that shoppers decide in the first eight seconds whether they feel comfortable in a particular supermarket, and some consumers base their opinions of the store on the outside store appearance.[53]

The store image is a function not only of advertising and promotional campaigns and of pricing strategies, but also of other non-price aspects such as layout, cleanliness, and sales efficiency.[54] In particular, some categories (e.g., dairy and produce) are important for a supermarket because they define the store's competitive positioning. If a store is positioned as a high-end gourmet, fresh produce store, it is essential that it pay significant attention to its produce department, making sure that there is sufficient variety and that the category is particularly appealing. The produce section is important because studies show that this category has the highest purchase rate, that is, the highest percentage of people purchasing in the category, given they entered the category.[55] If a store wants to be known for its low prices, then it is important for the store to maintain a low-price position in certain key categories. Industry executives typically believe that consumers specifically remember the prices of a few select categories that they purchase frequently, for example, milk or soft drinks.

Therefore, stores that want to maintain an image of low prices must have low prices particularly in those categories in which consumers tend to be highly sensitive to competitive differentials.[56]

Because the first thing consumers see when entering a store can frame their perceptions of the store, displays placed immediately inside the front entrance are considered strategically important. A store that wants to give the impression of first-class service may have a concierge desk up front, as a big, prestigious supermarket in Los Angeles does. On the other hand, a store that wants to project an image of low pricing may place exceptional sale items near the first aisle or may try to foster a warehouse environment. A store that is trying to stimulate consumers' interest in high-profit, entertaining, fancy categories may lead off with that kind of display. One upscale supermarket in a well-to-do suburb changes the lead-in display to reflect seasons, and often leads with fun categories, such as Halloween candy, back-to-school supplies, rich chocolates, Christmas specialties, and so forth, carefully selected to slow the shopper down and encourage browsing.

As the food retailing business gets more intense, grocers are turning to sophisticated micromarketing techniques to target specific consumers within their stores. In addition to store-wide strategies, such as the pricing and service strategies already mentioned, many supermarkets are concentrating on appealing to individual consumers.

TARGETING THE INDIVIDUAL SHOPPER

The ultimate approach to enticing shoppers into supermarkets would be if grocers could customize their marketing programs to appeal to the needs of individual consumers. If a particular consumer was not coming to the store as often as s/he used to, the grocer could provide that consumer with a special incentive to entice a return visit. On the other hand, a frequent shopper would be rewarded for his or her loyalty with special price discounts, or with special privileges.

Specific Micromarketing Strategies

Although this kind of pinpointed, targeted marketing is not widespread yet, grocers are beginning to identify each shopper's purchasing behavior and to respond accordingly. For example, Pathmark, in New York, monitored 16,000 transactions and found that many of their shoppers used check cashing cards every time they made a purchase in the store. By entering the number on the shopper's check cashing card into the register and the total amount spent on each shopping trip, Pathmark created a purchase history for each customer. Pathmark then targeted the inactive shoppers with special coupons to try to get them back into their store. Of the inactive customers, 18 percent—more than 1,150 customers—came back to the store to redeem their coupons.[57]

Snyder Foods in Oklahoma also implemented a micromarketing program they called the Consumer Specific Pricing (CSP) system. This supermarket chain stopped distributing coupons or double coupons through local newspapers. Instead, the stores distributed coupons directly to their shoppers based on their particular shopping habits. Loyal customers were provided with better discounts on coupons than infrequent shoppers. The store also stopped charging very low prices to everyone for Thanksgiving turkeys. Instead, they rewarded their most loyal customers with a coupon for a free turkey, moderately loyal customers received a coupon offering a large discount off the regular price, and infrequent shoppers received smaller discount coupons. Walk-in customers who had no strong relationships with the supermarket paid the full retail price.[58]

Sometimes these micromarketing programs can be expensive, because they generally involve administrative costs, as well as the general cost of managing and analyzing the information. Depending upon the supermarket, these costs can make the program unattractive. On the other hand, some supermarkets have found that the costs are mitigated because they allow the supermarket to reduce their mass advertising dollars significantly. The other benefit of micromarketing is that the information about various consumers' shopping patterns provides a competitive advantage.[59]

Methods of Gathering Information About Consumers

There are four basic ways that a supermarket can collect information about the shopping habits of consumers:[60]

1. Sweepstakes: A relatively inexpensive way to get information about customers is for a grocer to implement a sweepstakes program. In this kind of program, shoppers are encouraged to enter a sweepstakes to win a certain multiple of their purchase amount. The shopper records his or her name, address, telephone number, and amount of purchase. This method is the least expensive, but also provides the least comprehensive data.

2. Frequent shopper programs: The second method is similar to a frequent flyer program in the airlines. Here, at each purchase occasion the shopper is given a certain number of stamps depending upon how much is spent. The stamps are accumulated by the shopper until a certain amount have been collected. Then the shopper can redeem the stamps for discounted items or discounts off of total purchases, as one example. This simple method provides data on who the store's customers are and how much they spent on each shopping trip.

3. Tracking check transactions: A third way for a supermarket to capture data about its shoppers is through tracking of check transactions. Every time a shopper wants to cash a check, s/he is asked to provide a check cashing card. Then, when checks are used for purchase, a grocer can collect the date of purchase and the amount purchased for each household identification number. If check cashing cards are not routinely used, the grocer can alternatively collect the shopper's phone number before ringing up each shopping trip. In either case, a purchase history with shopping trip frequency and amount spent per trip would be accumulated.

In recent years, supermarkets have finally begun accepting credit cards. In 1994, 63 percent of supermarkets accepted credit cards.[61] Credit cards, or ATM cards, also potentially allow grocers to record a purchase history for a specific identification number. This is not being done at this time, but it is a possibility for the future.

4. UPC bar-code data: Finally, the most high-tech form of customer identification is the bar-coded plastic card. These shopping cards are issued to consumers. Generally, the supermarket provides incentives, such as discounts off special items in the store and check cashing privileges, to get their consumers to present these cards at every purchase occasion. This method is the most expensive but provides the opportunity to collect the most information. For example, the grocer can scan the shopper's card, and then record each item—or SKU (stockkeeping unit)—purchased at each shopping trip. This tells the grocer exactly when and what each shopper is purchasing.

This shopper information can be linked back to store data indicating what items were available in the supermarket at the time of purchase and at what prices, and what promotional deals were offered. Using this kind of data, the grocer can determine price and promotional sensitivities for each household, measure shopping patterns, and determine the most effective marketing schemes. Ideally, this is the best system, but practically this amount of data is too expensive and too cumbersome for grocers to manage effectively. The grocer may prefer just to collect the amount spent per shopping trip, or perhaps the amount spent per department in the supermarket, or maybe even the amount spent per category.[62]

COMPETING WITH OTHER TYPES OF RETAILERS

The changing competitive marketplace has meant that supermarkets not only face competition from other supermarkets, but they face competition from other types of retailers as well. In particular, as mentioned in Part One of the book, mass merchandisers such as Wal-Mart and Kmart have increasingly begun to stock grocery products, building supercenters that focus on giving the consumer what they want at the lowest possible price. Category killers, such as Toys 'R' Us and Petco, also have such large assortments and such low prices that shoppers are buying products, such as diapers and pet food, in them that they used to purchase in supermarkets.

Importance of Non-Grocery Categories

The non-grocery categories, such as health and beauty care, general merchandise, and prepared foods, were typically not given much floor space in supermarkets. These categories are high margin/low turn categories, compared to the standard grocery categories of low margin/high turn. But supermarkets are increasingly devoting more floor space to these categories because of the threat of other retailers. One supermarket official called the nonfood categories, "the battleground of the '90s between supermarkets and discount stores." Supermarkets have to stay ahead in these categories in order to compete against the competition from other types of retail outlets.[63]

One primary non-grocery category is household and beauty aids/general merchandise (HBA/GM). *Supermarket Business* interviewed more than 2,600 consumers to learn how they decide whether to buy their health and beauty care products in a supermarket versus another channel. They found that consumers say that the most important factors in deciding where to buy these kinds of goods are price, convenience, selection, and variety. Other factors, such as advertising, size of package, and convenience of one-stop shopping, were less important to the purchase decision. In general, consumers perceive that health and beauty care products are more expensive in supermarkets, and there is less of a selection there as well.

The kind of health and beauty care products that are more likely to be purchased in a supermarket are staples, such as oral care, hair care, and deodorants. The study also found that men were more likely to buy health and beauty care products in a supermarket than were women.[64] Although the reasons for the different behavior between the genders were not probed, it is possible that women were more likely to be familiar with several different types of stores, and their corresponding prices and variety.

Supermarkets have been paying a lot of attention to the HBA/GM departments in order to try to change customer's perceptions. For example, the 31-store Big V supermarkets headquartered in Orange County, New York have been improving their nonfood categories in the store. In one Big V supermarket located in Monroe, New York, the center of the store houses a 500-square-foot video section featuring 2,000 titles. Directly behind the video section is the health and beauty care category. Emphasizing price and value, more than 400 private label HBA items are available. The price savings attributed to purchasing a private label over a national brand are also highlighted by shelf markers.[65]

Baby Products

Another key non-grocery category for supermarkets is baby products. Parents of young children are particularly attractive customers for supermarkets because they buy lots of merchandise throughout the store. Given the profitability of this segment, mass merchandisers and category killers such as Toys 'R' Us also cater to these shoppers. Supermarkets cannot afford to lose this business, so it is essential that they capture the key categories (e.g., baby products) that appeal to this segment.

Traditionally, baby products were located in nonfood, low-traffic areas of the supermarket, but now these products are generally placed in high-traffic grocery areas.[66] In addition, some supermarkets are using "baby clubs" to target the parents of young children. Baby clubs offer parents special incentives to make purchases in the baby aisle. Raley's supermarket, for example, targets shoppers with baby care needs and sends them coupons for specific products along with an invitation to join the program. When the shopper makes purchases in targeted baby categories, they are issued "Baby Bucks" which, when accumulated, can be redeemed for gift certificates to the store.[67]

Just as important as deciding what categories to bolster in an effort to keep parents from shopping at competing outlets is deciding where it does not make as much sense to compete. For example, although supermarkets have typically carried toys, most industry experts believe that it would be futile for the supermarkets to try to compete against category killers, such as Toys 'R' Us, in most toy categories. Supermarkets are probably not the first place consumers consider when they want to buy toys. Supermarkets have the best chance of competing in this category if they specialize in a "subset" of the toy category, or if they focus on toys that are most likely to be purchased on impulse.[68]

Time-Saving Services

Retailers face competition not only from other retailers, such as mass merchandisers who offer groceries, but also from other retailers who sell substitutes for groceries. Because convenience is becoming more of an issue for American consumers, they are more likely to eat out than to cook at home. Therefore, another competitor for grocery stores is fast-food restaurants. To respond to this threat, supermarkets have added large prepared foods sections to their deli departments. Prepared foods are attractive to supermarkets not only because they attract time-pressured customers, but also because that category offers very high margins. The average gross margin for hot take-out foods is 53.4 percent and the net margin is 41.5 percent[69] (for example, health and beauty care, formerly considered a very high margin category, averaged gross margins of 27.6% in 1993).[70]

One-stop shopping is another way that supermarkets can compete with other retailers—by making the supermarket experience as convenient as possible for shoppers. An emerging trend is a growing number of supermarkets that offer services. Some supermarkets now offer postal services, travel services, copying, fax, and even printing and typing services, to provide the advantage of convenience and one-stop shopping for busy customers who place a big premium on being able to get all of their errands accomplished in one place. Banks have also started to open up branches in supermarkets. Many supermarkets already have access to automatic teller machines (ATMs), but the trend is to start putting other banking services into supermarkets.[71]

Defender Sizes

Another problem for supermarkets in competing with mass merchandisers and category killers is that the latter have a very strong low-price image that supermarkets sometimes have trouble matching. One reason this perception is hard to change is that supermarkets do not tend to carry the larger sizes or club packs. Consumers seem to believe that small-sized packages have higher unit prices (although that is not necessarily true). Even when supermarkets have a lower unit price on a small size of Advil, for example, the consumer's perception of value is not as great as if the supermarket had put a low price on a larger sized product. Traditionally supermarkets have been reluctant to carry the larger sizes,[72] but competition from the alternative formats has become so intense that this has started to change. Many supermarkets now feature special aisles in which consumers can purchase larger, club-sized packages of some items.

Endnotes

1. Hartley, Robert F. (1986), *Marketing Mistakes*, 3rd Edition, New York: John Wiley & Sons, 217.

2. Stiven, Kristine (1989), "Future Store? It's . . . Black-and-White for Format Leader, A&P's James Wood," *Advertising Age* (May 8), S-17, S-18.

3. Tordjman, Andre (1988), "A Review of the United States Food Retailing Industry," *International Journal of Retailing*, 3 (4), 55–69.

4. Food Marketing Institute (1987), "Superstore Formats of the Future," *Progressive Grocer*, Food Marketing Institute, Washington, DC, December 1986, April 1987.

5. Loro, Laura (1994), "H-E-B, Wegmans Freshen Up Stale Image of Grocery," *Advertising Age*, 65 (May 2), S-15.

6. Loro, Laura (1994), "Doing What Comes Naturally," *Advertising Age*, 65 (August 8), 22.

7. Wallace, David J. (1989), "Convenience Stores Push Fast-Lane Pace," *Advertising Age* (May 8), S-16, S-17.

8. Wallace, David J. (1989), "Convenience Stores Push Fast-Lane Pace," *Advertising Age* (May 8), S-16, S-17.

9. Tordjman, Andre (1988), "A Review of the United States Food Retailing Industry," *International Journal of Retailing*, 3 (4), 55–69.

10. Frederick, Joanne (1995), "Supercenters: The Threat du Jour," *Grocery Marketing* (March), 14–17.

11. Consumer Reports (1993), "Survival Guide to the Supermarket," *Consumer Reports*, Vol. 58, No. 9 (September), 559–570.

12. Hortman, Sandra McCurley, Arthur W. Allaway, J. Barry Mason, and John Rasp (1990), "Multisegment Analysis of Supermarket Patronage," *Journal of Business Research*, 21 (November), 209–223.

13. Arnold, Stephen J., Tae H. Oum, and Douglas J. Tigert (1983), "Determinant Attributes in Retail Patronage: Seasonal, Temporal, Regional, and International Comparisons," *Journal of Marketing Research*, 20 (May), 149–57.

14. Hortman, Sandra McCurley, Arthur W. Allaway, J. Barry Mason, and John Rasp (1990), "Multisegment Analysis of Supermarket Patronage," *Journal of Business Research*, 21 (November), 209–223.

15. Hortman, Sandra McCurley, Arthur W. Allaway, J. Barry Mason, and John Rasp (1990), "Multisegment Analysis of Supermarket Patronage," *Journal of Business Research*, 21 (November), 209–223.

16. Arnold, Stephen J., Tae H. Oum, and Douglas J. Tigert (1983), "Determinant Attributes in Retail Patronage: Seasonal, Temporal, Regional, and International Comparisons," *Journal of Marketing Research*, 20 (May), 149–57.

17. McAlister, Leigh and Michael J. Zenor (1992), "The Impact of Retailer Differences on Promotional Response: A Link Between Unusual Levels of Support and Unusual Levels of Response," University of Texas at Austin Working Paper.

18. Raftery, Dan (1993), "Trim the Deadwood," *Progressive Grocer* (September), 42–43.

19. Woolf, Brian (1994), "Measured Marketing: A Tool to Shape Food Store Strategy: Using Electronic Marketing to Create Loyal Customers," a study conducted for the Coca-Cola Retailing Research Council.

20. Kahn, Barbara E. and David C. Schmittlein (1989), "Shopping Trip Behavior: An Empirical Investigation," *Marketing Letters*, 1 (1), 55–69.

21. Kahn, Barbara E. and David C. Schmittlein (1992), "The Relationship Between Purchases Made on Promotion and Shopping Trip Behavior," *Journal of Retailing*, 68 (3), 294–315.

22. Tordjman, Andre (1988), "A Review of the United States Food Retailing Industry," *International Journal of Retailing*, 3 (4), 55–69.

23. Heinbockel, John E. and Israel M. Ganot (1995), "Quarterly Supermarket Statistical," *Goldman Sachs: U.S. Research, Retailing: Food and Drug*, December 15.

24. Hoch, Stephen, Xavier Dreze, and Mary E. Purk (1994), "EDLP, Hi-Lo, and Margin Arithmetic," *Journal of Marketing*, 58 (October), 16–27.

25. Information Resources, Inc. (1993), *Managing Your Business in an EDLP Environment*, Chicago: IRI.

26. Hoch, Stephen, Xavier Dreze, and Mary E. Purk (1994), "EDLP, Hi-Lo, and Margin Arithmetic," *Journal of Marketing*, 58 (October), 16–27.

27. Mulhern, Francis J. and Robert P. Leone (1991), "Implicit Price Bundling of Retail Products: A Multi-product Approach to Maximizing Store Profitability," *Journal of Marketing*, (October), 63–76.

28. Nagle, Thomas T. (1987), *The Strategy and Tactics of Pricing*, Englewood Cliffs, NJ: Prentice-Hall.

29. Gibson, Richard (1993), "Broad Grocery Price Cuts May Not Pay," *Wall Street Journal* (May 7), B1, B8.

30. Mulhern, Francis J. and Robert P. Leone (1990), "Retail Promotional Advertising: Do the Number of Deal Items and the Size of Deal Discounts Affect Store Performance? *Journal of Business Research*, 21 (November), 179–94.

31. Walters, Rockney G. and Scott B. MacKenzie (1988), "A Structural Equations Analysis of the Impact of Price Promotions on Store Performance," *Journal of Marketing Research,* 55 (April), 17–28.

32. Nystrom, Harry, Jans Tamsons, and Robert Thams (1975), "An Experiment in Price Generalization and Discrimination," *Journal of Marketing Research*, 12 (May), 177–81.

33. Alba, Joseph W., Susan M. Broniarczyk, Terence A. Shimp, and Joel E. Urbany (1994), "The Influence of Prior Beliefs, Frequency Cues, and Magnitude Cues on Consumers' Perceptions of Comparative Price Data," *Journal of Consumer Research* (September), 21, 219–235.

34. Kumar, V. and Robert P. Leone (1988), "Measuring the Effect of Retail Store Promotion on Brand and Store Substitution," *Journal of Marketing Research*, 25 (May), 178–85.

35. Lal, Rajiv and Carmen Matutes (1994), "Retail Pricing and Advertising Strategies," *Journal of Business*, 67 (3), 345–371.

36. Nagle, Thomas T. (1987), *The Strategy and Tactics of Pricing*, Englewood Cliffs, NJ: Prentice-Hall.

37. Hess, James and Eitan Gerstner (1987), "Loss Leader Pricing and Rain Check Policy," *Marketing Science*, 6 (Fall), 358–374.

38. Walters, Rockney and Scott McKenzie (1988), "A Structural Equation Analysis of the Impact of Price Promotion on Store Performance," *Journal of Marketing Research*, 25 (February), 51–63.

39. Dreze, Xavier (1994), "Loss Leaders: Store Traffic and Cherry Picking," Doctoral dissertation, University of Chicago.

40. Mulhern, Francis J. and Robert P. Leone (1991), "Implicit Price Bundling of Retail Products: A Multi-product Approach to Maximizing Store Profitability," *Journal of Marketing* (October), 63–76.

41. Mulhern, Francis J. and Robert P. Leone (1991), "Implicit Price Bundling of Retail Products: A Multi-product Approach to Maximizing Store Profitability," *Journal of Marketing* (October), 63–76.

42. Garry, Michael (1993), "Making it on Supermarket Row," *Progressive Grocer* (December), 65–68.

43. Hoch, Stephen, Xavier Dreze, and Mary E. Purk (1994), "EDLP, Hi-Lo, and Margin Arithmetic," *Journal of Marketing*, 58 (October), 16–27.

44. Shore, Andres and Gary Giblen (1992), "Household Products and Cosmetics: Everyday Low (or "Value") Pricing: An Idea Whose Time Has Come," *Paine Webber* (October 13).

45. Tordjman, Andre (1988), "A Review of the United States Food Retailing Industry," *International Journal of Retailing*, 3 (4), 55–69.

46. Adams, Michael (1991), "The Udder Delights of Stew," *Successful Meetings,* 40 (March), 59–61.

47. "A Stellar Performance" (1994), *Supermarket Business* (July), 89, 93.

48. Garry, Michael (1993), "Making it on Supermarket Row," *Progressive Grocer* (December), 65–68.

49. Litwak, David (1993), "Standing the Test of Time," *Supermarket Business*, 48 (May), 87–95.

50. Johnson, Bradley (1993), "Supermarkets Take Position," *Advertising Age*, 64 (May 10), S-1, S-4.

51. Raphel, Murray and Neil Raphel (1994), "Everybody Sells!" *Progressive Grocer*, 73 (May), 21–22.

52. Ingram, Bob (1994), "At Minyard, 'Big D' Stands for Diversity," *Supermarket Business* (May), 41–48.

53. Von Bergen, Jane M. (1994), "Updating the Shopping List," *The Philadelphia Inquirer*, September 20, C1, C2.

54. Doyle, Peter and Ian Fenwick (1974-975), "How Store Image Affects Shopping Habits in Grocery Chains," *Journal of Retailing*, 4 (Winter), 39–52.

55. *Progressive Grocer* Special Report, The Marsh Super Study (December 1992) 6–67.

56. "Retailer Reactions to Competitive Price Changes," (1994), *Retailing Review*, University of Florida, Center for Retailing Education and Research, (Fall), RR3-RR5. (Based on a summary of an article by Peter R. Dickson and Joel E. Urbany from the *Journal of Retailing*).

57. "For Customer Data, It's In the Cards; Using Check Cashing Cards to Determine Customer Base," (1988), *Supermarket News,* 38 (May 9), 74.

58. Mogelonsky, Marcia (1994), "Please Don't Pick the Cherries: How Supermarketers Use Electronic Price Scanning to Build Store Loyalty," *Marketing Tools* (September/October), 10–13.

59. Woolf, Brian (1994), "Measured Marketing: A Tool to Shape Food Store Strategy: Using Electronic Marketing to Create Loyal Customers," a study conducted for the Coca-Cola Retailing Research Council, 3.

60. Woolf, Brian (1994), "Measured Marketing: A Tool to Shape Food Store Strategy: Using Electronic Marketing to Create Loyal Customers," a study conducted for the Coca-Cola Retailing Research Council.

61. Boyd, Malia (1994), "New Directions in Supermarkets," *Incentive* (November), 41–45.

62. Woolf, Brian (1994), "Measured Marketing: A Tool to Shape Food Store Strategy: Using Electronic Marketing to Create Loyal Customers," a study conducted for the Coca-Cola Retailing Research Council, p. 15–19.

63. Mendelson, Seth (1994), "A Conflict of Interest," *Supermarket Business* (May), 143–144.

64. "To End a Trend," (1994), *Supermarket Business* (September), 155–159.

65. "Supermarket Nonfoods Business: The Home," (1994), *Supermarket Business* (October), 91-94.

66. Snyder, Glenn (1994), "Category Switching Expands GM/HBC's Role," *Progressive Grocer* (April), 27–38.

67. "Turning Traffic Into Transactions," (1994), a study funded by the American Greetings Research Council with the cooperation of Food Marketing Institute.

68. "Is Mainstream But a Dream?" (1994), *Supermarket Business* (February), 67–68.

69. "Sales Manual/Top Performers: What's Hot," (1994), *Progressive Grocer* (July), 69–82.

70. Litwak, David and Nancy Maline (1993), "Who Said HBC Wasn't Perishable?" *Supermarket News* (May), 137–144.

71. "Rethinking the Service Counter," (1994), *Supermarket Business* (April), 65–66.

72. "Don't Cry Over Spilt Cash," (1994), *Supermarket Business* (February), 50–54.

9

How Do Consumers Decide What Categories to Buy?

Once a consumer has decided to go shopping, and then has decided which supermarket to visit, the next item of business is deciding what groceries to buy. Some purchase decisions are likely to be made in advance (planned purchasing) and some are likely to be made in the store (unplanned purchasing). Some purchases may even be made on impulse, without a conscious, or even rational, reason.

The likelihood of unplanned purchasing should be of particular interest to retailers because these decisions are being made in the store, thus in-store marketing and merchandising are critical. Research shows that over 60 percent of the buying decisions in a supermarket are unplanned.

Individual factors affect whether unplanned purchases will be made, specifically, whether or not consumers are familiar with the shopping environment, whether or not they are under time pressure, and whether or not they are shopping alone. All have been shown to affect the number of unplanned purchases.

There are also things that the grocer can do to alter consumers' purchasing habits. First, the layout of the supermarket itself can affect whether consumers are likely to walk down certain aisles, and this in turn affects what they are likely to purchase. Second, the in-store activities of the manufacturers can also increase unplanned purchasing and change general purchasing habits. Manufacturers can introduce new products, or change their pricing and promotional habits—activities that affect purchase rates greatly. Even more directly, manufacturers can sponsor in-store promotional programs or provide in-store demonstrations or food sampling to help increase purchasing.

Finally, atmospherics—changes in the sensory aspects of the retail environment—have also been shown to have some effect on purchasing. Atmospherics such as ambient odor, music, or visual changes in the decor can influence how much time consumers spend in the store, and their mood when they are there. These factors, in turn, seem to

have some relationship to the kinds of items purchased and the inci-
dence of unplanned purchasing.

CONSUMERS' PURCHASING HABITS

Once a consumer has decided which retail market to enter, then s/he has to decide what items to buy. If the decision regarding what to buy has been made in advance, before entering the store, then marketing activities, such as television or newspaper advertising, will probably have some influence on what will be bought. If the decision regarding what to buy is made in the store, then clearly in-store marketing activities, such as merchandising, store layout, and in-store promotions, will influence the purchasing process much more.[1]

Studies have shown that over 60 percent of the time, the buying decision for grocery products is actually made in the store.[2, 3, 4] Thus, it is very important for the retailer to understand how the supermarket environment can influence those decisions.

Planned Decisions

Purchase decisions that are made before entering the store are called planned decisions. A consumer can plan to buy a specific branded item (e.g., Hebrew National Hot Dogs), or can plan to buy in a specific product category (e.g., hot dogs), or can plan to buy in a product class (e.g., luncheon meat).[5] The more specific the planned purchase, the less likely the consumer is to be influenced by in-store activity. If a consumer plans to buy a specific item, then the job of the retailer is only to make sure that purchase occurs. Reasons a consumer may not purchase as originally intended include: (1) discovering that the price for the product is too high, or (2) learning that the product is not in stock, or (3) being unable to find the product in the store. In each case, the consumer may forego the original purchase and buy something else, or not make a purchase at all.

Looking at consumers' shopping lists is one way researchers have attempted to analyze the types of decisions consumers make in advance. There is some disagreement as to what percentage of shoppers use shopping lists, with estimates ranging from 22 to 75 percent. A Gallup study that interviewed about 4,220 shoppers across the United States found that 55 percent of consumers said they come into the supermarket with a shopping list. Items that were most likely to be on their shopping lists included milk, refrigerated items, bakery-fresh bread, and ready-to-eat cereal. Of the top items on shoppers' lists, they planned to buy 10.5 items and actually bought 19.8 items.[6] Other studies concur with the Gallup study indicating that staples (i.e., milk and eggs) are more likely to be planned purchases, or on shopping lists, than are new products or nonstaples (candy, desserts).[7]

The use of shopping lists does not, of course, preclude buying decisions being made in the store. In addition, the shopping list may merely list a product class purchase, for example, "buy meat," or a need, "get something for dinner," rather than a specific branded item or product category. A survey[8] was conducted among shoppers at several supermarkets in the United States to determine how precise shopping lists generally were. Lists were collected from 129 shoppers. The average number of items on the lists was 22 (mode 18), ranging from a minimum of five items to a maximum of 112. Less than 2 percent of the items listed were needs or general product classes (e.g., meats), with the rest being product categories (72%) or specific brand names (26%). The percentage of brand names listed (versus just a product category) varied by product category. Product categories that don't tend to be heavily marked by brand names, such as carrots, steak, or chicken, had a very small percentage of brand names listed, as would be expected. Product categories with very high levels of brand activity—beer, cereal, household cleaners, and personal care products, for example—were likely to be noted by a brand name.

Some surveys of shoppers revealed that those who are more likely to use shopping lists are more educated, more likely to have teenagers in the home, and more likely to own their own homes. One study, conducted in New Zealand on 279 consumers, found that grocery shoppers with lists purchased on average seven fewer items and spent $13.13 less than their "non-list" counterparts.[9]

Unplanned Purchases

From the retailers' point of view, unplanned and impulse purchases may represent a bigger opportunity, because they are the decisions being influenced in the store. Impulse purchases have been defined as purchases in which a consumer experiences "a sudden, often powerful and persistent urge to buy something immediately."[10] Unplanned purchases, on the other hand, are decisions that are made in the store and not prior to entering the store.[11] Thus, all impulse purchases are unplanned, but not all unplanned purchases are impulsive.

As with the planned purchases, there is a continuum of unplanned or impulse purchases as well.[12] On one end of the continuum is pure impulse buying that breaks the normal buying pattern, and is probably relatively rare. On the other end of the continuum is intended unplanned buying that occurs when the shopper comes into the store with some specific purchases in mind, but ends up purchasing a different brand, size, or flavor than the one originally intended as a function of in-store activity. In the middle is reminder or suggestion unplanned buying, in which something sparks the memory of the consumer and encourages a purchase that wasn't originally intended on this shopping trip. These types of purchases generally are not out-of-the-ordinary type purchases.[13]

Several factors will increase the probability that a consumer purchases an item that s/he had not originally planned on purchasing.[14] First, impulse or unplanned items tend to be lower priced (e.g., specials on candy or crackers) and a particularly good price can dramatically increase the likelihood. Placing items in high-traffic areas (e.g., at the end of an aisle) or featuring a big red arrow pointing out a particular product can also increase the likelihood of unplanned purchasing. Second, if a product is easy to store and/or carry, then it is more likely to be purchased without advanced planning. Anything that requires special handling or difficult storage (e.g., large-sized boxes of detergent or diapers) generally requires planning. Finally, the ready access of cash through ATM machines, often located right in the supermarket, and the ubiquitous use of credit cards have also increased the amount of unplanned purchasing.

Impulse Purchases

True impulse purchases are made spontaneously and are completely unpremeditated, when there is an urge to buy something "out of the blue."[15] The consumer purchases impulsively because s/he feels a need for possession, a need that is often rationalized, such as, "Well, I don't really need this, but it will make me feel better if I buy it," or "The price is too good to resist, I must get it." Another common feature of impulse purchases is that they are usually made in haste and without much thought. Sometimes this results in feelings of regret following an impulsive purchase. Some impulsive purchase behavior has been characterized as foolish by economists and immature by psychologists.[18]

Items that retailers think will generally be purchased impulsively are placed near the cash register. The average length of time in the checkout line is eight minutes,[19] plenty of time to glance at the miscellaneous items that are frequently located there: candy, gum, magazines, batteries, eyeglass kits, and so forth. All are low-priced goods that one might not have purchased anyway, and probably wouldn't have made a special trip to purchase.

The effectiveness of placing impulse items near the cash register was empirically tested in a convenience store in New Jersey.[20] The store manager noticed that his customers were typically ignoring his well-stocked candy aisle because their attention was focused on getting to the walk-in coolers in the back, where the eggs, milk, and drinks were stored. When the store manager moved the candy aisle to the exit aisle, he found a 40 percent increase in sales. A study on confection purchasing indicated that whereas candy is usually about tenth on a customer's list of items to buy when entering a convenience store, it rises to about second by the time a customer is ready to leave. This increase *only* occurs, though, if the candy selection is made visible when the customer is getting ready to leave. If the customer does not see the candy, it is not purchased.

In supermarkets, placing magazines near the cash register has contributed to increased sales. Today, about 50 to 60 percent of total single-copy magazine sales are estimated to come from the supermarket channel. The magazines are generally sold through the persuasion of the cover of the magazine. Referring to the list of the top ten magazines sold in supermarkets in 1993,[21] it seems likely that some of these are impulse purchases—particularly those in the middle and end of the list.[22]

Top 10 Magazines Sold in Supermarkets in 1993

1. TV Guide
2. Woman's Day
3. Family Circle
4. National Enquirer
5. Star
6. Cosmopolitan
7. People
8. Good Housekeeping
9. First for Women
10. Woman's World

FACTORS THAT INFLUENCE IN-STORE PURCHASE DECISIONS

In studying consumer decision making, researchers have found three variables that affect whether consumers are likely to make unplanned purchases. These factors are: (1) the environment, which involves the consumer's knowledge of the store and the store layout, (2) the amount of time the consumers has available for shopping,[23] and (3) whether the consumer is alone or accompanied by someone else.[24]

Knowledge of Supermarket

Consumers often come into a supermarket with a plan of how they want to shop. When they are familiar with the layout of the supermarket, where different products are located and where different brands are within a product class, then their shopping process is generally guided by memory and requires minimal effort. In this familiar environment, the consumer is more likely to purchase the items that s/he was planning to purchase. The consumer is likely to shop either entirely out of habit or, because the environment is not taxing, s/he may notice more in-store information—such as price comparisons or comparisons among brands.[26, 27]

When the environment is unfamiliar, consumers must spend more effort to find what they want. Thus, consumers are less likely to make in-store detailed comparisons among brands and/or prices because it would be too taxing. Consumers are more likely, however, to respond to simple in-store cues because of more attention being paid to the environment, and thus more unplanned purchasing should occur.[27, 28]

Effects of Time Pressure

The average supermarket trip takes shoppers about 45 minutes to accomplish.[29] When the shopper is rushed and does not have the full time needed to shop comfortably, s/he usually feels stressed. Under stress, consumers are not as able to remember information (such as what brand they bought last, or what a fair price is) unless it is particularly well known to them. Further, they cannot take in as much in-store information.[30] In addition, under time pressure consumers are motivated to complete the shopping trip as soon as possible, and thus are less likely to respond to in-store promotions, and are likely to trade off accuracy (i.e., buying items at a reasonable price or buying exactly the items desired) for speed (i.e., getting out of the store as quickly as possible).[31]

As we have noted, lack of store knowledge increases unplanned purchasing, but this effect is moderated by the amount of time the consumer has to spend shopping. Unplanned purchasing in unfamiliar environments is more likely to happen when the consumer has sufficient time to shop. When consumers are under time pressure and are unfamiliar with the store, they are more likely to buy within the planned product categories, but they may also switch brands or make substitutions, due to difficulty in locating the originally intended item. When consumers are in a familiar store and have sufficient time to shop, they are most likely to shop carefully, and switching from original plans may occur because of in-store price and brand comparisons. In a familiar store, time-pressured consumers are most likely to buy exactly what they planned on purchasing.[32]

Influence of Others in the Purchase Decision

Supermarket shopping is not always a solitary activity. Fewer than half of shoppers shop alone.[33] In many cases, the shopping companions are children. Children can be very influential in the buying process and can easily increase the number of unplanned purchases.

In one study conducted on grocery shoppers in New Zealand, shoppers who were accompanied by children spent an average of 11 percent more time in the supermarket and spent $30 more per shopping trip than those who were unaccompanied. Of course, these findings can mean a lot of things. Perhaps the accompanying children encourage the shopper to spend more time in the store and, consequently, to spend more money. Or, more likely, an unaccompanied shopper is more apt to live alone than one who is accompanied by children, and that too could explain the shorter time in the store and the smaller grocery bill. These results, though, do mirror other studies that found that shoppers accompanied by children spend more time in the stores.[34]

Another survey, conducted by Simmons Market Research Bureau,[35] again showed that young children were influential in the buying process for some supermarket products. Children's influence was stronger in some of the categories in which they tend to consume, such as cereals, cookies, candy, gum, soft drinks, frozen pizzas, and boxed macaroni and cheese. Just because children consume in a category does not necessarily mean that they are involved in the purchase decision. Children's involvement in categories such as hot dogs, frozen dinners, or canned spaghetti was slight, even though these are categories that are frequently consumed by children. The latter product classes are not as intrinsically interesting to the children and manufacturers have not (yet) gone out of their way to promote to children.

Percentage of Survey Respondents Indicating That Children Were Involved in Purchase Decision, by Product

Cereals	47%
Cookies	38%
Candy	35%
Gum	35%
Soft drinks	25%
Frozen pizzas	25%
Boxed macaroni and cheese	25%

Supermarkets tend to make items readily accessible to children in those categories in which children are known to have influence. Items in these categories tend to be placed on lower shelves or at the cash register. A survey conducted by the Center for Science in the Public Interest found that high-sugar cereals tended to be placed at eye level for children, while the more nutritious cereals that appealed to adults were placed on higher shelves.[36] Manufacturers also design packaging to cater to children in certain product categories. Yogurt manufacturers have changed their packaging to appeal especially to children, as have some soft drink manufacturers—and cereals have always used cartoon and popular television characters on their packages to catch children's eyes.

LAYOUT OF THE SUPERMARKET

What are the variables that retailers can use to influence in-store purchasing? The key objective of the retailer is to keep the customer in the store longer and to notice and respond to more of the in-store promotions. One way to do this is through the store layout. The layout of the store, the way the product categories are arranged within the store, and the way the shelves are arranged within the categories can affect whether or not consumers buy certain products.

By changing the store environment periodically, shoppers can become more susceptible to in-store cues. This is more likely to be effective, however, if consumers have enough time to shop. To reduce feelings of time pressure and irritation, and to make the shopping experience easier, retailers can make aisles wider and in-store information easy to read and understand.[37]

Traditional Supermarket Layout

One of the salient characteristics of the early supermarkets (around 1914–1917) was the concept of self-service, rather than relying on grocery clerks to get products for consumers. Early reactions to this self-service concept were not enthusiastic; trying to find products all over the store was difficult for consumers who were used to having help. So, a store in Pomona, California arranged all the items in the store in alphabetical order and called itself Alpha Beta.[38] An alphabetical layout might make sense rationally, or as a first-cut solution, but it proved to be difficult to implement.

The general layout of the supermarket that emerged, and is now considered traditional, is one in which the consumer enters the store through the produce section, where there are attractive displays. The meats section is generally in the back of the store; the dairy section, where necessary staples such as milk and butter/margarine reside, is on the opposite side of the store, and the grocery items are in the middle.

The food aisles of the supermarket, literally the "meat and potatoes" of the business, generate more than 50 percent of the total sales

---

The Top 12 Categories in Terms of Sales for 1993

1. Meat, 15–20%
2. Fresh produce, 7%
3. Carbonated soft drinks, 4.8%
4. Milk, 4.4%
5. Cold cereal, 3.9%
6. Cigarettes, 3.8%
7. Fresh bread/rolls 3.0%
8. Cheese, 2.8%
9. Chips and snacks, 2.6%
10. Beer and ale, 2.4%
11. Juice (non-refrigerated) 2.1%
12. Frozen dinner and entrees, 2.0%

---

in the store. The top 12 categories in terms of sales for 1993 are all food categories, except for cigarettes.[39]

Center Aisles versus Periphery

The basic model of a supermarket may be a result of Department of Agriculture studies that were run in 1964. These studies found that in test stores where the perishable items were placed in center aisles rather than on the periphery, the number of items purchased and the amount spent declined. The test consumers did not spend less time in these experimental stores, but they were less likely to walk around the whole store, tending instead to go directly to the center of the store to purchase what they needed. The study concluded that both the time spent shopping and the distance traveled within the store determine how much money is spent. A generalized merchandising rule that has emerged, therefore, is that staples should be distributed throughout the supermarket, forcing consumers to walk through as much floor space of the store as possible.[40]

Researchers have studied consumers' mental maps to learn more about merchandise placement. In one experiment conducted in the early 1980s, academic researchers studied these mental maps for the location of different items in supermarkets. They studied two super-markets in Davis, California—one was a branch of a national chain and the other was a store owned locally. Regular customers were shown floor plans of the two supermarkets and asked to recall where different product categories were located in each store. Items located in the peripheral aisles were recalled more accurately and more fre-quently than items located in the central aisles.

The explanation for this result is not clear-cut because the product categories and locations of the categories were not independent. One way to disentangle this confound was to find product classes that were in a central location in one supermarket and a peripheral loca-tion in the other. Four product categories fit this criterion. When those four product categories were located in the peripheral aisles, their location was accurately remembered significantly more often than when the same product categories were located along the cen-ter aisles. One reason for the poor recollection of items in the center of the store is that people tend to remember best the first things that they see (primacy) or the last things that they see (recency), with the central items the least well-remembered or learned.[41]

Supermarkets have also experimented with video cameras and surveillance equipment in order to track how consumers travel through stores. Researchers who studied 1,600 shoppers found that consumers traveled heavily through the periphery of the store, which accounted for 80 percent of the traffic, but were much less likely to travel down the stores' inner aisles, which drew only 13 to 30 percent of the traffic. Another study found that at some of these inner aisles that stock groceries, consumers park their carts at the end of an aisle and walk down the aisle, picking up a few items and carrying them back to their carts. From the supermarket's point of view, this behavior may be less than optimal because consumers may be prone to purchase less from these inner aisles because they are limited by what they can carry back to their carts.[42]

Just because an area of the store generates strong consumer traffic doesn't necessarily translate into big sales transactions. The bakery department is one such area of the grocery store that can generate a great deal of traffic, but many customers may be just looking or smelling, rather than purchasing. A study by the Food Marking Institute showed that while 77 percent of consumers walk through the bakery department, only a third of them make purchases.[43]

Strategic Changes in Layout

Some grocers have started breaking away from traditional store layouts in order to direct traffic strategically into high-margin areas of the store, or to create synergy among product purchases. For example, one Arizona supermarket traced consumer traffic in the store and discovered that only 18 percent of the grocery store consumers traveled down the greeting cards aisle. This aisle was considered important because it generated high margins. The store owner experimented with the store layout, placing the greeting card aisle between two high-traffic departments, the floral department and the peanut-butter-and-jelly aisle. In the new location, the greeting cards display was visited much more often by consumers and sales jumped 40 percent in the next quarter. This same grocer is now studying how to increase traffic for its own store-brand products by placing them in frequently traveled locations such as key end-of-the-aisle display shelves.[44]

A relatively new layout design in supermarkets is to separate the fresh perishables sections of the supermarket from the grocery and nonfood aisles. The perishable sections include featured deli counters, pizza, prepared foods, service meat and seafood, a coffee bar, floral, snack bar, and the in-store bakery. For example, Randall's New Generation store in Houston, Texas opened in 1989 with this format. The store was separated into two parts, one side had the fresh perishables and the other grocery and nonfood aisles. The decor in the two sides was different, with the grocery side more stark and brightly lit and the perishable foods side featuring muted lighting, tiled floors, and wood decor. The format worked well for the store and helped Randall's reach a whole new customer base. Some in the industry are labeling this new format a "food court" within the supermarket.[45]

Cross Merchandising

Cross merchandising is a promotional technique that ties a promotion for one product to the promotion of another. Cross merchandising has been used frequently by manufacturers. For example, Duncan Hines might include a coupon for its frosting in a cake mix box, or Rice Krispies might include a coupon for Marshmallow Fluff in its cereal box.

Manufacturers and retailers have also begun experimenting with in-store cross promotions to encourage consumers to travel from high-traffic areas to low-traffic areas. Pepsi-Cola Co. has been testing some in-store advertising programs that advertise their soft drink brands in the high-traffic bakery department and advertise their snack and chip products (Frito-Lay) in the coffee aisles.[46]

Systematic experiments to determine the effectiveness of cross merchandising have been conducted.[47] In one, researchers experimented by using a "draw" category—one with high visibility and/or high frequency of purchase—to encourage purchase of a "target" item. Four different promotional techniques were used to test the effectiveness of cross merchandising:

1. Control, which offered a temporary in-store price reduction for the target item
2. Traditional, which involved an in-store cross-promotion between complementary categories (e.g., a baking sheet as the "draw" and a measuring cup as the "target")
3. In-aisle, which involved an in-store cross-promotion within a given aisle but between different categories (e.g., soap as the "draw" item and toothpaste as the "target")

   4. Traffic building, which involved an in-store cross promotion between a high-traffic category and a low-traffic category (e.g., bath tissue as the "draw" item and shampoo as the "target")

This experiment was carefully conducted so that the price promotions on the target items were comparable, and the difference was in how the "draw" category was used. Across the country, 210 stores participated and 20 cross-merchandising tests were conducted. In each test, the targeted category was a HBC/GM item.

The control, or in-store coupon promotion, increased the target item sales by 80 percent as compared to historical non-promotion baselines. The traditional and in-aisle cross-merchandising techniques performed equivalently to the control group. The traffic building promotions improved sales of the target item 15 percent over the control. This suggests that increased sales in the HBC/GM categories can occur by linking the purchase of seemingly unrelated items where one is in a high-traffic area and the other is in a low-traffic area.[48]

In some instances in the study, the traffic-building cross merchandising was not so effective. When the physical distance between the draw item and the target item was too far in the store, then the cross-merchandising techniques were not as effective. In addition, using a slow-moving category, such as flour, was not as effective as a draw category. The best draw items were from categories in which there was a great deal of traffic, such as bath tissue or laundry detergents. Target categories that work better with cross merchandising are those that are purchased more frequently, such as hair care, film, and soap. Categories that are purchased less frequently, such as oral care, vitamins, and laundry baskets, work less well as the target category in traffic-building tests.[49]

An experiment involving shelf reorganization[50] was run in two categories, oral care and laundry care. Shelf allocations were rearranged to increase the sales of slower moving goods by making them more prominent. In oral care, the primary product, toothpaste, is purchased by most households with an average interpurchase time of about two months. On the other hand, toothbrushes are purchased by most households, but not as frequently, with average interpurchase times of about 4 to 6 months. In the laundry category, the primary product, detergent, is purchased by most households approximately every two months, but fabric softener is only purchased by about 65 percent of the households. By making the slower moving products more prominent within the category as compared to the better-moving primary products, the hope was to increase sales. The changes in the oral care category increased sales of toothbrushes by 8 percent and profits in the category by 6 percent; the laundry care category resulted in a 4 percent increase in sales and profits. We don't know if these changes reflect short-term changes in behavior due to the novel display or if these changes would persist over time.

IN-STORE ACTIVITIES OF MANUFACTURERS

One obvious factor that influences unplanned purchasing and purchasing in general in a product category is the in-store activity generated by the manufacturers in the category. For example, when manufacturers manage to move beyond mindless "me-too" proliferation to introduce truly innovative new products, categories can grow explosively.

New Products
Four of the five top-performing grocery categories in 1994, defined by percent change in sales from the previous year, were characterized by the introduction of some truly innovative new products.

Top Five Grocery Category Performers (1994 Sales)	
Soup	+6.43%
Breakfast foods	+5.79%
Baby foods	+5.10%
Juice	+3.99%
Cookies/crackers	+3.21%

In canned soup, much of the growth in the category was attributed to a stream of new products, such as healthy soups, ethnic soups, and seasoned soups. In breakfast foods, four of the best-selling new food products overall in 1994 were cereals, including Rice Krispies Treats, Banana Nut Crunch, Quaker Toasted Oatmeal, and General Mills' Ripple Crisp. In juice, much of the growth was due to the sales of the new fruit-flavored drinks, spurred on by the success of Snapple—a new product that really revved up the category. In cookies and crackers, growth was attributed to the craze for fat-free products, like the Snack Well items. Nabisco, the leader in the category, and Keebler, the number two in the category, introduced reduced- and low-fat versions of most of their cracker and cookie products.

Only in baby foods was the success of the category due mostly to higher sales of a mature product, formula. But even in this category, as the baby population levels off, new products will be introduced. Gerber has already extended the baby food category by introducing Hispanic-oriented foods, larger size juices, and yogurt juices.[51]

Price/Promotional Strategies

Another manufacturer-driven activity that affects sales in a category are changes in price and promotional strategies. As mentioned previously, the breakfast foods category had a number of new products that helped spur sales growth. In addition, growth in this category was also due to changes in price and promotional strategies. For example, prior to 1994, ready-to-eat cereals were characterized by such strategies as heavy couponing, free samples, and buy-one, get-one-free offers. Private labels also saw great growth spurts. The big news in this category in 1994 was the announcement by General Mills that they were going to lower the list prices on eight of their leading brands, and reduce other promotional activities such as couponing and buy-one, get-one-free offers.[52] Similarly, in 1996, cereal prices came down again with the price moves by Post, Kellogg, and General Mills. Kellogg's price cuts brought their prices down to the levels of the late 1980s. The price cuts were designed to spur higher rates of growth in the category.

In-Store Promotions

Another way that manufacturers can influence sales in a category is by generating in-store promotional materials. ACTMEDIA is a company that sells in-store promotions to the manufacturers. ACTMEDIA works out arrangements with the retailers to lease out "space" or "in-store media" to manufacturers. ACTMEDIA provides in-store marketing promotions, such as "shelftalkers"—signs on the shelves, or freezer markers—on in-store freezers. They also have "pop radio," an in-store broadcasting network that plays live-radio formatted entertainment and combines advertising and price-feature promotions. "Instant coupon machines" pop out a coupon at the shelf that can be redeemed immediately at the cash register. ACTMEDIA calls all of these promotional devices the "theater-in-the-store." They claim that their tests have documented an average sales increase of 8 percent for products using ACTMEDIA advertising programs. Their advertising claims that their promotions are targeted to the consumer's moment of decision and therefore help create an incentive for the consumer to try the product, or switch away from their brand to a new brand.[53]

Effects of Food Sampling

Another way to keep consumers in the store is to give them free food. Food sampling uses the old sales tactic of baiting consumers with the lure of a free taste. The free sample alleviates any perceived risk if consumers are afraid to try new products, or new versions of old products. Sampling also creates awareness for the manufacturer. In addition, sometimes consumers feel obligated to buy if they tried a sample.

In general, supermarkets have been very amenable to sampling because it has traditionally been funded by the manufacturer, and ends up helping both the manufacturer and the retailer by selling more product. Sampling in supermarkets can also benefit the retailer in other ways. When a lot of sampling and demonstrations are going on around the store, the atmosphere of the supermarket changes—into more of a indoor food fair. Sometimes this can take on enormous proportions. For example, ShopRite in Lincoln Park, New Jersey has a three-day Samplefest with more than 60 booths offering 80 to 100 products for customers to sample. The Samplefest focuses on a different department each year, one year it was produce, the next it was seafood. The store owner predicted that a volume increase of 5 percent emerged from Samplefest and that growth continues from that level.[54]

Changing the sampling into a whole event can also move a lot of product for the manufacturer. For example, Cadbury Schweppes Diet Sunkist brand of soft drink was distributed in 3-ounce cups at a special event using a Diet Sunkist van and an inflatable can of soda to attract attention. Customers who purchased a certain amount of soda in the supermarket received a Diet Sunkist T-shirt. There were also games in an outdoor display by the van. Sunkist reported that as a result of this demonstration, 625 cases of soft drinks sold in six hours—the single largest movement ever for the brand.[55]

A survey of bakery directors representing 6,000 supermarkets showed that well-planned sampling programs increased sales and profits, and enhanced customer relations. In addition, sales were 27 percent higher when the demonstrator mentioned the price of the item and asked the customer to make the purchase. Demonstrating an item that was also being advertised and featured in the newspaper increased the effectiveness of the sampling results by 300 percent.[56]

There are several companies that work with manufacturers to help advertise, promote, and display products within the grocery store. For example, Point of Sale employs 2,000 demonstrators who work as independent contractors. These demonstrators go into supermarkets in the Midwest and organize in-store sampling or demonstrations. Sometimes these demonstrators are also encouraged to talk about the product and gather consumer reaction.[57]

ATMOSPHERICS IN THE STORE

Atmospherics—the conscious designing of the retail environment to create pleasant, emotional, sensory effects—can serve several purposes. Atmospherics, such as bright lights and color, festivities, and music, draw attention to the supermarket and bring in customers. The manager of Super Foodtown in New Jersey, for example, changed the entrance of his store so that customers entered and got a panoramic view of the produce department, an inviting display of color, dramatic lighting (he dropped, warm, white spotlights on the fruits and vegetables), and wide aisles. To encourage browsing, the manager left his produce in loose displays rather than prepackaging them. The strategy worked: the percent of total store sales attributed to the department increased and gross margin was maintained.[58]

Atmospherics can also be used to send a message. If a supermarket wants to create an upscale image, it might have classical music playing and hardwood floors. Or, atmospherics can be used to create a mood—a pleasant environment that makes people happy to be there.[59] Harris-Teeter opened a super foodstore in Atlanta, Georgia that is marketed as ". . . living, interactive theater, where the customer truly becomes a part of supermarketing."[60] The supermarket is targeted for people who really love food and who want a sensuous shopping environment that also provides a social atmosphere. This supermarket has 30 in-store chefs, an espresso bar as big as a convenience store, and a Caesar salad island.

When atmospherics make the store environment more pleasant, consumers are likely to spend more time in the store. It is hoped that if consumers are persuaded to spend more time in the store, and are feeling happy, more money will be spent.

Influence of Mood on Shopping Behavior

Although there is a lot of folk lore about how atmospherics affect purchase behavior, there is little conclusive scientific evidence. One reason is because the effects of atmospherics can be difficult to quantify, are likely to be transient, and will only subtly influence purchase behavior within the store.[61]

One study showed that atmospherics within the environment can affect purchase intentions in two ways. First, atmospherics could affect whether the consumer feels happy or unhappy in the environment. This store-induced pleasure seemed to have some effect on the extent to which a consumer purchased beyond what s/he had planned to purchase. Second, atmospherics could affect consumers by the degree in which the consumer feels excited or aroused by the environment. The arousal that the in-store environment can create seems to affect the amount of time spent in the store and the willingness to interact with sales people.[62]

Another study showed that positive mood increases variety seeking by consumers. In this laboratory study, where the influence of positive mood on purchasing behavior could be isolated,[63] researchers found that when subjects were in an experimental condition where positive mood was induced (through the unexpected gift of a bag of colorful candies wrapped with ribbons), they were more likely to seek variety in their choice of products than were subjects who were in a control or neutral condition. From other measures collected at the time of the experiment, the researchers concluded that positive mood improved the consumers' anticipation that happy or positive events would occur, and also encouraged people to elaborate more in their thinking. The subjects in the positive mood conditions anticipated higher enjoyment levels from consuming these items than did the subjects in the neutral condition. Thus, a fun-filled, festival-like supermarket environment can encourage consumers to choose novel items, or items different from the normal pursuits. If the retail environment becomes too stimulating, it can have the opposite effect. If too much is going on, consumers may try to simplify things and may respond by purchasing with product categories in a more routine fashion, choosing less variety. In this case, more limited assortments would be acceptable.[64]

The outcome of the shopping experience also depends upon the level of consumer involvement. Other studies testing how mood influenced shopping were conducted in department store settings, but the findings may generalize. In one department store study, the effects of mood were found to be moderated by the level of involvement in the shopping experience and by whether the experience was perceived to be positive or negative. When the shopping experience was perceived to be positive, and the consumers were involved, shopping intentions were the highest. Shopping intentions were measured by asking questions such as how much time you were likely to spend shopping, to buy other items, and so on.[65]

In another department store study,[66] researchers tried to establish whether pleasure induced by the store environment could influence shopping behavior. Before entering the department store, shoppers were asked to estimate the time that they planned to shop and the amount of money they planned on spending. After the shoppers had been shopping for five minutes, the researchers asked them to rate their feelings on a 12-item scale that measured both pleasure and arousal. At the end of the shopping trip, the amount of time the shoppers had spent in the store and how much money they had spent was noted. Shoppers who scored higher on the pleasure and arousal scales or, in other words, shoppers who were happier and in a higher arousal state, were found to spend more time in the store and to spend more money than intended.

These studies suggest that if the shopping environment is pleasant and encourages shoppers to enjoy themselves, shoppers may linger more in the store, may spend more money, and may purchase more unusual items or purchase more variety in their overall selections. Thus, it makes some sense for supermarket retailers to attempt to link these concepts of pleasure and arousal to specific environmental factors that can be influenced.[67] The environmental factors that have been studied include color, odor, and in-store music.

Influence of Color

A review of the literature on the marketing implications of color[68] in retail store design indicates that color has been used to get the consumer's attention. In one study, subjects were more drawn to or aware of warmer colors, such as red and yellow, in the store environments, but paradoxically found the red environments to be unpleasant and less attractive than the cooler colored environments (e.g., blue/green).[69]

Another set of studies constructed to resolve that paradox show that the effects of color should be evaluated on two dimensions, an arousal dimension and an evaluative dimension. Colors that have been found to be the most arousing include red and blue, the extremes of the color spectrum, while the colors in the middle of the spectrum, green and yellow, are less arousing. Colors that are evaluated as positive include the cooler colors such as blue and green, whereas the warmer colors such as red and orange are evaluated less positively. Thus, red is judged as a color that is arousing, but perhaps not as positive. Red may be especially useful where impulse purchasing is warranted.[70]

In a simulated retail setting where the task was to purchase a television, the effect of color on purchase intentions in the retail environment was specifically studied. Red and blue were used because they are on the extreme opposites of the color spectrum. In the red store, more shoppers postponed selection of a television and were willing to spend less money than shoppers in the blue store. Also, more shoppers in the blue store than in the red store selected the most expensive television. The color treatments did not affect the amount of time consumers spent shopping. In a second experiment involving a simulated furniture store, subjects in the blue environment indicated a greater intention to shop, browse, and purchase in the simulated store than subjects in a red environment. These two experiments showed more positive consumer reactions to blue retail environments than to red retail environments. The effects seemed to be driven at least in part by the fact that the blue environment was perceived to be more pleasant and the red environment was viewed as more negative and unpleasant.

It should be noted that most of these empirical results about the influence of color on purchasing behavior were found with regard to the purchase of durables and thus may not extend to food products. Some supermarket products may benefit from the warm emotional meaning or the excitement that the color red can also generate. In any event, these results indicate that color in the retail environment can influence consumer behavior.[71]

Influence of Fragrance

Another marketing technique that has been used to change the atmosphere of the store is the introduction of pumped-in aromas into the store environment. The aromas, such as the musky aroma that newborn babies get from their mothers, has been pumped into the air-conditioning systems in supermarkets in England. In another store in England, the smell of Christmas puddings and brandy was pumped into the nonfood areas in December in an effort to get consumers in the holiday spirit. At Easter, some stores pump in the aroma of chocolate. Aroma "vendors," such as Marketing Aromatics, a London firm, suggest that odors can work on three different levels. First, they may relax the consumer; second, they may stir up memories or associations with certain products; finally, they may serve as an aromatic logo or brand name, so that the consumer associates a specific store with a specific scent.[72]

Once again, scientific studies have shown subtler effects of ambient odor on consumer shopping behavior. Unlike the commercial claims about the effects of smell, academic studies tend to be done in the laboratory with very careful control. The point of these studies is to isolate the effect of odors on behavior, mood, and thinking.

A review of the findings about the effect of odor on general human behavior[73] identified some evidence that pleasant fragrances can sometimes increase alertness,[74] facilitate the recall of happy thoughts and memories,[75] and improve the performance of laboratory subjects on certain cognitive tasks, such as unscrambling words and decoding messages.[76] In addition, some evidence shows that pleasant fragrances influence these behaviors, at least to some degree, because they put people in a positive mood.[77, 78, 79]

There has also been some research conducted specifically in shopping environments to test the effect of pumping odors into the atmosphere on purchasing behavior. The research has shown that putting pleasant smells into the atmosphere of a store will significantly increase the amount of time consumers spend in the store,[80, 81] but there has been no evidence that the ambient odor increases the numbers of items purchased or the total amount spent.[82]

In another study,[83] researchers found that effect of odor on decision making depended upon whether the odor was or was not congruent with the product class being considered. For example, when the smell of chocolate was pumped into the air, the effect of that odor on decision making depended upon whether the consumers in the study were choosing among chocolate products or among a non-candy product, such as flowers. When the smell matched the product class, the consumers appeared to be more cognitively flexible, and were more likely to seek variety in their choices in the category.

When the ambient odor was incongruent with the product class, consumers were less cognitively flexible, and revealed more brand loyal behavior. This finding is important because it suggests that odor may also be effective not only by influencing emotions, but by influencing the cognitive processes and by serving as a way to make certain memories more accessible to the consumer.

Influence of In-Store Music

Music is probably one of the most frequently used atmospherics to change the environment of the store. A summary of the literature[84] shows that sales in various retail environments depend on the type of music that is played. In supermarkets, studies found that higher sales per consumer were generated when Muzak was played as compared with contemporary music or no music.[85] Across all the empirical work, the general finding is that any improvement in sales was also correlated with customers spending longer times in the store—either because they moved slower or because they stayed in the store for a longer time.

As with many of these other atmospherics, a lot of folklore exists about how they work and influence purchase behavior, but not a lot of scientific evidence exists to support these beliefs.[86] One survey[87] conducted on 52 retail stores of various types found that although there was no scientific proof for these beliefs, 76 percent of the store managers thought that their customers purchased more when background music was playing, and 82 percent of them thought that the music helped put customers in a better mood. Their customers also believed these findings. In the same study, the 63 percent of customers of these retail stores who were surveyed said that they either "purchased more" or "probably purchased more" when background music was playing in stores, and 70 percent indicated that they preferred stores that played music. In another survey of over 200 customers of a New York area supermarket, 77 percent of the customers indicated that they preferred background music while they shopped and 67 percent felt that this indicated that the store managers cared about their customers.[88]

There has been some scientific support for the influence of music on consumer behavior. Researchers[89] found that customers spent significantly less time in stores when the music was loud compared to when the music was soft, although there was no significant difference in sales or in the customers' reported levels of satisfaction. Another experiment conducted in a medium-sized supermarket located in the southwestern United States[90] found that if the tempo of instrumental music played in the background of a supermarket was slowed down, the pace of the in-store traffic flow also slowed down. The slower pace music stimulated an even slower pace than no music at all, although this difference was not statistically significant. This slower pace also resulted in increases in per capita expenditures in the store as compared to faster pace music. Interestingly, when the customers were asked questions as to whether they were aware of the music playing or if they could recall what music was playing, there was no difference among any of the experimental groups (i.e., slow-paced music, faster-paced music, or no music). It was suggested that supermarkets should keep in-store music at a slow pace to encourage customers to spend more time in the store, and hopefully to purchase more while there. In restaurants, or perhaps in the food court areas of the supermarket, the tempo of the music might be faster to encourage customers to move through the process more quickly and allow more customers to be served.

Endnotes

1. Bettman, James R. (1979), *An Information Processing Theory of Consumer Choice*, Reading, MA: Addison-Wesley.

2. Whalen, Bernie (1995), "Retail Customer Service: Marketing's Last Frontier," *Marketing News*, (March 15), 16, 18.

3. "Turning Traffic Into Transactions," (1994), a study funded by the American Greetings Research Council with the Cooperation of Food Marketing Institute.

4. Kollat, D. T. and R. P. Willet (1967), "Customer Impulse Purchasing Behavior," *Journal of Marketing Research*, 4, 21–31.

5. Kollat, D. T. and R. P. Willet (1967), "Customer Impulse Purchasing Behavior," *Journal of Marketing Research*, 4, 21–31.

6. Shermach, Kelly (1995), "Study: Most Shoppers Notice P-O-P Material," *Marketing News*, (January 2), 27.

7. Kollat, David T. and R. P. Willet (1969), "Is Impulse Purchasing Really a Useful Concept for Marketing Decisions?" *Journal of Marketing*, 33 (January), 79–83.

8. Spiggle, Susan (1987), "Grocery Shopping Lists: What Do Consumers Write?" in *Advances in Consumer Research*, Vol. 14, Melanie Wallendorf and Paul F. Anderson, Eds.., Provo, UT: Association for Consumer Research, 241–245.

9. Thomas, Art and Ron Gardland, (1993), "Supermarket Shopping Lists," *International Journal of Retail & Distribution Management*, 21 (2), 8–14.

10. Rook, Dennis W. (1987), "The Buying Impulse," *Journal of Consumer Research*, 14 (September), 189–199.

11. Iyer, Easwar S. (1989), "Unplanned Purchasing: Knowledge of Shopping Environment and Time Pressure," *Journal of Retailing*, 65 (Spring), 40–57.

12. Stern, Hawkins (1962), "The Significance of Impulse Buying Today," *Journal of Marketing*, 26 (April), 59–62.

13. Spiggle, Susan (1987), "Grocery Shopping Lists: What Do Consumers Write?" in *Advances in Consumer Research*, Vol. 14, Melanie Wallendorf and Paul F. Anderson, Eds., Provo, UT: Association for Consumer Research, 241–245.

14. Stern, Hawkins (1962), "The Significance of Impulse Buying Today," *Journal of Marketing*, 26 (April), 59–62.

15. Rook, Dennis W. (1987), "The Buying Impulse," *Journal of Consumer Research*, 14 (September), 189–199.

16. Rook, Dennis W. (1987), "The Buying Impulse," *Journal of Consumer Research*, 14 (September), 189–199.

17. Rook, Dennis W. (1990), "Is 'Impulse Buying' (Yet) a Useful Marketing Concept?" Working Paper, Northwestern University, (May).

18. Rook, Dennis W. (1990), "Is 'Impulse Buying' (Yet) a Useful Marketing Concept?" Working Paper, Northwestern University, (May).

19. Staten, Vince (1993), *Can You Trust a Tomato in January?* New York: Simon and Schuster.

20. Dwyer, Steve (1993), "C-Store Merchandising: For Candy Consumers, Seeing is Buying," *National Petroleum News* (September), 50–52.

21. "Supermarket Nonfoods Business: Minding Your Magazines," (1994), *Supermarket Business* (December), 61–66.

22. "Supermarket Nonfoods Business: Minding Your Magazines," (1994), *Supermarket Business* (December), 61–66.

23. Park, C. Whan, Easwar S. Iyer, and Daniel C. Smith (1989), "The Effects of Situational Factors on In-Store Grocery Behavior: The Role of Store Environment and Time Available for Shopping," *Journal of Consumer Research*, 15 (March), 422–433.

24. Belk, Russell W. (1975), "Situational Variables and Consumer Behavior," *Journal of Consumer Research*, 2 (December), 157–63.

25. Park, C. Whan, Easwar S. Iyer, and Daniel C. Smith (1989), "The Effects of Situational Factors on In-Store Grocery Behavior: The Role of Store Environment and Time Available for Shopping," *Journal of Consumer Research*, 15 (March), 422–433.

26. Iyer, Easwar S. (1989), "Unplanned Purchasing: Knowledge of Shopping Environment and Time Pressure," *Journal of Retailing*, 65 (Spring), 40–57.

27. Park, C. Whan, Easwar S. Iyer, and Daniel C. Smith (1989), "The Effects of Situational Factors on In-Store Grocery Behavior: The Role of Store Environment and Time Available for Shopping," *Journal of Consumer Research*, 15 (March), 422–433.

28. Iyer, Easwar S. (1989), "Unplanned Purchasing: Knowledge of Shopping Environment and Time Pressure," *Journal of Retailing*, 65 (Spring), 40–57.

29. Shermach, Kelly (1995), "Study: Most Shoppers Notice P-O-P Material," *Marketing News* (January 2), 27.

30. Park, C. Whan, Easwar S. Iyer, and Daniel C. Smith (1989), "The Effects of Situational Factors on In-Store Grocery Behavior: The Role of Store Environment and Time Available for Shopping," *Journal of Consumer Research*, 15 (March), 422–433.

31. Isenberg, Daniel J. (1981), "Some Effects of Time-Pressure on Vertical Structure and Decision Making in Small Groups," *Organizational Behavior and Human Performance,* 27 (February), 119–134.

32. Park, C. Whan, Easwar S. Iyer, and Daniel C. Smith (1989), "The Effects of Situational Factors on In-Store Grocery Behavior: The Role of Store Environment and Time Available for Shopping," *Journal of Consumer Research*, 15 (March), 422–433.

33. Staten, Vince (1993), *Can You Trust a Tomato in January?* New York: Simon and Schuster, p. 31.

34. Thomas, Art and Ron Gardland, (1993), "Supermarket Shopping Lists," *International Journal of Retail & Distribution Management*, 21 (2), 8–14.

35. Berkowitz, Harry (1993), "Marketers Assess Buying Power of Children," *The Philadelphia Inquirier*, September 8, C7.

36. Staten, Vince (1993), *Can You Trust a Tomato in January?* New York: Simon and Schuster, p. 52.

37. Iyer, Easwar S. (1989), "Unplanned Purchasing: Knowledge of Shopping Environment and Time Pressure," *Journal of Retailing*, 65 (Spring), 40–57.

38. Staten], Vince (1993), *Can You Trust a Tomato in January?* New York: Simon and Schuster. p. 20–23.

39. Figures for first two categories are taken from Great Atlantic and Pacific Tea Co. stores. Figures for the next 10 categories are based on Information Resources Inc.'s InfoScan service as reported in "What's in the Bag," by Kathleen Deveny, *Wall Street Journal* (October 26, 1993).

40. Staten, Vince (1993), *Can You Trust a Tomato in January?* New York: Simon and Schuster, 33–34.

41. Sommer, Robert and Susan Aitkens (1982), "Mental Mapping of Two Supermarkets," *Journal of Consumer Research*, 9 (September), 211–215.

42. McCarthy, Michael J. (1993), "James Bond Hits the Supermarket: Stores Snoop on Shoppers' Habits to Boost Sales," *Wall Street Journal: Market Place*, (August 25), B1, B8.

43. McCarthy, Michael J. (1993), "James Bond Hits the Supermarket: Stores Snoop on Shoppers' Habits to Boost Sales," *Wall Street Journal: Market Place* (August 25), B1, B8.

44. McCarthy, Michael (1993), "James Bond Hits the Supermarket: Stores Snoop on Shoppers' Habits to Boost Sales," *The Wall Street Journal: Marketplace* (August 25), B1, B8.

45. Litwak, David (1993), "Standing the Test of Time," *Supermarket Business*, 48 (May), 87–95.

46. McCarthy, Michael (1993), "James Bond Hits the Supermarket: Stores Snoop on Shoppers' Habits to Boost Sales," *The Wall Street Journal: Market Place* (August 25), B1, B8.

47. "Turning Traffic Into Transactions," (1994), a study funded by the American Greetings Research Council with the Cooperation of Food Marketing Institute.

48. "Turning Traffic Into Transactions," (1994), a study funded by the American Greetings Research Council with the Cooperation of Food Marketing Institute.

49. "Turning Traffic Into Transactions," (1994), a study funded by the American Greetings Research Council with the Cooperation of Food Marketing Institute.

50. "Turning Traffic Into Transactions," (1994), a study funded by the American Greetings Research Council with the Cooperation of Food Marketing Institute

51. "Sales Manual/Top Performers: What's Hot," (1994), *Progressive Grocer* (July), 69–82.

52. "Sales Manual/Top Performers: What's Hot," (1994), *Progressive Grocer* (July), 69–82.

53. ACTMEDIA (1992), "ACTMEDIA: The In-store Marketing Network," sales brochure, Norwalk, CT.

54. Duff, Mike (1989), "A Moveable Feast," *Supermarket Business* (July), 9A–12A.

55. Eisman, Regina (1993), "Giving Away the Goods," *Incentive* (May), 39–44.

56. Weller, Ed (1992), "Sampling Sells," *Progressive Grocer* (October), 121.

57. "Grocers Say Best Place to Influence Consumers is in the Store," (1993), *Marketing News* (August 30), 7.

58. Simmons, Tim (1994), "If They Stay, They'll Pay," *Supermarket Business* (February), 103–107.

59. Kotler, Philip (1973-1974), "Atmospherics as a Marketing Tool," *Journal of Retailing*, 49 (Winter), 48–64.

60. "Don't Die Until You've Seen this Store!" (1994) *Supermarket Business* (January), 27–33.

61. Donovan, Robert J. and John R. Rossiter (1982), "Store Atmosphere: An Environmental Psychology Approach," *Journal of Retailing*, 58 (Spring), 34–57.

62. Donovan, Robert J. and John R. Rossiter (1982), "Store Atmosphere: An Environmental Psychology Approach," *Journal of Retailing*, 58 (Spring), 34–57.

63. Kahn, Barbara E. and Alice M. Isen (1993), "The Influence of Positive Affect on Variety-Seeking Among Safe, Enjoyable Products," *Journal of Consumer Research*, 20 (September), 257–270.

64. Menon, Satya and Barbara E. Kahn (1995), "The Impact of External Context on Variety-Seeking in Product Choices," *Journal of Consumer Research* (December), 285–295.

65. Swinyard, William R. (1993), "The Effects of Mood, Involvement and Quality of Store Experience on Shopping Intentions," *Journal of Consumer Research*, 20 (September), 271–280.

66. Donovan, Robert J., John R. Rossiter, Gilian Marcoolyn, and Andrew Nesdale (1994), "Store Atmosphere and Purchasing Behavior," *Journal of Retailing,* 70 (3), 283–294.

67. Baker, Julie, Michael Levy, and Dhruv Grwal (1992), "An Experimental Approach to Making Retail Store Environmental Decisions," *Journal of Retailing*, 68 (Winter), 445–460.

68. Bellizzi, Joseph A. and Robert E. Hite (1992), "Environmental Color, Consumer Feelings and Purchase Likelihood," *Psychology and Marketing*, 9 (September/October), 347–363.

69. Bellizzi, J. A., A. E. Crowley, and R. W. Hasty (1983), "The Effects of Color in Store Design," *Journal of Retailing*, 59, 21–45.

70. Crowley, Ayn E. (1993), "The Two-Dimensional Impact of Color on Shopping," *Marketing Letters,* 4 (1), 59–69.

71. Bellizzi, Joseph A. and Robert E. Hite (1992), "Environmental Color, Consumer Feelings and Purchase Likelihood," *Psychology and Marketing*, 9 (September/October), 347–363.

72. "Electronics Wage Hidden War on Shoppers," (1993), *The Sunday Times* (London, England), (October 24), 9.

73. Baron, Robert A. and Marna I. Bronfen (1994), "A Whiff of Reality: Empirical Evidence Concerning the Effects of Pleasant Fragrances on Work-Related Behavior," *Journal of Applied Social Psychology*, 24 (13), 1179–1203.

74. Warm, J. S. W. N. Dember, and R. Parasuraman (1991), "Effects of Olfactory Stimulation on Performance and Stress in a Visual Sustained

Attention Task," *Journal of the Society of Cosmetic Chemists*, 12, 1–12.

75. Ehrlichmann, Howard and Jack N. Halpern (1988), "Affect and Memory: Effects of Pleasant and Unpleasant Odors on Retrieval of Happy and Unhappy Memories," *Journal of Personality and Social Psychology*, 55 (5), 769–779.

76. Baron, Robert A. and Marna I. Bronfen (1994), "A Whiff of Reality: Empirical Evidence Concerning the Effects of Pleasant Fragrances on Work-Related Behavior," *Journal of Applied Social Psychology*, 24 (13), 1179–1203.

77. Baron, Robert A. and Marna I. Bronfen (1994), "A Whiff of Reality: Empirical Evidence Concerning the Effects of Pleasant Fragrances on Work-Related Behavior," *Journal of Applied Social Psychology*, 24 (13), 1179–1203.

78. Baron, Robert A. (1990), "Environmentally Induced Positive Affect: Its Impact on Self-Efficacy, Task Performance, Negotiation and Conflict," *Journal of Applied Social Psychology*, 20 (March), 368–384.

79. Ehrlichmann, Howard and Jack N. Halpern (1988), "Affect and Memory: Effects of Pleasant and Unpleasant Odors on Retrieval of Happy and Unhappy Memories," *Journal of Personality and Social Psychology*, 55 (5), 769–779.

80. Knasko, Susan (1989), "Ambient Odor and Shopping Behavior," *Chemical Senses*, 14 (94), 718.

81. Teerling, A., R. R. Nixdorf, and E. P. Koster (1992), "The Effects of Ambient Odours on Shopping Behaviour," from the abstracts of the 10th Congress of ECRO, August 23–28, Munich Germany, 155.

82. Knasko, Susan (1989), "Ambient Odor and Shopping Behavior," *Chemical Senses*, 14 (94), 718.

83. Mitchell, Deborah, Barbara E. Kahn, and Susan Knasko (1995), "There is Something in the Air: The Effects of Congruent or Incongruent Ambient Odor on Consumer Decision Making," *Journal of Consumer Research*, 22 (September), 229–238.

84. Yalch, Richard and Eric Spangenberg (1990), "Effects of Store Music on Shopping Behavior," *The Journal of Consumer Marketing*, 7 (Spring), 55–63.

85. Ware, Jeff and Gerald L. Patrick (1984), "Gelson's Supermarkets: Effects of MUZAK Music on the Purchasing Behavior of Supermarket Shoppers," MUZAK Research Report.

86. Millman, R. E. (1982), "Using Background Music to Affect the Behavior of Supermarket Shoppers," *Journal of Marketing*, 46 (3), 86–91.

87. Burleson, G. L. (1979), "Retailer and Consumer Attitudes Toward Background Music," unpublished paper, Department of Business Administration, University of Texas at El Paso.

88. Linsen, M. A (1975), "Like Our Music Today, Ms. Shopper?" *Progressive Grocer*, 56 (October), 156.

89. Smith, Patricia Cane and Ross Curnow (1966), "Arousal Hypotheses and the Effects of Music on Purchasing Behavior," *Journal of Applied Psychology*, 50 (3), 255–256.

90. Millman, R. E. (1982), "Using Background Music to Affect the Behavior of Supermarket Shoppers," *Journal of Marketing*, 46 (3), 86–91.

10

How Do Consumers Decide Which Brands to Buy within a Product Category?

Once a consumer has decided to buy within a particular product class, then the decision as to which specific item or brand to purchase must be made. A brand will not be chosen at all if it is not in the consumer's consideration set—the set of items that a consumer is considering for a purchase. How do brands get into a consumer's consideration set? This decision is based both on factors that occur before the consumer enters the store, as well as influencing factors within the store. A consumer learns about brands outside of the store through many cues. For example, the consumer may have been exposed to advertising, or may be familiar with certain brand names through past experiences with other product classes, or may have heard about particular brands through word of mouth. Sometimes a consumer's preference for a brand is formed inside of the store. In this case, packaging, shelf layout, shelf facings, pricing patterns, and forced comparisons between brands can all affect brand choice.

The information that a consumer gathers about a brand—such as the brand name, nutritional information, packaging cues, or word-of-mouth recommendations—and the way this information is recorded in memory can influence consumers' preferences for brands, and whether the brand will be considered for purchase. The presence of store brands, or private label brands, on the shelf can also influence decision making.

If consumers were optimal decision makers, then the formation of different consideration sets would not affect the final product purchased. Consumers would always choose their more-preferred brand regardless of which other brands were considered at an earlier stage. But many times, consumers don't care enough to insure that they are choosing optimally. Rather, they frequently use simplifying rules to narrow down the brands that they are considering. Research has shown that as the composition of consideration sets vary, so does the final choice.

CONSUMERS' CONSIDERATION SETS

Once a consumer decides to buy in a particular category on a specific shopping trip, he or she then has to decide which brand to buy. Sometimes the brand decision and the product category decision are made simultaneously. For example, the consumer's shopping list may read, "buy Tide," rather than just "buy detergent." In many categories, however, the brand decision is not made at the same time as the product category decision. When this is the case, given the enormous number of choices within each category, the consumer generally makes the decision in stages. First, the consumer considers a set of brands that are acceptable using relatively simple criteria. Then the consumer chooses one from this set to purchase, usually applying a more detailed analysis.[1] This "phased decision making"[2] helps simplify the decision process.

The first phase of this decision-making process, or the initial set of acceptable choices, has been labeled a "consideration set"[3, 4, 5] or an "evoked set."[6, 7] The items may change over time; the consumer may delete or add items to the set at will. The final or static consideration set, or the alternatives that are considered just prior to purchase, has been called the "choice set,"[8] and consists of fewer, more differentiated alternatives.

Formation of Consideration Sets

Observations of consumers' shopping patterns reveal that consumers spend very little time making each specific purchase decision in the supermarket. Consumers spend an average of 12 seconds from the time the shelf is approached to the time the item is placed in their carts, and they only examine 1.2 brands on average.[9] This lack of time in making decisions suggests that consumers are not using only physical stimuli to make their choices, but rather are also relying on memory.

Pure "stimulus-based choices,"[10] or decisions that are made based only on information that is physically present at the time the consumer is making a decision and do not depend on any factors in consumer's memory, are relatively rare. Most supermarket product categories are mature and consumers have a long history with them, so past experiences are generally brought into the store. For example, a particular brand name may be familiar, thus causing the consumer to consider that item more carefully; or past experiences with a brand or a friend's recommendation may come to mind again, influencing the purchase.[11] On the other hand, pure "memory-based choices," where all the information necessary to make the decision is recalled from memory and no in-store cues are processed, are also rare, as it is hard for consumers to ignore all in-store cues.

Composition of Consideration Sets

The number of brands considered before a final choice is made varies a great deal. The size of the consideration set depends on the costs involved in evaluating a number of different alternatives (such as thinking costs, search costs, or opportunity costs) versus the benefits involved with a larger set of options.[12] Generally, the size and composition of a consideration set depends upon how consumers categorize their shopping needs and how familiar a consumer is with the various brands in the category. The composition of the consideration set also may be affected by which brands are on promotion.[13, 14]

There are two types of classification schemes, natural versus ad-hoc. The goal that a consumer has for a particular shopping need can affect the way s/he goes about acquiring information about the possible alternatives.[15] On one hand, the consumer can classify the need by product category, such as "fruit" or "ketchup." This has been labeled a "natural" classification scheme, as opposed to an "ad-hoc" classification scheme which consumers construct spontaneously for use in special instances. An example of an ad-hoc classification scheme might be "possible foods for a Mexican dinner," or "things to take on a picnic."[16] In purchasing for an ad-hoc goal, consumers are more likely to be influenced by in-store promotional cues and less likely to rely on memory, unless they have extensive experience with the particular goal.[17] If a consumer plans to buy products described by a natural classification scheme, the consideration set is more likely to be composed of items from memory, and less likely to be influenced by in-store features.[18] These differences in the composition set will be more pronounced when the consumer is under time pressure.

Because consumers respond more to in-store cues when they are thinking about ad-hoc categories, supermarkets have begun to organize some of their departments in these types of categories, rather than in the traditional categories. For example, some supermarkets now have aisles labeled "ethnic foods." Even more specifically, some supermarkets create an "Italian food" aisle, or prepare special "Fourth of July" or other holiday displays.

Even within natural or traditional categories, the way brands are displayed on the supermarket shelf can affect how consumers gather information about them,[19] and thus whether or not the consumer considers a particular brand. For example, most typical supermarket shelves cluster the same name brand products together. In the yogurt category, for example, most supermarkets put all the flavors that Dannon offers together, then all the flavors that Yoplait offers together, and so on. This type of display encourages consumers to think first about which brand they want to choose, and then decide which flavors to buy within that branded line. If the products had been displayed with all of the strawberry yogurts together, then all the lemon-lime yogurts, and so forth, consumers would most likely choose which flavors they wanted first, and then choose which brand name they would most like for that particular flavor. The first type of display will likely encourage consumers to buy the same brand for the different flavors, while the second type of display is more likely to result in consumers purchasing different brands.[20]

These differences in choice patterns as a result of how the items are displayed within a category can be illustrated quite dramatically by observing differences in the way meats are merchandised in United States as compared to Australia or Japan. In the United States, meats are generally displayed by species—chicken, beef, lamb—and then by the anatomy of the animal within the species. In Australia and Japan, the meat department is arranged by usage or by preparation—microwaved, braised, grilled. In addition, the labeling of the meat is more descriptive. For example, they might label a cut a "10-minute herbed beef roast." Recipes are also visible on the package or near the package. This type of merchandising exposes shoppers to a greater variety of meats within a particular cooking style and results in more variety in consumers' meat purchasing.[21]

Consumer familiarity with brands affects which ones are considered. For some brands, a consumer has extensive experience, both direct and indirect.[22] Other brands are completely unfamiliar or unknown. Familiar brands are more salient to the consumers; they are noticed first on the shelf and are more likely to be part of a consideration set. Further, brands that are noticed first tend to inhibit the recognition of other brands. Finally, the more familiar a consumer is with a brand the less likely the consumer is to misidentify it or to attribute characteristics of another brand to it (or vice versa). These factors are particularly important if a consumer is under time pressure and is susceptible to considering items that "stand out" from the competition on the shelf.[23]

IMPORTANCE OF BRAND NAME

Because brand familiarity affects whether or not a brand is considered, the brand name itself is one of the key factors in consumer purchasing decisions. A brand has positive "customer-based brand equity" if consumers react more positively to marketing activity for the brand, as opposed to the way they would respond if the same marketing activity was applied to an unnamed or generic product.[24]

The first goods to be branded were grocery items. The first food to receive a brand name was Underwood Deviled Ham in 1843.[25] Here, a brand name insured that the consumer would get the same quality and consistency time after time. This benefit was so great that branded products could charge a premium price. The concept of branding then spread to other supermarket products, such as chicken—*Perdue* chicken and *Tyson* chickens; produce—*Dole* pineapples, *Sunkist* oranges, *TomAHtoes* tomatoes, and *Chiquita* bananas; and dairy—*Kraft* cheese and *Sealtest* milk. These brand names not only insure consistent quality but they also enhance the product's value by strengthening the association of brand name with the specific product.[26] So when one thinks of peanuts, for example, *Planters* may immediately come to mind, and thus that brand may more likely be purchased.

From the consumer's point of view, a brand name is generally a strong influence on purchase if three elements are in place. First, the consumer must have a positive evaluation of the brand name. Second, the brand name must be easy to remember and be strongly associated with the product category. The ease with which the name is remembered when a consumer thinks of a category will depend on the frequency with which the consumer has seen the brand associated with the category, how recently the consumer has seen the brand associated with the category, and the salience of these connections to the consumer. In addition, a strong association with the category will depend on how similar the brand is to others in the category and also how prototypical the brand is to the category.[27] For example, Coke is seen as a prototypical soft drink, and thus will easily come to mind when the category "soft drinks" is evoked. Finally, the brand image and evaluation must be consistent over time.[28] In particular, a very strong brand name is one in which a consumer holds favorable associations that are unique to that brand and imply an advantage over other brands.[29]

Brand Extensions

Given that a strong brand name can influence purchase, many firms spend a great many advertising dollars building up their brand names. Once that kind of money is invested in a brand name, there is usually a desire to amortize that investment over more than one product. There are two ways that a firm can extend the value of its brand name. The first way is through line extensions, where the firm uses the brand name on other products in the same product category. For example, Kellogg's uses their brand name on their corn flakes product, on their Frosted Flakes, and on their Rice Krispies. The second way is through brand extensions or category extensions where the brand name is used on products in a category different from the original one upon which the brand name was built. For example, Dole was creating brand extensions when they used their brand name not only on pineapple (the original use) but also on frozen desserts, refrigerated beverages, and fresh package vegetables.[30] The advantage of these kinds of brand extensions is that the consumers immediately recognize the brand name and hopefully will transfer the benefits associated with the original product to the new product.[31]

Brand extensions are not always successful though. Sometimes the extension can threaten the positive benefits associated with the original brand product. The risks appear to be greater for extensions that are perceived to be moderately typical of the family brand, that is, extensions that are consistent with some expectations about the original brand name product but not others.[32] For example, the Carnation Company was considering extending its brand name Friskies to a new product that was to be a contraceptive dog food, called Lady Friskies, but tests showed that the new product would adversely affect sales of the original Friskies dog food.[33] Similarly, some industry analysts think that the successful introduction of Miller Lite beer in the United States may have harmed the perceptions of the flagship beer Miller High Life by causing consumers to think the original beer was less hearty.[34] Brand extensions can also dilute the power of the brand name if a brand name is used on too many products. Finally, brand extensions can also confuse the consumer if the new product has different associations connected to the brand name than the associations connected with the original product.[35]

Three factors need to be in place for a brand extension to be effective.[36] First, the consumer must perceive that the associations with the brand name fit the new product.[37] So, for example, using the Kodak brand name on a new introduction in the ice cream category would not be an effective brand extension. Second, the new item must be at least comparable, but preferably superior, to other items in the category. Putting a strong brand name on a "copycat" product may not be a strong enough incentive to get consumers to try the product.[38] Third, the benefits that are being transferred from the brand name to the new item must be desirable in the category. So, for example, Campbell's found out that it was not a good idea to put their brand name on a new spaghetti sauce product because consumers thought the sauce would be too watery.[39]

Brand extensions can also help to strengthen the original brand by clarifying the business definition and strategic advantages. For example, by using the brand name "Weight Watchers" on several products, the image of the whole product line was fortified and clarified.[40]

Co-Branding

Co-branding, or partnering around new products, is a growing trend in the supermarket. Two powerful brand names doubling up can seek greater influence in the supermarket. The arrangement among the marketers varies, but generally the partners share research and development costs, slotting fees, and advertising and promotion budgets.[41]

There are different degrees of partnership. Some of the arrangements are for one-time-only commitments, such as when Disney promoted its movie, *Lion King,* by allowing scenes from the movie to be printed on Nestle's candy bars. There are also limited-time promotions, such as when Grey Poupon was promoted in advertising Subway sandwiches. There is also ingredient branding, such as Skippy peanut butter in Delicious cookies[42] and Kellogg's Pop Tarts with Smucker's fruit filling.

As with brand extensions, there are both benefits and hazards to co-branding. By including two brands, consumers expect the advantages of both to be evident in the product—potentially a strong selling point. In addition, combining brand names can expand product market boundaries. For example, if a pizza company such as Pizzeria Uno was trying to increase consumption of pizza by promoting it as a breakfast food, it might name its new breakfast pizza, "Eggo Pizza by Pizzeria Uno." By capitalizing on the Eggo brand name that is already associated with breakfast food, Pizzeria Uno may have an easier time convincing the consumer to experiment.[43]

On the other hand, if the co-branded product fails, then the reputation of the original brand name may suffer. The other problem is one of confusing the customer—if the two brands have different images, the customer may not understand the relationship. Finally, there is always the risk of overexposure, which can dilute the quality image of a brand.[44]

PRIVATE LABEL BRANDS

Private label brands, or store brands, are the retailers own "brand." Many chains, such as Safeway, offer different tiers of private label brands: Safeway's Bel-air, Town House, and Lucern brands compete with premium products while their Marigold and Gardenside lines are more price oriented.[45] Private label brands can be exclusive retailer programs such as A&P's Ann Page, or they can be manufactured by a third party, such as Loblaws.[46]

Private label brands are different from generic brands. Generic brands are the no-name products that frequently appear in nondescript black-and-white packaging. Although generics received a lot of attention when they were first introduced in the early 1970s, they were never a serious threat to branded products because of their perceived inferior quality and packaging. Private label brands, on the other hand, have achieved much greater success. The private label brands have achieved increased product quality, superior packaging, and sometimes even advances in innovation.[47]

Private label brands usually mean higher profits for the retailers. Retailer margins on private labels can be 20 to 30 percent higher than on national brands.[48] These store brands can also build store loyalty—any retailer can sell Procter & Gamble products, but only A&P can sell its private label brands. In addition, private label brands are the only brand name that occurs consistently throughout the store across many product categories. Private labels are guaranteed full distribution in all the stores in a supermarket chain and are frequently provided with good shelf placement.[49]

Growth of Private Label Brands

Private label brands are becoming more popular in the United States. The market share of private label brands generates about 14 percent of the total supermarket revenue over the last decade, and 18 percent of all units sold.[50] Private label brands, on the other hand, have made greater headway in Europe. By some accounts, private label brands represent as much as 32 percent of supermarket volume in Britain and as much as 24 percent in France.[51] In Canada, private label brands account for 25 percent of sales. The largest selling brand of chocolate chip cookies in Canada is Loblaws' private label, President's Choice.[52] President's Choice, once only available in Canadian stores, is now available in hundreds of U.S. supermarkets.[53]

One reason for the greater market share of store brands in Europe and Canada than in the United States is that in Europe and Canada the major supermarket chains are national. For example, in France and in Britain, the top five chains represent 65 percent and 62 percent of grocery sales respectively. In Canada, Loblaws alone controls 27 percent of the supermarket business. In the United States, there is less concentration. The top five chains in the United States account for less than 20 percent of the overall supermarket business. In the United States, the supermarket business is more regional, dominated by many medium-sized grocery chains. In addition, in Canada and Europe there are fewer national brands on the market and the extent of product assortment (e.g., sizes, packaging, flavors, etc.) is much less than in the United States. The U.S. market is also much bigger than any of the other country markets, thus creating better economies of scale for advertising and production for manufacturers.

These factors suggest that the competition among manufacturers is more intense, and the retail chains are individually weaker in the United States than in England, France, or Canada. These supply-side factors suggest that the growth of private labels, although strong in the United States, will likely remain lower here than in England, France, or Canada, at least for awhile. However, as the supermarket business begins to fall to national mass merchandisers, such as Wal-Mart who in 1996 was ranked the fourth largest food retailer on *Supermarket News*'s top 75 list,[54] the U.S. landscape may begin to resemble the European market more closely.[55]

Success of Private Label Brands vis-à-vis National Brands

In the United States, in spite of the success of store brands and in spite of their lower prices, store brands generally continue to be less preferred by consumers as compared to national brands. Most evidence shows that American consumers will continue to buy national brands if the price is right.[56]

The performance of private labels varies a great deal, however, by category. In 1989, store brands accounted for 65 percent of sales of frozen green and wax beans, but for only 1.1 percent of sales of personal deodorants.[57] In some categories, the share of private label is growing dramatically: In P&G's biggest business, disposable diapers, the share of private label rose from 21 to 31 percent in just two years (1991 to 1993).

Several research studies have tried to identify the factors that contribute to the success of private label brands in a category. One study,[58] using aggregate-level store data across 180 categories, found that the determinants of success for private labels in any particular category depended upon the quality that consumers attributed to the store brand, and the activity of the retailers and manufacturers. Private label brands appeared to perform better in categories where the objective quality of the store brands was higher and where there was little variability in quality in these store brands. Interestingly, the study found that the depth of the price cut of the store brand, as compared to national brands, was not significant. In addition, promotion intensity had no impact. A low price, in and of itself, was not a sufficient reason for purchasing the store brand.

Based on the European experience, private label brands had greater penetration in product categories where there was (1) less advertising, (2) less innovation, and (3) bigger price premiums for the national brands.[59]

Supply-side activities affect the success of private labels as well. Because retailers have to promote, brand, and coordinate production for the store brands, they are more likely to take on these additional costs in categories where there is more expected profitability. Thus, all else being equal, retailers are more likely to develop and support private label brands in large categories with high profit potential. The manufacturers of the national brands also play a role. In categories where there is a great deal of advertising support for national brands[60] and where there is high price competition among many competing national brands,[61] private labels are less likely to succeed. On the other hand, if there is high price competition between national brands and store brands, then private labels brands are more likely to succeed.[62] A department that sees that highest percentage of private labels is the dairy department. Dairy, with its commodity orientation and lack of national brand strength, contributes almost three times its share of private label sales. In 1994, 64 percent of egg sales, 58 percent of milk sales, and 30 percent of cottage cheese/sour cream were private label.[63]

An experiment was conducted on 1,500 shoppers[64] to measure consumer response to private label brands. The experiment found that one reason for the continued advantage of national brands with regard to private label brands is that consumers seem to evaluate brands primarily by extrinsic cues (such as price, brand name, and packaging), rather than by intrinsic characteristics (such as the ingredients and taste of the product). In the experiment, the shoppers tasted various products that were either identified as a national brand or a store brand. What the shoppers did not know was that in half the cases, the private label brands were actually labeled as national brands, and vice versa. In the other half of the cases, the brands were labeled accurately. The results showed unequivocally that consumers evaluated the private label brands as lower quality even when the actual products tasted were national brands labeled as private label brands. Conversely, the consumers rated the national brands as higher quality even when those brands were actually store brands in disguise. These results show that consumers are using the extrinsic factors to guide their choice and are inferring that the quality of the private label brands is low because of the low price and lack of brand name. The study also revealed, congruent with the previously discussed study, that consumers seemed by and large to be more interested in quality than in value for the money.

These results suggest that private label brands might perform better if they were positioned on their quality rather than on their low price. Today's store brands can generally hold up to this kind of positioning. *Consumer Reports* has repeatedly tested and compared private label brands to the other brands and " . . . found them to be good, sometimes as high in quality as the national-brand alternatives—or even higher."[65] Many supermarkets are now trying to capitalize on the strong quality of some of their private labels. For example, in a Laneco supermarket in New Jersey, consumers were asked to do a taste test of the private label and the name brand product right in the store. The store manager found that this in-store demonstration was a very effective way to convert customers. In the Foodbasket IGA in Wyoming, supermarket employees go to local schools to show kids the quality and quantity they get with private labels as compared to national brands.[66]

GATHERING INFORMATION ABOUT SPECIFIC BRANDS

In addition to brand name, there is other information that a consumer may need in order to make a decision as to which brand to buy. Sometimes consumers get information about the characteristics or attributes of brands within a category before they enter the store through advertising, word-of-mouth, or direct experience. Other times consumers get information about attributes of a brand at the point of sale because the retailer or the manufacturer provide that information.

Legislation has standardized some of the conveyance of information. Retailers started providing unit price information in the 1970s, and in 1990, manufacturers started labeling the nutritional information of their products in a standardized way. When the information is not standardized, consumers need to infer or interpret the facts in order to form judgments. In addition, it is much more difficult to gather the information when it is not standardized.

Collecting the information is costly, so consumers are only likely to do so if they perceive there is some benefit. The costs of collecting information are the time and effort needed to acquire all the relevant information, the time needed to comprehend all the information that is collected, and the knowledge to know what action to take as a result of the findings.[67] The way the information is presented to the customer can affect how and if the consumer uses it.

Effects of Information Format

Several research studies have looked at how various information formats affect consumers' behavior. In general, the research studies find that when the costs of using the information are reduced, the consumers are more likely to use the information, and that information is more likely to affect purchasing.

Ease of use of information makes a difference to the consumer. Although unit price information is presented to the customer on the shelf underneath each brand, it is frequently very difficult to use. Sometimes the brands are not located directly above the proper unit pricing label. Even if the procedure is accurately done, it is still difficult for the customer to get all the relevant pricing information about all possible alternatives to consider, and then make the appropriate trade-offs.

Customers would use the pricing information much more if the procedure were made easier. For example, if all the pricing information about brands within a category was listed in one place, with the unit prices ranked from lowest to highest, consumers could much more easily decide whether the higher-priced goods were worth the additional money.[68]

Retailers may not always want to make the choices easy for the consumer. Products that yield higher margins are likely to be the ones that fare poorly if pricing information is made transparently clear. On the other hand, when the pricing comparison is to the advantage of the retailer, as when retailers are trying to convince consumers of the worthiness of a store brand, then the pricing information is generally more systematically conveyed. The store brand is frequently placed to the right of the competing national brand with the differences in prices highlighted. The comparison makes the price information quite clear and easy to use.

Effort-reducing displays of information can affect consumers' product choices. Another study[69] tested how the posting of a simple list of nutritional information affected purchase behavior. Most evidence indicates that shoppers perceive sugar in cereal to be negative and try to reduce their sugar consumption.[70] Therefore, the researchers posted, right in the cereal aisle, information about the sugar or sucrose content for all the brands of breakfast cereals. The information about the cereals was listed alphabetically and in order of how much sugar each cereal contained. The average sugar content of all brands of cereal sold, and the market shares of high- and low-sugar cereals were measured before, during, and after the posting of the information.

The results were quite compelling. While the posters were up in the store, consumers bought cereals with less sugar than cereals they bought before the posters were put up. Surprisingly though, the consumers returned to their old habits after the posters were removed. The effect of the information was only influential when it was present at the time of purchase.

One experiment looked at the effects of information presented in advertising. In this interesting natural experiment, researchers were able to study how health information presented in advertising could affect behavior. In October 1984, the Kellogg Company, with the cooperation of the National Cancer Institute, began an advertising campaign to point out the health benefit connection between eating fiber and controlling the incidence of colon cancer. This was a telling campaign, because previous to this time, there was a government regulation against health claims by a food product. The relaxation of the ban allowing the Kellogg Company to advertise this health benefit was a major event in the cereal market, and a sufficiently isolated event for the study of how information in advertising may or may not change behavior.[71]

Kellogg's advertising not only attempted to educate the public about the health benefits of fiber, but also promoted their own brand of fiber cereal, All-Bran. By the end of 1985, Kellogg had extended the fiber–cancer advertising to some of its other brands of cereals, and other competitors had also begun to focus on the fiber theme. In addition, the increased attention to the fiber–cancer link, and the right to advertise this link, led to the development of new fiber-based cereals on the market.

The Federal Trade Commission analyzed this period to see how consumers reacted to the relevant new health information. The analysis was done in two stages. First, the study looked at consumers' response to the health-related information when producers were prohibited from advertising, and then the study looked at the consumer response a year after the advertising had been in place. The interest was first, in whether the dissemination of the scientific knowledge itself changed purchase behavior, and second, how advertising affected this transmission of the health-related benefits and affected purchase behavior.[72]

Looking at consumer response before the Kellogg advertising campaign began, the FTC found that significant costs to the consumer must be overcome in order for them to respond to new health-related information. First, the consumer had to find out about the information, then understand the information, and then change food consumption habits to increase the use of fiber-based cereals. They study found that there was great heterogeneity in the value individuals placed on health, and these differences affected the desire of consumers to collect and use the relevant information. All else being equal, the people who were in general more sensitive to health-related concerns were more likely to eat high-fiber cereals in any event. The newly-released scientific information did not change their behavior. Consequently, in the pre-advertising period, the consumption of higher-fiber cereals was relatively constant.

The FTC study then looked at the effect of a year of cereal-producer advertising. The evidence clearly demonstrated that the consumption of fiber cereal increased once the ban on health-claims advertising was removed. The data indicate that advertising increased fiber cereal consumption because it reduced the cost of acquiring the information by those consumers who were not likely to read about the health benefits in other media. Thus the advertising changed behavior for those consumers who were not likely to hear about the cancer–fiber link except through the advertising, but did not change the behavior of those who had learned about the health benefit through other means.

More generally, this study shows that consumers are likely to respond to information provided by advertisers that has value to them, but the cost of acquiring that information may be high. Consumers are not likely to seek out information actively, but may respond if the cost of acquiring the information is lowered.

Limits on Information Processing

One concern with providing information to the consumer is that the amount of information that the consumer confronts in the supermarket can be considerable. Just the information supplied to the consumer at the point of sale is impressive. For example, there are approximately 150 national brands of instant breakfast cereal on the market, and the typical supermarket carries anywhere between 60 and 90 brands. In addition, each package could provide much more information to the consumer. Usually the packages contain pictorial or graphical information in addition to almost 100 separate items of information.[73]

Obviously, although information is helpful, the decision maker can be flooded with *too* much information, which in turn may affect the quality of the decision. Some empirical evidence suggests that too much information can cause consumers to spend more time analyzing the information, to become confused or stressed, and sometimes to pay less attention to the most pertinent, relevant information. Therefore, if the information is overwhelming, consumers can actually make poorer decisions given more information.[74, 75]

Consumers may not actually experience information overload in most supermarket contexts. This is not because there isn't more than enough information available to swamp the consumers, but because it has been found empirically that consumers stop taking in information before it overloads them. In other words, consumers usually just evaluate a small amount of information present in the environment when making decisions.

Therefore, the key question is: Because consumers are not likely to take in all the information available to them, what information do they process?[76] Are they looking at the most important, relevant attributes? Empirical results suggest that experienced consumers are better able to pay attention to the attributes that are predictive of product performance compared to inexperienced consumers (with a product category),[77] but there are still biases in the way information is taken in.

Consumers must be able to access and use accurately the information provided to them. One problem with information provided to the consumer, either through advertising or through in-store cues (such as packaging or shelf markers) is that it is not always recalled or interpreted correctly. Sometimes the information that is conveyed is deliberately misleading, as when a manufacturer states the product is "less fattening" than a substitute, but this only true because the portion sizes are much smaller. Other times the information is purposely vague and the consumer interprets it in a more positive light than originally stated, such as when a manufacturer calls the product "not expensive" and the consumer interprets that as "inexpensive."[78] Even when the information is accurately represented, consumers do not always understand it or believe it. Only one-third of the consumers surveyed by the Food and Drug Administration (FDA) understood that the ingredients recorded on a food product label are listed in order of their weight.[79]

Consumers also infer information about product attributes that is not always accurate. For example, based on an overall evaluation of a brand, a consumer may infer certain characteristics about the brand (halo effects).[80] Thus, if consumers evaluate a brand overall as a high quality one, they may infer that it is nutritious even if it is not. Consumers may also evaluate a brand based on its similarity to another brand. So a consumer may assume that a new or unfamiliar brand has the same ingredients as a brand with which they are more familiar.[81] Consumers may infer characteristics about a brand because they believe certain attributes are likely to occur together. For example, consumers often think that higher prices are associated with higher quality. While this is sometimes true, it is not always true.

Consumers sometimes say one thing and behave in an inconsistent way. For example, 94 percent of Americans say that they are at least somewhat concerned about nutrition. In particular, they are concerned with fat, salt content, cholesterol levels, and sugar intake.[82] Consumers know that they should be concerned with nutrition, and thus they want nutritional information made public and healthy alternatives available. But just because they want these nutritional alternatives available does not mean that their presence will affect purchase behavior. As a Wendy's executive stated in a *Forbes* article,[83] "Folks feel better eating a bacon cheeseburger when they're looking at a healthy salad bar with fresh vegetables."

There are also biases in the way consumers take in information. Consumers tend to take in information that is consistent with what they already believe. Confirmation bias, or the tendency for consumers to take in information that confirms what they already think and disregard information that challenges preconceived notions, is a very strong phenomenon. If a consumer thinks highly of an in-store bakery, s/he is likely to remember all of the instances of tasting superior products and forget the times that the confections were not up to par. It is difficult, therefore, to change consumers' strongly held opinions about certain brands and products because evidence to the contrary tends to be ignored.

Consumers are also more sensitive to very vivid, unique, or otherwise salient information and may neglect to observe more subtle cues.[84, 85, 86] This may result in more importance being inappropriately placed on the salient cues. One study showed that by changing the vividness of a piece of information, the influence that information had on later judgments varied. The more vivid fashion the information was portrayed, the more likely it was to be incorporated in the later judgment.[87] In addition, it has been shown that consumers overestimate the relative risk of events if they are more salient or newsworthy, because these events come to mind very easily and thus are overgeneralized.[88, 89, 90] This can explain the extreme reactions consumers sometimes show to relatively low-risk hazards, such as alar on apples,[91] or fear about tampering with over-the-counter drugs resulting from the hysteria when one or two Tylenol packages were adulterated.

Changes in the way items are described, or framed, can affect consumers' judgments. Researchers found that when respondents were asked to choose between the same ground beef that was labeled either as "75% lean" or as "25% fat"—descriptors that are technically equivalent—consumers chose the beef labeled as "75% lean" as being superior to the beef that contained "25% fat."[92] This response pattern persisted even after tasting the meat, although the magnitude of the effect decreased.[93]

Although these types of biases in information gathering are very common and can be very strong, it has been demonstrated that consumers who are made aware of the potential for bias in their judgments will display less bias and often improve their decision making dramatically.[94, 95] In the supermarket context, analyses such as those done in *Consumer Reports* can help consumers recognize the possible sources of bias that could be influencing their decisions. Experimental work has shown, though, that consumers are more likely to be influenced by the corrective reporting if the discrepancy in information is large rather than slight.[96]

FINAL CHOICE OF ONE SPECIFIC BRAND

At some point, the consumer has to choose which brand of all the ones considered to put in the shopping cart. Easy decisions are those where one brand in the consideration set dominates all others. More typically, one brand will be better on one attribute, say taste, while another may be better on a different attribute, say lower price. When there is not a clear dominant alternative to pick, consumers will have to decide how to make trade-offs among the different factors in order to make a decision. The normative rules of decision making suggest that a consumer should use all of the relevant information available and make explicit trade-offs. In other words, a consumer should decide to what extent s/he may be willing to trade off less of one favored attribute or dimension for more of another favored dimension.[97]

Simplifying Heuristics

More typically in supermarket decisions, consumers use simplifying choice rules or heuristics to make decisions either because it is too difficult to think about all the trade-offs or they prefer not to.[98] It is also not that important to most consumers that they make the best decision. Finally, during a single shopping trip, a consumer has to make many, many decisions, and it is likely, therefore, that the consumer will not want to spend too much time on any single decision.[99]

Generally, they just want to make a decision that meets some minimum requirements. For example, some consumers make decisions by using a "satisficing" rule.[100] Using this rule, consumers would consider the items in the consideration set one at a time as they came across them on the shelf. They would evaluate the characteristics of the first brand compared to some minimum standard, sacrificing the search for optimal selection. If the brand satisfied the minimum standard on each important attribute, then that brand would be chosen and no other brands would be evaluated. If the brand was below the minimum cut-off, then the next one in the consideration set would be evaluated.

Sometimes it is not possible to trade off one attribute for another even if the consumer wants to make an optimal decision. For example, if someone is allergic to nuts, then any food with nuts would be inedible, and there would be no discount in price that could make up for it. The consumer would screen out all alternatives that had nuts and consider the remaining options. That type of decision model has been labeled an "elimination-by-aspects" model, where options are totally eliminated if they perform poorly on a certain attribute.[101] A similar but opposite rule would consider the most important attribute, say price, and then pick the option that is the best on that attribute, the lowest-priced item in the category. If more than one option was best on that attribute, then the consumer might consider the second most important attribute, maybe type of package, and then pick the brand that is best on that attribute, and so forth. This rule is known as a lexicographic rule.[102]

Affect Referral

Another way that consumers make decisions in the supermarket is by relying on memory, a process which is known as "affect referral."[103] In this kind of decision making, consumers form attitudes or impressions at the time they first receive information. These first impressions are then stored in memory and later retrieved as a basis for judgment. Thus, when asked "What is your favorite brand of soup?" a consumer might respond "Campbell's," strictly relying on past favorable memories of that brand. Here, the consumer will not have given much thought to trading off the attributes or considering other brands currently available, or processing all the information—advertising, labels, prices—that might be available to help with the decision.

A similar theory to affect referral suggests that for decisions that are made repeatedly over time, and for which the consumer doesn't care that much about making an optimal decision, "choice tactics" are developed over time. In this view, it is assumed that the consumer uses a simplified choice rule, such as "buy the cheapest brand" or "buy the brand my friend recommended" initially. The product is then sampled and, if found satisfactory, there is an increased likelihood that this product will be chosen again. Through a series of trials which may involve positive, negative, or neutral evaluations, the post-purchase evaluation will stabilize over time and a very simple decision rule will emerge. Thus, on shopping trips, rather than thinking extensively about the pros and cons of each alternative, the shopper merely uses a simple "rule of thumb" to make the decision.[104]

An empirical test was done to assess this theory. Some researchers observed 120 shoppers in a supermarket in a major metropolitan area. Purchase behavior in one category, laundry detergents, was observed. Laundry detergents were chosen because there are a wide variety of brands available, the displays for the product within a supermarket are generally large, and the product is generally considered to be low risk for most consumers. On average in this category, consumers examined a very small number of packages (average = 1.42), and 72 percent of the consumers examined only one package; 83 percent of the consumers picked up only one package, and only 4 percent picked up more than two. The consumers took an average of 13 seconds from the time they entered the laundry detergent aisle to the time they made their decision. Given that the laundry detergent aisle is generally long, it took consumers almost the entire time allowed for the decision to arrive at the physical proximity of their chosen brand. Clearly, these data suggest that the majority of consumers were engaging in very little pre-purchase decision making when making a laundry detergent purchase.[105]

Influence of Context on Preferences

If consumers in the supermarket made optimal decisions, carefully considering all the trade-offs, then the process of forming a consideration set prior to making a final choice would not affect that final choice. Consumers would always choose their most preferred brand regardless of which other brands they considered in the process. Researchers studying actual consumer decisions find, however, that consumers' final choices do vary depending upon the way the initial consideration set is formed. The probability of a purchasing a specific brand will differ depending upon how many other brands are in the consideration set with it, and which other brands they are.[106, 107]

It is easy to see how the composition of the consideration set can influence the final choice, because consideration sets are so often formed using very simple criteria, such as: "Consider all the brands I've heard of," or "Consider all the brands on the middle shelf," or "Consider all the brands that are less than $1," or "Consider all the brands of cereal that are low in sugar." Given that the consideration sets are often formed in these less-than-optimum ways, it is obvious that the final purchase will depend on how the consideration set is organized.

Even when consumers are less arbitrary in forming consideration sets, the composition of the set of final possibilities can have subtle effects on choice. In many product classes consumers' preferences are unstable and may be susceptible to seemingly irrelevant influences.[108] This does not imply that consumers do not know what they want, but rather that consumers' preferences are not fixed and may change in response to the different ways the alternatives are presented, or to differences in the timing and quantity of purchase. Therefore, brand choices can be influenced without changing the actual preference for a brand per se, but merely by changing the contents of the consideration set.[109]

Two generalizations about the way consumers form preferences help to understand how the composition of the consideration set can affect the final choice.[110] The first generalization is that there is a tendency for consumers to prefer an alternative if it fares well in a comparison with other alternatives in the consideration set. Thus, a consumer will prefer an alternative more if it is in a consideration set that makes it look good by comparison, than if that same alternative is in a consideration set that does not have that feature. There is a popular optical illusion that illustrates this concept. Children are asked which center circle is larger, the one surrounded by small circles or the one surrounded by large circles. The optical illusion is that the two center circles are the same size, but the one surrounded by small circles looks larger. This generalization explains the "attraction effect" described in the next section.

The second generalization states that consumers do not like to choose an extreme option when tradeoffs are involved. They generally would rather choose an option that is intermediate on attributes than one that is extreme. This generalization explains the "compromise effect" described at the end of this chapter.

Both of these generalizations are less likely to hold when consumers have very strong preferences within a category. But in many categories, consumers' preferences are not so well-formed, and they frequently use the choice context to determine which item is the "best buy."[111] In some cases, the consumers are unaware of how the alternatives in a consideration set affect their choice; in other cases, they use the other options in the consideration set to justify their choice.[112]

Attraction Effect

Empirical testing has shown that adding a dominated alternative to a consideration set can increase the likelihood that a consumer will buy the alternative that dominates it.[113, 114] For example, consider a simple two-item category. One item, the "high end" item in the category, has a high price, fancy packaging, and presumably high quality taste. The other item, the "generic" item in the category, has a low price, plain packaging, and presumably the taste is not as high quality. If another high-end brand is added to the set, but is dominated by the first high-end brand—in other words, its taste and packaging are not as good, but its price is higher—there is some evidence that the presence of this dominated alternative will increase the likelihood that the consumer will choose the original high-end product. Similarly, if a dominated low-end product is added—a low-end product that has a higher price than the original generic—then the original "generic" will more likely be chosen. The idea here is that by adding the dominated alternative, the item that dominates it is made to appear more attractive, more clearly offering a better value, and increasing the likelihood that that item is chosen.[115]

This idea was tested in the marketplace by a mail-order company. The company had traditionally offered a bread-baking machine for $279. It subsequently added a more expensive machine for $429 that basically offered the same benefits as the cheaper machine. Few customers bought the new, more expensive alternative, but surprisingly, sales for the original bread-baking machine doubled![116]

Even more surprisingly, some research has shown that just a similar item to a consideration set, not necessarily one that is dominated, can increase the likelihood that the original item is chosen. For example, consider the category of potato chips and, for argument's sake, assume that the consumer considers two items within the category, plain potato chips and ripple potato chips. This research suggests that if the retailer can merely convince the consumer to consider another brands of ripple potato chips (for example, by using a special in-store display), the consumers' desire to purchase the original rippled potato chip is likely to increase.[117, 118]

Compromise Effect

Empirical testing has also shown that when decisions are difficult to make because a consumer has trouble trading off the value of one attribute for another, the inclusion of a "compromise" brand may help to simplify the decision because it is easier to justify the final choice.[119] For example, if a consumer is considering whether to buy an expensive brand of shampoo with special ingredients, or a cheaper brand of shampoo that does not have the special added ingredients, the decision centers upon whether or not the consumer thinks the special ingredients are worth the extra price. If this decision is difficult to make—that is, the calculation of exactly how much the special ingredients are worth—then the consumer may instead choose a compromise brand, or one that has fewer special ingredients (and thus is cheaper) than the expensive brand, but has more special ingredients than the cheapest brand (and thus is more expensive than that brand). Choosing the compromise brand when consumers are uncertain about their preferences is easier to justify because it reduces the conflict association with giving up one attribute (say, higher quality) for another attribute (say, lower price). The compromise brand may also be perceived as the safest choice because any error (e.g., not getting enough quality or paying too much) is minimized.[120]

Another explanation for why consumers tend to choose the middle brands rather than brands on either end of the continuum is that consumers try to determine their personal needs by comparing themselves to other consumers. Generally, consumers tend to think of themselves as "average" and therefore in circumstances when they don't really know their own preferences, they infer that their tastes would be consistent with the "average" brand or the compromise brand.[121]

Endnotes

1. Payne, John (1976), "Task Complexity and Contingent Processing in Decision-Making: An Information Search and Protocol Analysis," *Organizational Behavior and Human Performance*, 16 (August), 366–387.

2. Bettman, James (1979), *An Information Processing Theory of Consumer Choice*, Reading, MA: Addison-Wesley.

3. Lehmann, Donald R. and Yigang Pan (1994), "Context Effects, New Brand Entry, and Consideration Sets," *Journal of Marketing Research*, 21 (August), 364–374.

4. Bichal, Gabriel and Dipankar Chakravarti (1986), "Consumers' Use of Memory and External Information in Choice: Macro and Micro Perspective," *Journal of Consumer Research*, 12 (March), 382–405.

5. Nedungadi, Prakash (1990), "Recall and Consumer Consideration Sets: Influencing Choice Without Altering Brand Evaluations," *Journal of Consumer Research*, 17 (December), 263–276.

6. Shocker, Allan D., Moshe Ben-Akiva, Bruno Coccara, and Prakash Nedungadi (1991), "Consideration Set Influences on Customer Decision-Making and Choice: Issues, Models, and Suggestions," *Marketing Letters,* 2 (August), 181–198.

7. Lehmann, Donald R. and Yigang Pan (1994), "Context Effects, New Brand Entry, and Consideration Sets," *Journal of Marketing Research*, 21 (August), 364–374.

8. Shocker, Allan D., Moshe Ben-Akiva, Bruno Coccara, and Prakash Nedungadi (1991), "Consideration Set Influences on Customer Decision-Making and Choice: Issues, Models, and Suggestions," *Marketing Letters,* 2 (August), 181–198.

9. Dickson, Peter R. and Alan G. Sawyer (1990), "The Price Knowledge and Search of Supermarket Shoppers," *Journal of Marketing*, 54 (July), 42–53.

10. Lynch, John G., Jr., and Thomas K. Srull (1982), "Memory and Attentional Factors in Consumer Choice: Concepts and Research Methods," *Journal of Consumer Research*, 9 (June), 18–37.

11. Alba, Joseph W., J. Wesley Hutchinson, and John G. Lynch, Jr. (1991), "Memory and Decision-Making," in *Handbook of Consumer Re-*

search, edited by Thomas S. Robertson and Harold H. Kassarjian, New York: Prentice Hall.

12. Hauser, John R. and Birger Wernerfelt (1990), "An Evaluation Cost Model of Consideration Sets," *Journal of Consumer Research,* 16 (March), 393–408.

13. Currim, Imran, Robert J. Meyer and Nhan T. Le (1988), "Disaggregate Tree-Structured Modeling of Consumer Choice," *Journal of Marketing Research*, 25 (August), 153–65.

14. Fader, Peter S. and Leigh McAlister (1990), "An Elimination by Aspects Model of Consumer Response to Promotion Calibrated on UPC Scanner Data," *Journal of Marketing Research*, 28 (August), 322–332.

15. Huffman, Cynthia and Michael J. Houston (1993), "Goal-Oriented Experiences and the Development of Knowledge," *Journal of Consumer Research*, 20 (September), 190–207.

16. Barsalou, Lawrence (1983), "Ad hoc Categories," *Memory and Cognition*, 11 (3), 211–227.

17. Alba, Joseph W. and J. Wesley Hutchinson (1987), "Dimensions of Consumer Expertise," *Journal of Consumer Research*, 13 (March), 411–454.

18. Alba, Joseph W., J. Wesley Hutchinson, and John G. Lynch, Jr. (1991), "Memory and Decision-Making," in *Handbook of Consumer Research*, edited by Thomas S. Robertson and Harold H. Kassarjian, New York: Prentice Hall.

19. Bettman, James R. and Kakkar, P. (1977), "Effects of Information Presentation Format on Consumer Information Acquisition Strategies," *Journal of Consumer Research*, 3, (March) 233–240.

20. Simonson, Itamar and Russell S. Winer (1992), "The Influence of Purchase Quantity and Display Format on Consumer Preference for Variety," *Journal of Consumer Research*, 19 (June), 133–138.

21. Zbytniewski, Jo-Ann (1992), "Going Global with Meat," *Progressive Grocer*, (December), 78–79.

22. Alba, Joseph W. and J. Wesley Hutchinson (1987), "Dimensions of Consumer Expertise," *Journal of Consumer Research*, 13 (March), 411–454.

23. Alba, Joseph W., J. Wesley Hutchinson, and John G. Lynch, Jr. (1991), "Memory and Decision-Making," in *Handbook of Consumer Research*, edited by Thomas S. Robertson and Harold H. Kassarjian, New York: Prentice Hall.

24. Keller, Kevin Lane (1991), "Conceptualizing, Measuring and Managing Customer-Based Brand Equity," Marketing Science Institute Working Paper #91–123, October 1991.

25. Staten, Vince (1993), *Can You Trust a Tomato in January?* New York: Simon and Schuster, pp. 122–123.

26. Farquhar, Peter H. (1989), "Managing Brand Equity," *Marketing Research* (September), 24–33.

27. Nedungadi, Prakesh (1990), "Recall and Consumer Consideration Sets: Influencing Choice without Altering Brand Evaluations," *Journal of Consumer Research*, 17 (December), 263–276.

28. Farquhar, Peter H. (1989), "Managing Brand Equity," *Marketing Research* (September), 24–33.

29. Keller, Kevin Lane (1991), "Conceptualizing, Measuring and Managing Customer-Based Brand Equity," Marketing Science Institute Working Paper #91–123, October 1991.

30. Stern, Aimee L. (1985), "New Payoff from Old Brand Names," *Dun's Business Month* (April), 42–44.

31. Farquhar, Peter H. (1989), "Managing Brand Equity," *Marketing Research* (September), 24–33.

32. Loken, Barbara and Deborah Roedder John (1993), "Diluting Brands Beliefs: When Do Brand Extensions Have a Negative Impact?" *Journal of Marketing*, 57 (July), 71–84.

33. Tauber, Edward M. (1981), "Brand Franchise Extension: New Product Benefits from Existing Brand Names," *Business Horizons*, 24 (2), 36–41.

34. Keller, Kevin Lane (1991), "Conceptualizing, Measuring and Managing Customer-Based Brand Equity," Marketing Science Institute Working Paper #91–123, October 1991.

35. Aaker, David A. and Kevin Lane Keller (1990), "Consumer Evaluations of Brand Extensions," *Journal of Marketing*, 54 (January), 27–41.

36. Tauber, Edward M. (1981), "Brand Franchise Extension: New Product Benefits from Existing Brand Names," *Business Horizons*, 24 (2), 36–41.

37. Broniarczyk, Susan M. and Joseph W. Alba (1994), "The Importance of the Brand in Brand Extension," *Journal of Marketing Research*, 31 (May), 214–228.

38. Stern, Aimee L. (1985), "New Payoff from Old Brand Names," *Dun's Business Month* (April), 42–44.

39. Stern, Aimee L. (1985), "New Payoff from Old Brand Names," *Dun's Business Month* (April), 42–44.

40. Aaker, David A. (1991), *Managing Brand Equity*, Free Press.

41. Spethmann, Betsy and Karen Benezra (1994), "Co-Brand or be Damned," *BrandWeek* (November 21), 21–24.

42. Spethmann, Betsy and Karen Benezra (1994), "Co-Brand or be Damned," *BrandWeek* (November 21), 21–24.

43. Park, C. Whan (1994), "Strategic Implication of Branding Decision," presented at the 1994 AMA Doctoral Consortium at Santa Clara University, August.

44. "Brands Fight Back Against Private Labels," (1995), *Marketing News* (January 16), 8–9.

45. Consumer Reports (1993), "Survival Guide to the Supermarket," *Consumer Reports*, Vol. 58, No. 9 (September), 559–570.

46. Hoch, Stephen J. and Shumeet Banerji (1993), "When Do Private Labels Succeed?" *Sloan Management Review* (Summer), 57–67.

47. Kim, Peter (1993), "Restore Brand Equity!" *Directors and Boards*, (Summer), 21–29.

48. Hoch, Stephen J. and Shumeet Banerji (1993), "When Do Private Labels Succeed?" *Sloan Management Review* (Summer), 57–67.

49. Hoch, Stephen J. (1996), "How Should National Brands Think about Private Labels?" *Sloan Management Review* (Winter), 89–102.

50. Richardson, Paul S., Alan S. Dick, and Arun K. Jain (1994), "Extrinsic and Intrinsic Cue Effects on Perceptions of Store Quality," *Journal of Marketing*, 58 (4), 28–36.

51. Oster, Patrick, with Gabrielle Saveri and John Templeman (1993), "Procter & Gamble Hits Back: Its Dramatic Overhaul Takes Aim at High Costs—and Low-Price Rivals," *Business Week* (July 19), 20–22.

52. Hoch, Stephen J. and Shumeet Banerji (1993), "When Do Private Labels Succeed?" *Sloan Management Review*, (Summer), 57–67.

53. "Brands Fight Back Against Private Labels," (1995), *Marketing News* (January 16), 8–9.

54. Zwiebach, Ellict (1996), "SN's Top 75: How the Leading Supermarket Companies Ranked by Volume in 1995," *Supermarket News* (January 15), 92.

55. Hoch, Stephen J. (1996), "How Should National Brands Think about Private Labels?" *Sloan Management Review* (Winter), 89–102.

56. "How Consumers Evaluate Private Label Brand Quality" (1995), *Stores* (Winter), 1–2.

57. Hoch, Stephen J. and Shumeet Banerji (1993), "When Do Private Labels Succeed?" *Sloan Management Review* (Summer), 57–67.

58. Hoch, Stephen J. and Shumeet Banerji (1993), "When Do Private Labels Succeed?" *Sloan Management Review* (Summer), 57–67.

59. Glemet, Francois and Rafael Mira (1993), "The Brand Leader's Dilemma," *The McKinsey Quarterly*, Number 2, 3–15.

60. Hoch, Stephen J. and Shumeet Banerji (1993), "When Do Private Labels Succeed?" *Sloan Management Review* (Summer), 57–67.

61. Raju, Jagmohan S., Raj Sethuraman, and Sanjay K. Dhar (1995), "The Introduction and Performance of Store Brands," *Management Science*, 41 (June), 957–973.

62. Raju, Jagmohan S., Raj Sethuraman, and Sanjay K. Dhar (1995), "The Introduction and Performance of Store Brands," *Management Science*, 41 (June), 957–973.

63. McNair, Bill (1994), "My Brand – Your Brand: Co-existence and Collaboraton in the Dairy Case," a Neilsen presentation at the International Dairy/Deli/Bakery Association, June 7.

64. Richardson, Paul S., Alan S. Dick, and Arun K. Jain (1994), "Extrinsic and Intrinsic Cue Effects on Perceptions of Store Quality," *Journal of Marketing,* 58 (4), (October), 28–36.

65. Consumer Reports (1993), "Survival Guide to the Supermarket," *Consumer Reports*, Vol. 58, No. 9 (September), 559–570.

66. Rigney, Peter (1994), "How Do You Promote Private Label?" *Progressive Grocer* (August), 162.

67. Russo, J. Edward, Richard Staelin, Catherine A. Nolan, Gary J. Russell, and Barbara L. Metcalf (1986), "Nutrition Information in the Supermarket," *Journal of Consumer Research*, 13 (June), 48–70.

68. Russo, J. E. (1977), "The Value of Unit Price Information," *Journal of Marketing Research*, 14, 193–201.

69. Russo, J. Edward, Richard Staelin, Catherine A. Nolan, Gary J. Russell, and Barbara L. Metcalf (1986), "Nutrition Information in the Supermarket," *Journal of Consumer Research*, 13 (June), 48–70.

70. General Mills (1980), "A Summary Report on U.S. Consumers' Knowledge, Attitudes and Practices About Nutrition," prepared by Maracom Research Corp., published by General Mills, Inc. Minneapolis, MN.

71. Ippolito, Pauline and Alan D. Mathios (1990), "Information, Advertising, and Health Choices: A Study of the Cereal Market," *Rand Journal of Economics*, 21 (Autumn), 459–480.

72. Ippolito, Pauline and Alan D. Mathios (1990), "Information, Advertising, and Health Choices: A Study of the Cereal Market," *Rand Journal of Economics*, 21 (Autumn), 459–480.

73. Jacoby, Jacob (1984), "Perspectives on Information Overload," *Journal of Consumer Research*, 10 (March), 423–435.

74. Jacoby, Jacob, Carol A. Kohn, and Donald E. Speller (1973), "Time Spent Acquiring Information as a Function of Information Load and

Organization," *Proceedings of the American Psychological Association's 81st Annual Convention*, Washington, DC, 8, 813–814.

75. Maholtra, Naresh K. (1982), "Information Load and Consumer Decision Making," *Journal of Consumer Research*, 9 (March), 419–430.

76. Jacoby, Jacob (1984), "Perspectives on Information Overload," *Journal of Consumer Research*, 10 (March), 423–435.

77. Johnson, Eric J. and J. Edward Russo (1984), "Product Familiarity and Learning New Information," *Journal of Consumer Research*, 11 (June), 542–549.

78. Alba, Joseph W., J. Wesley Hutchinson, and John G. Lynch, Jr. (1991), "Memory and Decision-Making," in *Handbook of Consumer Research*, edited by Thomas S. Robertson and Harold H. Kassarjian, New York: Prentice Hall.

79. Mueller, William (1991), "Who Reads the Label?" *American Demographics*, (January), 36–40.

80. Beckwith, Neil and Donald R. Lehmann (1975), "The Importance of Halo Effects in Multi-Attribute Models," *Journal of Marketing Research*, 12 (August), 265–275.

81. Loken, Barbara, Ivan Ross, and Ronald L. Hinkle (1986), "Consumer 'Confusion' of Origin and Brand Similarity Perceptions," *Journal of Public Policy and Marketing*, 5, 195–211.

82. Miller, Cyndee (1993), "U.S., European Shoppers Seem Pleased with their Supermarkets," *Marketing News* (June 21), 1.

83. Gutner, Toddi (1994), "Food Distributors," *Forbes* (January 3), 148–150.

84. Tversky, Amos and Daniel Kahneman. (1974). "Judgment under Uncertainty: Heuristics and Biases," *Science,* 185, 1124–1131.

85. Taylor, Shelley E. (1987). "The Availability Bias in Social Perception and Interaction," in Daniel Kahneman, Paul Slovic, and Amos Tversky (Eds.), *Judgment under Uncertainty: Heuristics and Biases.* New York: Cambridge University Press, 190–200.

86. Folkes, Valerie. (1988). "The Availability Heuristic and Perceived Risk," *Journal of Consumer Research,* 15 (June), 1323.

87. Reyes, Robert M., William C. Thompson, and Gordon H. Bower (1980), "Judgmental Biases Resulting from Differing Availabilities of Arguments," *Journal of Personality and Social Psychology,* 39 (July), 2–12.

88. Folkes, Valerie. (1988), "The Availability Heuristic and Perceived Risk," *Journal of Consumer Research,* 15 (June), 13–23.

89. Lichtenstein, Sarah, Paul Slovic, Baruch Fischhoff, Mark Layman and Barbara Combs (1978), "Judged Frequency of Lethal Events," *Jour-*

nal of Experimental Psychology: Human Learning and Memory, 4 (November), 551–578.

90.   Tversky, Amos and Daniel Kahenman (1973), "Availability: A Heuristic for Judging Frequency and Probability," Cognitive Psychology, 5 (2), 207–232.

91.   Alba, Joseph W., J. Wesley Hutchinson, and John G. Lynch, Jr. (1991), "Memory and Decision-Making," in Handbook of Consumer Research, edited by Thomas S. Robertson and Harold H. Kassarjian, New York: Prentice Hall.

92.   Levin, Irwin P., Richard D. Johnson, Craig P. Russo, and Patricia J. Deldin (1985), "Framing Effects in Judgment Tasks with Varying Amounts of Information," Organizational Behavior and Human Decision Processes, 36 (December), 362–377.

93.   Levin, Irwin P. and Gary J. Gaeth (1988), "How Consumers are Affected by the Framing of Attribute Information Before and After Consuming the Product," Journal of Consumer Research, 15 (December) 374–378.

94.   Hoch, Stephen J. (1988). "Who Do We Know: Predicting the Interests and Opinions of the American Consumer," Journal of Consumer Research, 15 (December), 315–324.

95.   Russo, J. Edward and Paul J. H. Schoemaker (1989), Decision Traps: The Ten Barriers to Brilliant Decision-Making and How to Overcome Them, New York: Simon and Schuster.

96.   Corfman, Kim P. and Barbara E. Kahn (1995), "The Influence of Member Heterogeneity on Dyad Judgment: Are Two Heads Better than One?" Marketing Letters, 6 (1), 23–32.

97.   Keeney, R. L. and Raiffa, Howard (1976), Decisions with Multiple Objectives: Preferences and Value Tradeoffs, New York: Wiley.

98.   Hogarth, Robin M. (1987), Judgment and Choice (2nd Ed.), New York: Wiley.

99.   Hoyer, Wayne D. (1984), "An Examination of Consumer Decision Making for a Common Repeat Purchase Product," Journal of Consumer Research, 11 (December), 822–829.

100.   Simon, Herbert A. (1955), "A Behavioral Model of Rational Choice," Quarterly Journal of Economics, 69, 99–118.

101.   Tversky, Amos (1972), "Elimination by Aspects: A Theory of Choice," Psychological Review, 79, 281–299.

102.   Payne, John, James R. Bettman, and Eric J. Johnson (1993), The Adaptive Decision Maker, New York: Cambridge University Press.

103. Wright, Peter (1975), "Consumer Choice Strategies: Simplifying vs. Optimizing," *Journal of Marketing Research*, 11, 60–67.

104. Hoyer, Wayne D. (1984), "An Examination of Consumer Decision Making for a Common Repeat Purchase Product," *Journal of Consumer Research*, 11 (December), 822–829.

105. Hoyer, Wayne D. (1984), "An Examination of Consumer Decision Making for a Common Repeat Purchase Product," *Journal of Consumer Research*, 11 (December), 822–829.

106. Kahn, Barbara E., William L. Moore and Rashi Glazer (1987), "Experiments in Constrained Choice," *Journal of Consumer Research*, 14 (June), 96–113.

107. Glazer, Rashi, Barbara E. Kahn, and William L. Moore (1991), "The Influence of External Constraints on Brand Choice: The Lone-Alternative Effect," *Journal of Consumer Research*, 18 (June), 119–127.

108. Simonson, Itamar (1993), "Get Closer to Your Customers by Understanding How They Make Choices," *California Management Review* (Summer), 68–83.

109. Nedungadi, Prakash (1990), "Recall and Consumer Consideration Sets: Influencing Choice Without Altering Brand Evaluations," *Journal of Consumer Research*, 17 (December), 263–276.

110. Simonson, Itamar and Amos Tversky (1992), "Choice in Context: Trade-off Contrast and Extremeness Aversion," *Journal of Marketing Research*, 29 (August), 281–95.

111. Simonson, Itamar and Amos Tversky (1992), "Choice in Context: Trade-off Contrast and Extremeness Aversion," *Journal of Marketing Research*, 29 (August), 281–95.

112. Simonson, Itamar (1989), "Choice Based on Reasons: The Case of Attraction and Compromise Effects," *Journal of Consumer Research*, 16 (September), 158–74.

113. Huber, Joel, John W. Payne, and Christopher P. Puto (1982), "Adding Asymmetrically Dominated Alternatives: Violations of Regularity and the Similarity Hypothesis," *Journal of Consumer Research*, 9 (June), 90–98.

114. Huber, Joel and Christopher P. Puto (1983), "Market Boundaries and Product Choice: Illustrating Attraction and Substitution Effects," *Journal of Consumer Research*, 10 (June), 31–44.

115. Tversky, Amos and Itamar Simonson (1993), "Context-Dependent Preferences," *Management Science*, 39 (10), 1179–1189.

116. Simonson, Itamar (1994), "Shoppers' Easily Influenced Choices," *New York Times* (November 6), 11.

117. Huber, Joel, John W. Payne, and Christopher P. Puto (1982), "Adding Asymmetrically Dominated Alternatives: Violations of Regularity and the Similarity Hypothesis," *Journal of Consumer Research*, 9 (June), 90–98.

118. Simonson, Itamar and Amos Tversky (1992), "Choice in Context: Trade-off Contrast and Extremeness Aversion," *Journal of Marketing Research*, 29, 281–295.

119. Simonson, Itamar (1989), "Choice Based on Reasons: The Case of Attraction and Compromise Effects," *Journal of Consumer Research*, 16 (September), 158–74.

120. Simonson, Itamar (1989), "Choice Based on Reasons: The Case of Attraction and Compromise Effects," *Journal of Consumer Research*, 16 (September), 158–74.

121. Wernerfelt, Birger (1995), "A Rational Reconstruction of the Compromise Effect: Using Market Data to Infer Utilities," *Journal of Consumer Research*, 21 (March), 627–633.

11

How Do Consumers Respond to Retailers' Merchandising, Pricing, and Promotional Strategies?

Retailers have many merchandising decisions to consider when trying to sell groceries to consumers. Merchandising decisions include: (1) how much space to allocate to a category and to a brand within a category, and where the space allocated to the brand should be located (e.g., top shelf versus bottom shelf, etc.), (2) the add/drop decision—whether to bring a new item into the store and then whether to drop it when other new items appear, (3) the pricing decision, and (4) the promotion decision.

To be profitable, retailers need to manage their category shelf-space allotments based on an understanding of the way consumers shop. Shelf space that is designed to follow historic customer shopping patterns generates more sales and is more profitable. Assortment also matters in shelf space allocation decisions. Larger assortments offer more variety, but they can confuse the customer if there is too much redundancy. Retailers can improve profitability by ridding their shelves of duplicated items.

Once retailers have decided on the assortment of brands within a product category, they then need to consider the pricing decisions. Consumers relate to price in three primary ways. First, consumers must be aware of the price. Although price is a very important criterion for making purchase decisions, some research has shown that frequently consumers buy out of habit and cannot recall the absolute price paid for specific items purchased. Second, consumers generally judge whether or not a price is reasonable by comparing it to a reference price. The reference price may be available at the point of sale, for example, a regular price compared to a sale price, or competitive prices. Or, the reference price may be one that consumers store in memory. If the purchase price is below or at the reference price, then the price appears reasonable. If the purchase price is above the reference price, it may appear unreasonable. The third way consumers relate to price is *by responding to price increases and decreases. It has been shown that consumers are more negatively troubled by price increases than they are delighted by price decreases.*

Finally, a retailer must consider whether to offer short-term price promotions. Three types of price promotions are used frequently in the supermarket: coupons, issued by manufacturers and retailers; in-store displays, either end-aisle or mid-aisle; and features, in which key prices are featured for certain brands in newspaper advertising or in-store flyers.

CONSUMERS' RESPONSE TO MERCHANDISING

Shelf space is one of the scarcest resources in a supermarket. A typical supermarket will stock more than 45,000 different items or stocking keeping units (SKUs).[1] A supermarket has to decide how much space to allocate to a category, how much space to allocate to each brand within the category, and where that brand should be placed within the category (e.g., top shelf versus bottom shelf, left side versus right side, etc.). In addition, every time a new product is introduced, a retailer has to decide whether or not to add that new product and whether or not to drop an existing product.

The space allocation decision is crucial because it is directly tied to retailers' sales. If a consumer comes into the store to buy a specific brand but it is out of stock, the sale could be lost. Some analyses show that the shopper does not buy an alternate item on that same shopping trip 34 percent of the time. About half the time the consumer goes to another store to pick up the missing item, but sometimes decides not to buy it at all.[2] Therefore, slow-moving items should be allocated less space than faster-moving ones, especially if stock-outs are occurring for the faster-moving items.

An extensive study examining the problem of out-of-stock merchandise[3] showed that on a typical afternoon in an average supermarket, more than 8.2 percent of items in targeted categories were out of stock. The number climbs to 11 percent on Sundays when customer traffic is high and deliveries and in-store labor are limited. The problem is even more acute in the sales of advertised special items—retailers lose more than 15 percent of potential sales of advertised items due to out of stocks. The study concludes that the net impact of all of these out-of-stock conditions is to reduce consumer purchases by 3.1 percent per shopping trip.

Space Management

Obviously, it is important for the retailers to use the shelf space wisely, matching supply to demand. Criteria that are used to determine how much space should be allocated to a particular item include how fast the item moves off the shelf, the gross margin of the items, sales, and direct profitability (which would include costs associated with storing, transporting shelving, and labor-intensive merchandising activities, such as pricing or promotion, in addition to gross margin).[4]

It is important for supermarkets to manage their shelf space on a space-to-movement basis—that is, based on the way products move in a particular area rather than to have a standard chain-wide policy. An experiment[5] designed for Dominick's Finer Foods in Chicago compared a single chain-wide space management approach with one where space within categories was allocated based on historic purchase patterns of customers that frequented the store.

Sixty stores participated in the test. Half of the stores followed the standard, single, chain-wide shelf allocation approach. The other half of the stores had customized shelf allocations set up. The overall space assigned to each product category was the same in all 60 stores. In the stores where the shelf allocations were customized, however, Apollo (IRI) and Spaceman (Nielsen) commercial computer decision-support systems were used to design shelf space allocations based on average unit movement for the last 12 months, allocating more space to higher market share goods. This increased allocation to higher market share goods reduced stock-outs and attracted more attention to the category. Just by changing the shelf allocation to reflect the demographic movement in the stores, sales increased by an average of 3.9 percent compared to the stores following the single, chain-wide approach. This increase in sales could result in increased profits of up to $67,000 per year.

Researchers conducted a shelf reorganization experiment[6] to investigate whether positioning slower moving products more prominently within the category (i.e., taking the prime locations away from the faster moving products that did not need the special attention) could increase category sales. The experiment was conducted in two categories: oral care and laundry care.

In oral care, the primary product, toothpaste, is purchased by most households with an average interpurchase time of about two months. On the other hand, toothbrushes are also purchased by most households, but not as frequently, with average interpurchase times of about 4 to 6 months. In the experiment, toothbrushes were moved to the center of the category, a more prominent shelf location where the toothpaste had traditionally been. The toothpaste was moved to a less prominent location. The idea was that because consumers would be coming to the category to purchase toothpaste anyway, they would find that product even if it were a little more difficult to locate. On the other hand, having toothbrushes in a more prominent location was likely to increase impulse purchases. Compared to the traditional layout, the new approach increased sales of toothbrushes by 8 percent and increased overall profits in the category by 6 percent while not harming toothpaste sales.

In the laundry category, the primary product, detergent, is purchased by most households approximately every two months, but fabric softener is only purchased by about 65 percent of the households. Here, the researchers put the fabric softener in the middle of the laundry detergent section, between the powder and the liquid forms. This new positioning drew more attention to the slower moving fabric softener. The change resulted in a 4 percent increase in sales and profits as compared to the traditional layout.

Space management not only affects which categories to increase or decrease, and which brands within a category should get more or less space, but also affects shelf placement—how brands within a category should be placed on a shelf. A study[7] comparing different shelf locations within eight product categories—analgesics, bottled juices, canned soup, canned seafood, cigarettes, dish detergents, frozen entrees, and refrigerated juices—showed that the height of the shelf that the product was on mattered significantly. Products located at a shelf height of 51 to 53 inches off the floor had the most favorable position, and could command a significant increase in sales. This distance is just below eye level (for U.S. females average eye level is 59 inches and for men is 64 inches). There were no general conclusions as to the best position in horizontal placement—some brands did well located on the edge of a particular shelf and some did well in the middle.

The surprising results of the study[8] were that additional shelf facings did not significantly increase sales for these routinely purchased goods. The researchers found that position was much more important than number of facings. As long as a product had the minimum critical amount of shelf space (with that minimum required varying for different categories), returns from additional shelf space over and above that minimum were nonexistent. Increased shelf space or additional shelf facings could increase sales for some impulse products, however. "Spur-of-the-moment" decisions are more likely to happen if the stimulus is more noticeable and has more impact—something that is likely to be true if the product is given more space on the shelf.

Category Assortment and Perceived Variety

There are two factors that a retailer needs to consider when deciding how to allocate products within limited shelf space to maximize profit. The first factor, discussed previously, was how to allocate the space to the different categories and to the brands within the category. Another aspect that the retailer has to consider is how much variety to present in the category, in terms of brands, package forms, flavors, and sizes.

The retailer must be concerned with the consumers' perceived variety. When consumers come into a supermarket, they expect to find a wide variety of items offered so that there is a high likelihood that they will find what they want. Two elements contribute to perceived variety: the number of acceptable options (which may be connected to the size of the display) and the amount of desirable diversity among those items.

The mere number of options represents a type of variety. For example, an ice cream parlor that offers 31 flavors appears to offer more flexibility and variety than one that offers two or three flavors, regardless of what those flavors are.[9] In addition, consumers perceive bigger shelf sets to offer more variety than smaller shelf sets, even if the actual number of different options available in each shelf set is the same.[10]

Large assortments, though, can be negative. While on one hand they seem to offer more variety, on the other hand they can also be seen as daunting or confusing. Too large an assortment can be irritating to consumers who may then resort to simplistic decision rules to make a decision quickly. In fact, consumers who shop in supermarkets that tend to have very large assortments are more promotion sensitive than consumers who shop in markets with smaller assortments. Possibly this is because the promotions are used to screen down the large assortment into smaller manageable consideration sets.[11] Here the large assortments are making the consumers more price sensitive.

Perhaps a more important aspect of flexibility and perceived variety is the amount of desirable diversity. If shoppers see little or no differences among items in a product class, then the perceived variety will be quite low. Desirable diversity is a function of the acceptability of the items and the distinctiveness of those items. If two items that are equally preferred are added to an assortment, the item that is more unique will add a perception of more variety.[12]

Duplication of products within categories is another consideration for the retailer. A study conducted by the Food Marketing Institute[13] tried to determine how shoppers view variety in the grocery store. Although consumers believe supermarkets should carry a wide variety of brands, they seem to believe that the typical supermarket carries too many items. Rather than offering expansive choice, some large assortments were just considered replete with redundant choices. This redundancy or duplication in the category made the shopping more difficult. Retailers could improve profitability, reduce customer confusion, and yet maintain variety for consumers by ridding the shelf of duplicated items. This links back to what we said in Part One of this book—to survive, retailers must become more efficient; they must carry what consumers want, not what manufacturers pay them to carry.

What constitutes the most efficient assortment varies in different categories. In toilet tissue, ketchup, salad dressing, and laundry detergent, shoppers thought the categories had too many different sizes of goods. In deodorant, shoppers thought the redundancy could be reduced by removing some of the different forms of each brand. In toothpaste, the redundancy could be reduced by removing some of the different package-types of each brand. (Just to get an idea of how many different items there are in the toothpaste category—P&G has 63 different toothpaste brand-size items with the Crest brand name; Colgate has 58.) Finally, in spaghetti sauce the perception was that there were too many different styles of sauces.

Because stated opinions do not always match behavior, the researchers set up some experiments in three participating supermarket chains (24 stores in total). In half of the stores (test stores), the assortments were streamlined by the removal of those items that had been identified as being redundant. For example, in some categories, some of the superfluous sizes were removed, or in other categories, excessive packaging types were removed. In addition, researchers observed the shelf immediately following a period of heavy business and noted the items that were clearly slow movers. These, too, were removed. In the other half of the stores (control stores), the assortments were as usual. The total amount of product category space was the same in both sets of stores. Available space resulting from item removals was allocated to high-volume products in the test stores.

During the study, consumers were stopped in the aisles and asked to comment on the category that they had just shopped. Most consumers in the test stores either noticed no difference in the category or thought that the variety had been increased! Comparisons between the test stores, with the recommended duplicated items removed, and the control stores (business as usual), showed that sales increased by an average of 1.62 percent in the test stores.

Further support for these results comes from Procter & Gamble's recent reduction of stockkeeping units (SKUs) in their categories. P&G has been reducing some of the SKUs in their categories by 15 to 25 percent. They found that, in some categories, consumers perceived better assortment with 35 percent *fewer* SKUs.[14]

These results showed clearly that actual variety and perceived variety are not always the same thing. Actual variety can decrease while perceived variety increases. Thus, the number of brands can be reduced without affecting sales or consumers' perceptions of varieties. This observation links back to ECR Initiatives discussed earlier in the book and, in particular, to the notion of "efficient assortment."

Another ECR Initiative discussed earlier was "efficient promotion." To begin to understand how to make promotional offers simpler and more effective, it is important that the retailer know how consumers react to price and promotional incentives.

CONSUMERS' REACTIONS TO PRICE

Changing technologies have greatly increased a supermarket manager's ability to be flexible in pricing strategies. Using electronic shelf label systems, instead of the old paper labeling systems, it is now possible for store managers to adjust prices on supermarket shelves several times a day. With liquid crystal displays that exhibit alpha and numeric characters, supermarkets could have "hourly specials," or issue electronic coupons or messages.[15] If and when grocery shopping on the Internet becomes more common, flexible pricing might become the norm.

Most American supermarkets, however, are not yet at the point of changing prices hourly, but the pricing decision still is a crucial one. There are at least three major ways a consumer relates to price. First, there is price awareness—the ability of consumers to recognize and remember prices. Second, there is the impact of contextual influences on price—the way external or internal reference prices affect the consumer's evaluation of current prices. Third, there is price sensitivity—the degree of reaction consumers have to changes in price.[16]

Price Awareness

Price is clearly an important variable in making a decision about what to buy in the grocery store. When the purchase process becomes routinized though, shoppers tend to buy out of habit and may not pay too much attention to what they are doing, a practice that could be called "mindless shopping."

A study[17] was conducted to observe how aware shoppers were of the prices they were paying for items in the grocery store immediately after an item had been chosen. In this study, observers, masquerading as grocery inventory clerks, were stationed in supermarkets watching shoppers' choice patterns. The amount of time between when the shopper's attention turned to the shelf and when the item was placed in a shopping cart was recorded. In addition, the number of different items that were touched and inspected was also noted. After the shopper put the item in the cart, s/he was intercepted by the observer who asked: "Off the top of your head, without checking, can you tell me what the price is of the [product name] you just chose?" This interview occurred within 30 seconds of the time the item was placed in the cart. The shopper was also asked whether the price of the item selected was a regular or special price as well as a few other questions. Four product classes were chosen for the study: coffee, toothpaste, margarine, and cold cereal. The total number of shoppers interviewed was 802.

The average time between arriving at and departing from the product category was less than 12 seconds. In 85 percent of the purchases only the chosen brand was handled, and 90 percent of the shoppers physically inspected only one size. One in five shoppers (21.1%) did not offer a price estimate when asked; they had no idea what the price of the item was. Only about half of the shoppers were able to state the correct exact price, and only 55.6 percent gave an estimate within 5 percent of the actual price. A third of the shoppers (31.8%) gave an inaccurate estimate of the price, with these estimates generally coming in lower than the actual price. Almost all of the shoppers (93%), though, did know the relative price (i.e., higher, lower, or the same) of the brand chosen as compared to the other brands in the category.

Of the shoppers in the study, 29 percent of them chose an item that was being sold at a special price. Surprisingly, half of those shoppers did not know that the item they bought was being promoted. Those shoppers who knew they purchased an item at a special price claimed to undertake more search and price checking than did the shoppers who purchased regularly priced items, but their price estimates were no more accurate.

Just under 60 percent of all the consumers even claimed to have checked the price. Many consumers just picked items off the shelf and put them in their carts. This study shows that many consumers shop out of habit, and may not be very sensitive to small changes in the prices of each item chosen. It also suggests that many consumers may need some kind of nudge to pay more attention to price. It seems that coupons may be more effective at reaching a price-sensitive segment than in-store promotions,[18] because coupons insure that shoppers are aware that they are getting a promotional price.

A few years later, the basic results of this study were replicated by the trade magazine, *Supermarket Business*. The magazine staff conducted a survey of consumers to see how well they remembered prices of items in the supermarket. The study found that although consumers believed that they knew the prices of things they bought, they frequently did not. Consumers who shopped at EDLP supermarkets knew prices better than those who shopped at high-low priced stores.[19]

One reason that consumers may have trouble remembering exact prices is because of some of the pricing tactics that are frequently used in the supermarket. These tactics become so familiar that consumers may assume they are being used even when they are not actually in use. For example, many prices in the supermarket end in "9," so an item will be marked as .49 rather than as .50. The pricing strategy is based on the assumption that consumers will underestimate the price in the former case and overestimate the price in the latter case, so the perceived price difference is bigger than one cent.

In an experiment done to test this assumption, consumers were asked as they were leaving a supermarket to look at a large board with 12 product categories of goods on it. The items in these categories were shown with their prices. After the shoppers looked at the board they were asked to recall the prices they had just seen. Recall for prices ending with "9" was compared to the recall for prices ending with the digits 0 through 8. These results showed that the consumers did not significantly underestimate the 9-ending prices.

However, there was a tendency for the consumers to overestimate the prices of the non-9-ending goods. Generally, the mistake made was that the consumers assumed the last digit was 9 even when it wasn't—and thus were overestimating the actual price.[20] This study implies that consumers try to minimize the effort of the thinking about prices by truncating the right digit in their calculations; they just assumed the right-most digit was always a nine. In another study, prices ending with "9" were underestimated when they were recalled two days later. It is possible that consumers initially recalled the price correctly, but during the two-day delay dropped off the right-most digits.[21]

These studies suggest that an explanation for shoppers' low knowledge of price information is that they are just not paying that much attention to price at the point of sale. Consumers have some assumptions about the way items are priced, and they rarely check to see if these assumptions still hold.

Another explanation for shoppers' low knowledge of prices is that shoppers may notice prices at the point of sale but may not remember them once they move away from the shelf.[22] There is evidence that, although consumers do not remember actual absolute prices, they do remember the relative price positions of different brands.[23] It has been shown that consumers can remember the correct rank order of prices even if they can't remember the actual prices.[24]

Contextual Influences on Price

Extensive research on consumer behavior leads to the conclusion that consumers do not evaluate prices absolutely, but, rather, they evaluate them in relative terms. In other words, the pricing context matters. Many studies have found that when consumers compare the purchase price to a reference price, or a standard against which an evaluation can be made.[25] There are two kinds of reference prices, external and internal. Consumers may use both internal and external reference prices to evaluate value,[26, 27, 28, 29] and also to determine how much to buy.[30]

An external reference price is one that is presented in the marketing environment. For example, in supermarkets, sometimes the "regular price" is indicated next to a "sale price" in a shelf display. Here, the regular price is the reference against which the value of the sale is computed. Or, the reference price can be a competitor's price, against which the value of a specific brand is compared. External reference prices can also be mentioned in advertising.

Although consumers are sometimes skeptical of manufacturers' or retailers' intentions in providing an external reference price, there is evidence that these external reference prices do affect consumers' perceptions of the value of the offer.[31] These perceptions are mediated by consumers' familiarity with the brand, the type of store, and the consistency of the discounting claims. The more familiar a consumer is with the brand, the less the consumer is affected by the external reference price, and the more the consumer depends on his or her own sense of what the brand is worth. Similarly, if the store does not routinely promote brands and, therefore, if a particular promotion is perceived to be more special, then the external sale prices have more of an effect on the perceived value of the offering.[32]

An internal reference price[33] is one that is recorded in the consumer's memory. In this case, a specific price is remembered (perhaps not accurately[34]), or a price is remembered combined with past prices, and that internal reference price forms the standard against which other prices are compared.[35, 36] Empirical evidence has found that if a brand is frequently promoted, consumers tend to lower their internal reference price for that brand.[37, 38] In the extreme, the promoted price, rather than the regular price, may become the reference price for that brand.

Consumers seem to have a range of acceptance around their reference price as to what they think is a fair price.[39] Prices that fall within that range are acceptable and prices that fall above that range are rejected.[40] Sometimes consumers derive pleasure just from getting a good deal. In that case, the purchase has two components: one, the pleasure in just acquiring an item and paying for it, and two, the pleasure in purchasing that item at a very good price.[41] Taken in the extreme, this suggests that consumers may derive pleasure from buying a product on sale even if they do not particularly want the good purchased!

Consumers respond asymmetrically to price increases and decreases relative to their reference prices. There is a stronger aversion to increases than there is delight to decreases.[42,43] Several research studies across many different product classes find that consumers are less likely to purchase a product if the price is higher than an internal reference price, and more likely to purchase a product if the price is lower; *but* the decreases in purchasing due to higher prices are greater than the increases in purchasing due to lower prices.[44, 45, 46] This asymmetric finding suggests that marketers of products that experience large natural fluctuations in price, such as coffee and sugar, should attempt to smooth out those price fluctuations rather than pass along the more radical increases and decreases in price as they occur.[47]

These results also suggest that retailers should be very careful about price increases because they are regarded particularly adversely by consumers. Price increases may be inevitable, but retailers would probably have less trouble with consumers if the price increases were made in small increments. This would allow consumers to adapt to the higher prices slowly,[48] rather than shock consumers with one large price increase. Also, small increases may fall within a consumer's tolerance range around an internal reference price.[49]

Another way that prices can be increased without calling attention to the increased price is by maintaining the same price but giving the consumer *less*. During the early 1990s, when the economy was bad and consumer confidence was low, some manufacturers practiced something called "product downsizing," or as consumer advocates labeled it, "product shorting."[50]

Manufacturers who wanted to raise prices, but were fearful of a negative reaction on the part of consumers, would instead change the standard size of the package. The result of this practice is that supermarket shelves are now lined with many different sizes in each category. For example, ground coffees now come in "8-, 10-, 11.5-, 12-, and 13-ounce sizes" in addition to the regular 1-pound units. In the tomato sauce category, nine sizes can be found: "25-, 26-, 26¼-, 27½-, 28-, 30-, and 32-ounces."[51] Although some states have considered requiring manufacturers to alert consumers to changes in the size of their packaging (e.g., New York), currently manufacturers are not required to do so. When there are many different sizes within one category, it is more of an effort for consumers to compare prices. This difficulty tends to make consumers less price sensitive, which may provide another benefit to manufacturers. On the other hand, this practice is also very expensive for the manufacturers, and is not consistent with the ECR initiatives.

To be fair, manufacturers often have other reasons for the change in sizing of their units. For example, Procter & Gamble maintains that the size of their coffee cans changed because of technological advancement—the beans are higher yielding, such that 13 ounces of the new and improved coffee made the same number of cups of coffee as the old 16-ounce size did. Spokespeople from the baby food industry said that the change in sizes of the baby food containers from

7½-ounce jars to 6 ounces and 4½-ounce jars to 4 ounces here was due to parental demand. Parents felt that the past sizes were too large. Also, the smaller containers were easier to handle.

Another way to make price increases less noticeable would be to make the price comparisons difficult for a shopper to compute. For example, sometimes the larger-sized packages of a brand offer a better value, but not always. In the bath tissue category, the smaller sizes (4 packs) can be a better deal than the larger sizes (12–24 rolls) because of more price promotions on the smaller size. Researchers[52] experimented with a change in shelf display that made it more difficult for consumers to make price comparisons. The category was originally organized by brand, making comparison between the package sizes easier. In the experiment, the category was rearranged by package sizes, facilitating price comparisons among brands but making price comparisons among package sizes more difficult. This change in shelf layout produced a 5 percent increase in category sales and profits and the results held up for a test period of about 10 months.

Price Sensitivity

There is much variability among individuals in the degree of reaction to these increases or decreases in price. Price sensitivity, or the way consumers' purchase behavior responds to changes in price, has been shown to depend upon consumer characteristics, brand loyalty, and competitive market intensity. In some cases, price sensitivity is diminished and higher prices are actually preferred because price is seen as a signal of quality.

Price sensitivity has been shown to vary by demographics. A study of consumers in the Chicago area found a systematic relationship between sensitivity to prices for supermarket goods and certain consumer characteristics. In general, more educated consumers, and homeowners who had larger, more expensive homes and fewer income constraints, were less price sensitive. Consumers from larger families, and African-American and Hispanic consumers were more price sensitive.[53]

Brand loyalty also makes a difference. Consumers who are loyal to a particular brand are also less likely to respond to changes in the price of that brand than are consumers who are not particularly loyal. Consumers who are not loyal to a brand may only purchase that brand if the price is low enough. In contrast, loyal consumers presumably feel some need for the brand and thus are much more likely to choose it regardless of the price. These loyal consumers may not even particularly notice the price.[54]

On the other hand, the situation reverses when considering *how much* to purchase. Because the brand-loyal consumers generally feel the need for the product, they are more likely to increase the quantity that they purchase in response to a noticeable decrease in price. Non-loyal consumers who may be purchasing a brand because of the low price rather than because it is a favorite are less likely to increase the quantity they purchase.[55]

Price sensitivity also varies depending upon the competitive intensity of the geographic area. Supermarkets that are relatively isolated essentially have a captive market and, thus, those consumers out of necessity are less price sensitive. If several stores are located fairly close to each other, then price sensitivity among consumers in the area increases because consumers feel that they have a choice.[56] If the market is particularly competitive, as has been the case in the Los Angeles area, then consumers may become very price sensitive.

Price sensitivity is also diminished when price is perceived as a positive cue that signals the quality and prestige of the good. Results of a survey of 582 grocery shoppers in the western United States indicated that when price is seen as a cue for quality, consumers are prestige sensitive rather than price sensitive. When high price is seen as positive attribute, consumers are less likely to recall the actual price paid accurately and are more likely to use the price as a global indicator of high quality. They are also unlikely to use coupons or take advantage of other price promotions. More typically, when price is seen as negative, that is, as a cost or expense, consumers are more price sensitive, more likely to take advantage of promotional offers such as coupons or in-store sales, and are more likely to recall accurately the prices they paid for products.[57]

CONSUMERS' RESPONSE TO PRICE PROMOTIONS

The use of price promotions, or *temporary* price discounts offered to customers,[58] has increased by twelvefold over the last decade.[59] Manufacturers are now spending more money on promotions than on advertising.[60] Price promotions on brands within a category are used by retailers and manufacturers for a variety of reasons. One of the basic motivations for price promotions is to take advantage of differences in consumers' sensitivities to price by varying price levels across periods. If price promotions are random and unpredictable, then consumers who are not price sensitive will generally purchase at the regular price (unless they get lucky and hit a sale). Those consumers who are price sensitive will wait for the promotional period.

Manufacturers use consumer price promotions to generate interest and trial in new products, to increase short-term market share of a specific brand, to counter competitive activity, and to build product-line synergy. Price promotions are used by retailers to increase activity in a category, to increase sales of profitable brands, to extinguish unwanted inventory, to create a store image, or to bring customers into the store.[61]

Temporary price promotions cause a significant short-term sales spike for the brand being promoted.[62] This may be beneficial for the manufacturer in the short term. From the retailer's point of view though, the key question is whether price promotions increase overall sales for the product category, or if the increase in sales of a promoted brand comes at the expense of other brands in the category. Based on an analysis of 27 different product categories,[63] it was found that product *category* sales can increase as a result of price promotions on specific brands within the category. Deeper discounts in particular increased the variability in total category sales. If promotions were very frequent, however, overall category sales did not vary much as a result of the promotional activity. The implication is that overall category sales are most likely to increase if brand promotions within the category are deep but infrequent. However, as pointed out in Part One of the book, it is unlikely that deep, infrequent promotions can be sustained over time in a category. Why? Because promotion incentives create a prisoner's dilemma, as discussed earlier, driving manufacturers and retailers to more frequent promotion activity that does not benefit overall category sales.

Asymmetric Response to Price Promotions

Consumers have historically categorized brands in terms of price tiers. In supermarkets, the natural price tiers have been (1) national or premium, (2) moderate or private label, and (3) generic brands.[64] When this hierarchy is in place, consumers do not respond to price promotions for these different products in the same way. When premium or national brands are promoted, increased sales for the discounted premium brand come from consumers who usually buy other premium brands and from consumers who usually buy moderate/private label or generic brands. On the other hand, when moderate/private label or generic brands are discounted, increased sales generally do not come from consumers who normally buy premium brands, but rather from consumers who normally buy other moderate/private label or generic brands. Promoting premium brands generates more overall consumer reaction than promoting moderate/private label or generic brands.[65]

This asymmetry suggests that as long as those perceived price tiers exist, price promotions are more strategically advantageous to national or premium brands than they are to moderate or private label brands.[66] If national brands promote, then shoppers who normally buy private label brands are attracted. On the other hand, when private label brands promote, shoppers of national brands are not attracted. Temporary price promotions then become a very effective tool for national brands to use against private label success. In particular, if the promotion on national brands is rotated so that only one is being promoted at one time, the private label brand will always be under attack from some national brand.[67]

These historical patterns of price tiers may be changing, however, as the quality of private label brands increases. When the quality gap between private labels and national brands becomes small or even zero, then the asymmetric effects can switch. When the perceived quality between a national brand and private label brand is equal, then the private label promotional price can be extremely attractive and the promotions can actually be more effective on private label brands than on national brands.[68]

Can Price Promotions Undermine Brand Preferences?

Although price promotions can clearly increase sales in the short term, there has been some speculation that there might be a longer-term negative impact on brand preferences once the promotion is retracted. In another words, when the promotion is retracted, not only are the incremental sales lost that were gained because of the price cut, but loyal purchasers of the brand at the regular, higher price will now defect as well.

The fear is that consumers would become adjusted to the sale price, and would respond negatively when the price is raised again to its original pre-promotion levels. As mentioned previously, one reason for this effect is that the consumer's internal reference price for the brand may shift closer to the promoted price, and thus the original price would be perceived as being too high. There is also some evidence that price promotions "teach" consumers to buy only on promotion – thus heightening price sensitivity.[69]

Another reason some researchers believe that promotions could hurt the long-term sales of products is that the consumers see the price as a signal for quality.[70, 71, 72] Because there is asymmetric information in the marketplace—the seller knows the quality of the good for certain, but the buyer must infer it from external signals such as price—the buyer may assume that a high price is signaling a high quality good, and a low promotion price is signaling lower quality. Therefore, when a consumer sees a product go on sale, the consumer assumes there is something wrong with it, and will not buy the product again at its regular price. In simple words, "you get what you pay for"—a brand that has to promote must have something wrong with it.

These long-term, post-promotion negative effects on brand preferences or brand evaluations are not as likely to occur, however, if consumers are switching among brands in the marketplace for reasons other than for price (e.g., for the sake of variety). In addition, if many other brands in the marketplace are also promoting periodically, there is likely to be less negative reaction to any one brand promoting.[73]

There have been some explicit empirical tests of this proposed long-term post-promotion negative impact on brand evaluations.[74] So far, the empirical evidence has found that promotions provide a short-term lift in sales, but there does not seem to be strong follow-up negative repercussions in changing brand preferences. The lack of a negative effect may be at least partly attributable to the lack of involvement that consumers seem to exhibit when grocery shopping. In such a situation, the promotion will have the strongest effect right at the point of sale, but the effect should dissipate quickly, thus making longer-term negative effects unlikely.[75, 76]

Stockpiling

Retailers or manufacturers use temporary price promotions to build interest in their brands. Ideally, a consumer would purchase the product on sale and then purchase it the next time at the regular price. If, however, consumers purchase a great deal of product on sale and then keep it on inventory, they would be unlikely to purchase it later at regular price. The promotion then would not be increasing demand for the product (which is the retailers' or manufacturers' ultimate goal), but instead would be encouraging consumers to buy earlier and forego later purchases. This stockpiling effect would suggest that the peak in sales that occurs due to a short-term promotion would be followed by a trough in sales when the promotion is retracted. Some empirical evidence on supermarket shopping suggests that at the aggregate level, the stockpiling effect is relatively small.[77, 78] For individual consumers, however, stockpiling may be a very real decision.

If consumers were to stockpile, it would likely depend on their perceptions of two aspects of the promotion: the frequency and the amount of the discount. If promotions were frequent or if the amount of the discount was perceived to be insignificant, consumers would feel less of a need to stockpile.[79]

A survey of 400 shoppers in the metropolitan New York area assessed consumer perceptions of deal frequency, regular prices, and sale prices for a 12-week period to see how the consumers' attitudes related to actual data. On average, buyers of a specific brand were between two and five times more accurate on the sale price, regular price, and deal frequency of that brand than were nonbuyers of the brand. In addition, consumers who purchased the specific brand-size frequently were more likely to be accurate than consumers who purchased it infrequently.

Overall, there was reasonable accuracy in the recall of which specific brand-sizes were on sale during the 12-week period and which ones were not. Consumers were less accurate in recalling how frequent the sales were, but still more accurate than would have been the case had they been merely guessing. Consumers tended to overestimate the frequency of infrequently promoted brands and underestimate the frequency of brands that were promoted often. Less than half of the consumers who expressed an opinion were accurate in stating the deal price—38 percent of the responses were within 20 cents of the actual sale price.[80]

Certain consumers may be faced with the decision of deciding whether or not to stockpile when their brand is on sale. This is because some consumers are reasonably savvy about the promotional activity of brands that they purchase frequently, according to survey results. If they do decide to stockpile, they are then faced with the decision of how much to purchase. The optimal decision would be based on what they anticipate the future price of the good will be, how much they are likely to consume, whether they currently have any in inventory, the value of any alternative investments, and, finally, the costs of storing the good.[81]

As with many other decisions made in the supermarket, consumers are unlikely to calculate the exact optimal amount of a discounted item to purchase and store. They are more likely to rely on simplified rules that seem to work well enough. An experiment was conducted to uncover what simplified stockpiling rules consumers were likely to use in the supermarket. In the experiment, consumers tended not to think about how much of a good they had in inventory when a really good sale was present. The consumers found it difficult to "pass up a bargain" even when they knew they had enough of the product at home. If the promotions became too frequent, however, the consumers were less likely to stockpile in spite of the attractive discount. This suggests that even in product classes with constant consumption rates, savvy consumers are likely to respond to a really good deal by purchasing bigger quantities, as long as the promotions are not too frequent.[82]

Even if consumers decide not to stockpile a good on sale, they still may face the simpler decision as to whether or not to make a purchase at a specific time. Should they purchase strawberries now or wait for next week when they are likely to be on sale? If consumers choose to buy the product now, then there may be regret if it does go on sale next week. On the other hand, if they wait, there is a possibility that the sale will not materialize or, worse yet, the price of strawberries might increase.

If consumers are asked to think about how they would feel in the two situations should they make the wrong choice—in other words, would they feel more regret if they bought the strawberries now and it turned out that there was a sale next week, versus if they didn't buy the strawberries now and it turned out that the price increased the next week—they tend to indicate that they would feel more regret in the latter case. Therefore, forcing consumers to think about the possibilities of regret in the two circumstances makes them more likely to purchase earlier than to wait.[83]

TYPES OF CONSUMER PROMOTIONAL TOOLS

There are three major types of consumer promotional tools that are used in the supermarket. The first, and probably the most well-known kind, is couponing. Coupons can either be issued by the retailer or by the manufacturer. The second, most visible, way the retailer can promote items is through in-store special displays. There are end-aisle displays and mid-aisle displays. Frequently, the displays are marked by a "big red arrow" or some other graphic that calls attention to the shelf. Finally, the third way retailers can promote is by featuring certain brands and their prices in weekly newspaper advertising and in-store flyers.

Coupons

The first coupon dates back to 1895 when C. W. Post offered a coupon for its new Grape-Nuts cereal. Over the years, there has been an explosive growth in coupons, with over 300 billion distributed in 1992.[84] Coupons can be distributed by manufacturers or by retailers.

Manufacturers' coupons not only offer a price discount, but also provide a way to draw attention to the brand. Coupons can help create a brand image as well as provide an incentive for purchase. They can be used as a reminder device for products that are purchased by most households, but are purchased infrequently, such as shampoo, toothpaste, and disposable wraps. They also may be used as a targeting device for products that are bought very frequently but by a small proportion of households, such as baby supplies and pet foods. Finally, coupons can also be used as an effective price discrimination technique[85] for high-priced products such as diapers, coffee, and laundry detergent.[86]

The use of coupons requires handling costs on the part of consumers. They usually must cut, sort, and redeem the coupon in order to take advantage of the price incentive.[87] Most coupons are redeemed either at the time that they are distributed[88] or just before the expiration date.[89] Because of the effort involved in using coupons, the majority of consumers throw away coupons. In 1993, 300 billion coupons were issued and 293 billion were thrown away—only 7 billion were redeemed. According to Procter & Gamble,[90] from a manufacturers' point of view, couponing only make sense when a new product is being introduced, in response to competition, or to target a consumer base who won't purchase unless a coupon is issued.

Manufacturers' coupons are distributed through Sunday newspapers, magazines, through direct mail, in the supermarket, or in the package itself.

Newspaper-distributed coupons have been found to have a significant effect at increasing market share, but the effect varies from brand to brand. In a study of the instant coffee market, coupons did generate incremental sales, but not all redemptions were incremental.

Loyal users of the brands were disproportionately higher users of coupons. In addition, although coupons did increase market share for many brands, the increases in sales were generally not large enough to counterbalance the increased costs of the coupons. Thus, in many cases the coupons were not profitable, even when they did significantly increase sales.[91]

Package coupons are another type of manufacturer's coupons. There are three kinds of coupons that manufacturers may include with their brands:

1. Peel off coupons that are redeemed when the package is purchased
2. On-pack coupons that are a visible part of the packaging but are redeemed at a later purchase occasion
3. In-pack coupons that are not visible at purchase time and are redeemed at a later purchase occasion

Each year, approximately 11 billion coupons are distributed through brand packaging. The redemption rate for these types of coupons is about four times higher than when coupons are distributed through other means.[92] The key managerial function of these types of coupons is to build customer loyalty by establishing a link between one purchase occasion and the next. The peel-off coupons provide the highest incentive to purchase at the initial point of sale of the three types of package coupons, and are most likely to draw in consumers who may have purchased another brand if the coupon were not present. They are also the most likely to be redeemed. In-pack coupons do not provide any incentive at the point of sale because they are not visible, but they help retain previous customers. On-pack coupons do a little of both. They provide incentive for consumers at the point of sale because they are visible then, and they also help retain previous customers. An empirical study that compared the three types of package coupons found that on-pack coupons garnered the highest long-term market share (when the face value of all three coupons were the same) and higher profitability.[93]

In an effort to target to specific consumers more precisely, electronic coupons are now being used. In some supermarkets, manufacturers can have coupons delivered electronically at the cash register as the consumer pays for groceries. Catalina Marketing Corp., in Anaheim, California, provides a system to manufacturers that tracks a customer's purchases as they are scanned. Coupons are delivered right then based on what a consumer has purchased. If Pepsi has bought the service and the consumer has purchased Coke, Pepsi can have a coupon delivered that offers a special deal on Pepsi. Pepsi can also target their own customers with special promotions. In this way, the manufacturer can target directly to consumers who purchase soft drinks.

Catalina also offers a product called "Checkout Direct" in which a system tracks a check-paying customer's purchases over time though an identification number and provides coupons at the checkout that are based on the shopper's habits. As of 1993, electronically delivered coupons represented a very small percentage, less than 1 percent, of the total coupons distributed. Electronically delivered coupons have a better redemption rate than coupons distributed through the newspaper. The redemption rate of electronically delivered coupons is 9.8% versus 2.1% for coupons that are distributed through Sunday newspaper inserts.[94]

Another coupon-tracking system has been developed by database marketer Acu-Tra. Their product, CouponSelect, ties couponing to television advertising. The system was tested on 1,000 homes in San Diego. Subscribers to cable television fill out detailed demographic and brand preference questionnaires, and in exchange they get a black box that sits on top of their television and issues coupons on request. Specific television ads are encoded to trigger a coupon offer. If the viewers want that specific coupon, they hit a button on a remote which allows it to be printed. The coupon that is printed has a bar code that includes the household information and date, time, and channel that the ad aired.[95]

Coupons are also being distributed through the World Wide Web. Healthy Choice, for example, has a home page on the Web where consumers can print their own coupons. These coupons are subject to the same restrictions as other coupons.[96]

Coupons can also be distributed by retailers, who can issue their own coupons to the consumer in two ways. First, the retailer can provide coupons in their newspaper advertising or in their in-store flyers. These coupons must be cut out by the consumer and then redeemed at the checkout. They work similarly to the way coupons issued by the manufacturer work.

Alternatively, the retailer can provide in-store coupons, either off-the-shelf price discounts or in-store hanging coupons. Off-the-shelf price discounts are signaled at the shelf with signs such as "Bonus Buy" or "Super Saver," and the discounts are automatically deducted at the check-out. In-store coupons hang near the product on the shelf. The consumer must take a coupon and present it at the check-out in order to get the discount.[97]

Field tests comparing the two different types of in-store retailer discounts indicated that the store coupon hanging at the shelf leads to a 35 percent greater increase in sales than the "Bonus Buy"-type off-the-shelf discount. In addition, the store coupons were more profitable because the consumers did not always remember to redeem the coupons.[98]

One reason why the "Bonus Buy" type of discounts are less effective in generating increased sales than are the in-store coupons may be that consumers have become jaded to announcements of special sales. Therefore, when consumers see a sign touting a "Bonus Buy," they are suspicious as to whether or not the price is really a deal. On the other hand, when a coupon is presented, and if consumers remember to redeem it, they are certain they are getting some discount off the listed price.[99]

There are several common characteristics of coupon users. The general profile shows that heavy users of coupons are small households, with maybe one or two members, and typically the head of the household is 55 years or older, retired, and on a fixed income (with incomes over $25,000). Coupon users also tend to be less brand loyal and more price sensitive than the average consumer.[100]

A study based on 184 female shoppers examined attitudes towards the use of coupons.[101] The researchers found that many consumers clip coupons because they enjoy the process of clipping and redeeming them. Many respondents think of collecting and redeeming coupons as a hobby or game. Perhaps some of the reward here is the self-congratulatory feeling of having earned a price advantage due to a job well done.

Displays

Point-of-purchase displays have been shown to stimulate unplanned purchases[102] of exhibited brands. The displays may also serve as a reminder to purchase in the general product class even when the consumer chooses not to purchase the specific brand being displayed.[103] Displays are commonly used as a reminder for goods that are purchased by most households, but are purchased infrequently, such as baking ingredients, condiments, and holiday foods. Displays are also used for impulse items such as cookies, crackers, and salted snacks.[104]

Most displayed items are also accompanied by a promotion signal,[105] defined as a sign, marker, or other indicator of a promotion on the brand display. The promotion signals are used to get the consumers' attention. One of the interesting things about promotion signals is that they can frequently increase sales even when they are not accompanied by a price cut or coupon.

Procter & Gamble ran some experiments in Kmart and found that sales for coffee and toothpaste increased significantly when these products were placed outside their normal shelves on end-of-aisle display racks without any changes in price. Over a three-week period, sales for the toothpaste increased as much as 119 percent and sales for the coffee increased more than 500 percent in these alternative locations as compared to a matched period of time in the old locations.[106]

In another experiment,[107] researchers found that consumers who actively search and evaluate information in making purchase decisions are not influenced by a promotion signal that is not accompanied by an appropriate price cut. On the other hand, consumers who use simple cues in the environment to streamline their decision-making process are much more likely to be influenced by a promotion signal even if there is not an accompanying price cut.

In the experiment, the researchers asked 155 undergraduate students to complete a questionnaire that assessed their need for cognition. Individuals with high need for cognition are intrinsically motivated to seek out additional information in order to make decisions. Individuals with low need for cognition are less likely to engage in extensive decision making.

Two weeks later, the students were asked to make purchases in a simulated shopping environment. The environment was set up to look like a real grocery store. The product categories that were studied were toothpaste, peanut butter, and toilet paper. Some of the brands were priced regularly, some were marked with a promotion signal and were accompanied by a 15 percent price discount, and others were just marked with a promotion signal and no price discount.

Over all subjects, the presence of the real price discount increased sales significantly. There was a difference, however, in how the high versus low need-for-cognition students responded to the real versus signal-only promotions. The low need-for-cognition students responded to the real promotion condition and to the promotion signal condition, while the high need-for-condition students responded only to the real promotion condition.

The results of this lab experiment, P&G's Kmart experiments, and other experiments that have been run to test this phenomenon[108] suggest that retailers could generate increases in sales simply by placing a promotion signal on the shelf without significantly reducing the price of the good. Ethical and legal considerations preclude any clear deception, but these results suggest that a promotion signal accompanied by a minor price cut would be effective for some consumers. It is likely that if this tactic was used frequently, it would cease to be effective, as consumers may eventually become insensitive or learn the pricing trick.

Prices Featured in Advertising

Many times when a retailer lowers the price on a particular item, this item is featured in the stores' advertising that week, either in daily or weekly local newspapers or as a special circular distributed around the store.[109] The retailer is hoping to draw new consumers into the store by featuring lower-priced items. In addition, these lower-priced items may give the overall store an image of having better values. We should note, though, that not all feature ads advertise products that have price cuts. Sometimes retailers list items in ads with a small line of type and a regular price in order to comply with manufacturer contracts specifying advertising.

An empirical study of all different types of promotional tools found that only featured price-cut advertising affected purchase acceleration. In other words, price-cutting advertising could encourage consumers to come to the supermarket to purchase a featured brand sooner than they may have naturally come. On average there was a 10 percent reduction in the inter-purchase time due to featured advertising.[110]

One drawback to featuring special prices in advertising is that it focuses consumers' attention on price and increases their price sensitivity. There are several reasons for this effect. First, price advertising is likely to increase the importance of price as a criterion for making a decision about what to purchase. Second, the more information a consumer has about brands and their prices, the more easily consumers can make the appropriate trade-offs among different attributes. Finally, featuring low prices is likely to attract the more price sensitive consumers.[111]

In summary, one of the key initiatives of the Efficient Consumer Response program (ECR) is the call for "efficient promotion," or the suggestion that retailers simplify promotional efforts. Because promotions are unlikely to be completely eliminated in the near future, it is important for manufacturers and retailers to understand how the different promotional tools work and how consumers are likely to respond to each of the tools.

Endnotes

1. Dreze, Xavier, Stephen J. Hoch, and Mary E. Purk (1994), "Shelf Management and Space Elasticity," *Journal of Retailing,* 70 (4), 301–326.

2. Anderson Consulting (1996), "Where to Look for Incremental Sales Gains: The Retail Problem of Out-of-Stock Merchandise," a study conducted for the Coca-Cola Retailing Research Council, (January 16).

3. Anderson Consulting (1996), "Where to Look for Incremental Sales Gains: The Retail Problem of Out-of-Stock Merchandise," a study conducted for the Coca-Cola Retailing Research Council, (January 16).

4. Borin, Norm and Paul Farris (1990), "An Empirical Comparison of Direct Product Profit and Existing Measures of SKU Productivity," *Journal of Retailing,* 66 (Fall), 297–314.

5. Dreze, Xavier, Stephen J. Hoch, and Mary E. Purk (1994), "Shelf Management and Space Elasticity," *Journal of Retailing,* 70 (4), 301–326.

6. Dreze, Xavier, Stephen J. Hoch, and Mary E. Purk (1994), "Shelf Management and Space Elasticity," *Journal of Retailing,* 70 (4), 301–326.

7. Dreze, Xavier, Stephen J. Hoch, and Mary E. Purk (1994), "Shelf Management and Space Elasticity," *Journal of Retailing,* 70 (4), 301–326.

8. Dreze, Xavier, Stephen J. Hoch, and Mary E. Purk (1994), "Shelf Management and Space Elasticity," *Journal of Retailing,* 70 (4), 301–326.

9. Kahn, Barbara E. and Donald R. Lehmann (1991), "Modeling Choice Among Assortments," *Journal of Retailing,* 67 (Fall), 274–299.

10. Broniarczyk, Susan and Leigh McAlister (1994), "Arranging Category Displays to be Congruent with Consumers' Mental Representations: The Effect of Choice on Perceptions of Variety Offered," paper presented at the Association for Consumer Research Annual Conference, Boston, MA, 1994.

11. Bawa, Kapil, Jane T. Landwehr, and Aradhna Krishna (1989), "Consumer Response to Retailers' Marketing Environments: An Analysis of Coffee Purchase Data," *Journal of Retailing,* 65 (Winter), 471-495.

12. Kahn, Barbara E. and Donald R. Lehmann (1991), "Modeling Choice Among Assortments," *Journal of Retailing,* 67 (Fall), 274–299.

13. Williard Bishop Consulting Ltd., Information Resources, Inc., (1993), "Variety or Duplication: A Process to Know Where You Stand," a report prepared for the Food Marketing Institute.

14. From a speech by Steve David, Procter & Gamble Company, "The Changing Nature of Sales and product Supply," at the MSI conference, Evergreen Conference Center and Resort, Atlanta, GA, June 13–14, 1994.

15. Morton, Jerry (1993), "ESL: (Electronic Shelf Label Systems): Up and Running," *Progressive Grocer* (December), 23–24.

16. Sirvanci, Dr. Mete B. (1993), "An Empirical Study of Price Thresholds and Price Sensitivity," *Journal of Applied Business Research*, 9 (2), 43–49.

17. Dickson, Peter and Alan G. Sawyer (1990), "The Price Knowledge and Search of Supermarket Shoppers," *Journal of Marketing*, 54 (July), 42–53.

18. Narasimhan, Chakravarti (1984), "A Price Discriminantion Theory of Coupons," *Marketing Science*, 3 (Spring), 128–47.

19. Partch, Ken (1993), "It's the Customer, Stupid," *Supermarket Business* (June), 23–36.

20. "Do Consumers Underestimate 9-Ending Prices?" (1995), *Stores* (Winter), RR10, RR11.

21. Schindler, Robert M. and Alan R. Wiman (1989), "Effect of Odd Pricing on Price Recall," *Journal of Business Research,* 19 (November), 165–77.

22. Dickson, Peter and Alan G. Sawyer (1990), "The Price Knowledge and Search of Supermarket Shoppers," *Journal of Marketing*, 54 (July), 42–53.

23. Mazumdar, Tridib and Kent B. Monroe (1990), "The Effects of Buyers' Intentions to Learn Price Information on Price Encoding," *Journal of Retailing*, 66 (1), 15–32.

24. Zeithaml, Valarie A. (1982), "Consumer Response to In-Store Price Information Environments," *Journal of Consumer Research*, 8 (March), 357–369.

25. Urbany, Joel E., William O. Bearden, and Dan C. Weilbaker (1988), "The Effect of Plausible and Exaggerated Reference Prices on Consumer Perceptions and Price Search," *Journal of Consumer Research*, 15 (June), 95–110.

26. Biswas, Abhiji, Elizabeth J. Wilson, and Jane W. Licata (1993), "Reference Pricing Studies in Marketing: A Synthesis of Research Results," *Journal of Business Research*, 27 (July), 239–256.

27. Mayhew, Glenn E. and Russell S. Winer (1992), "An Empirical Analysis of Internal and External Reference Prices Using Scanner Data," *Journal of Consumer Research*, 19 (June), 62–70.

28. Rajendra, K. N. and Gerald J. Tellis (1994), "Contextual and Temporal Components of Reference Price," *Journal of Marketing*, 58 (January), 22–34.

30. Krishnamurthi, L., T. Mazumdar, and S. P. Raj (1992), "Asymmetric Response to Price in Consumer Choice and Purchase Quantity Decisions," *Journal of Consumer Research*, 19 (December), 387–400.

31. Kalyanaram, Gurumurthy and John D. C. Little (1994), "An Empirical Analysis of Latitude of Price Acceptance in Consumer Package Goods," *Journal of Consumer Research,* 21 (December), 408–418.

31. Lichtenstein, Donald R. and William O. Bearden (1989), "Contextual Influences on Perceptions of Merchant-Supplied Reference Prices," *Journal of Consumer Research*, 16 (June), 55–66.

32. Biswas, Abhijit and Edward A. Blair (1991), "Contextual Effects of Reference Prices in Retail Advertisements," *Journal of Marketing*, 55 (July), 1–12.

33. Winer, Russell S. (1986), "A Reference Price Model of Brand Choice for Frequently Purchased Products," *Journal of Consumer Research*, 13 (September), 250–6.

34. Kalyanaram, Gurumurthy and Russell S. Winer (1995), "Empirical Generalizations from Reference Price Research," *Marketing Science*, 14 (No. 3, Part 2 of 2), G161–G169.

35. Helson, Harry (1964), *Adaptation-Level Theory*. New York: Harper & Row.

36. Monroe, Kent (1973), "Buyers' Subjective Perceptions of Price," *Journal of Marketing Research*, 8 (November), 70–80.

37. Kalwani, Manohar U., Chi Kin Yim, Heikki J. Rinne, and Yoshi Sugita (1990), "A Price Expectations Model of Customer Brand Choice," *Journal of Marketing Research*, 27 (August), 251–262.

38. Mayhew, Glenn E. and Russell S. Winer (1992), "An Empirical Analysis of Internal and External Reference Prices Using Scanner Data," *Journal of Consumer Research*, 19 (June), 62–70.

39. Gabor, Andre and Clive W. J. Granger (1966), "Price as an Indicator of Quality: Report on an Enquiry," *Economica*, 46 (February), 43–70.

40. Monroe, Kent B. and Susan M. Petroshius (1981), "Perceptions of Price: An Update of the Evidence," in *Perceptions in Consumer Behavior*, Third Edition, Harold H. Kassarjian and Thomas S. Robertson, Eds., Glenview, IL: Scott Foresman and Company, 43–55.

41. Thaler, Richard (1985), "Mental Accounting and Consumer Choice," *Marketing Science*, 4 (Summer), 199–214.

42. Della Bitta, Albert J. and Kent B. Monroe (1974), "The Influence of Adaptation levels on Subjective Price Perceptions," in *Advances in Consumer Research*, Vol. 1, Scott Ward and Peter Wright, Eds., Urbana, IL, Association for Consumer Research, 359–369.

43. Kalyanaram, Gurumurthy and Russell S. Winer (1995), "Empirical Generalizations from Reference Price Research," *Marketing Science*, 14 (No. 3, Part 2 of 2), G161–G169.

44. Mayhew, Glenn E. and Russell S. Winer (1992), "An Empirical Analysis of Internal and External Reference Prices Using Scanner Data," *Journal of Consumer Research*, 19 (June), 62–70.

45. Putler, D. (1992), "Incorporating Reference Price Effects into a Theory of Consumer Choice," *Marketing Science*, 11 (Summer), 287–309.

46. Hardie, Bruce G. S., Eric J. Johnson, and Peter S. Fader (1993), "Modeling Loss Aversion and Reference Dependence Effects on Brand Choice," *Marketing Science*, 12 (4), 378–394.

47. Kalwani, Manohar U. and Chi Kin Yim (1992), "Consumer Price and Promotion Expectations: An Experimental Study," *Journal of Marketing Research*, 29 (February), 90–100.

48. Kalyanaram, Gurumurthy and Russell S. Winer (1995), "Empirical Generalizations from Reference Price Research," *Marketing Science*, 14 (No. 3, Part 2 of 2), G161–G169.

49. Kalyanaram, Gurumurthy and John D. C. Little (1994), "An Empirical Analysis of Latitude of Price Acceptance in Consumer Package Goods," *Journal of Consumer Research*, 21 (December), 408–418.

50. Marter, Marilynn (1994), "Measure for Measure?" *Philadelphia Inquirer* (April 6), F1, F5.

51. Marter, Marilynn (1994), "Measure for Measure?" *Philadelphia Inquirer* (April 6), F1, F5.

52. Dreze, Xavier, Stephen J. Hoch, and Mary E. Purk (1994), "Shelf Management and Space Elasticity," *Journal of Retailing*, 70 (4), 301–326

53. Hoch, Stephen J., Byung-Do Kim, Alan L. Montgomery and Peter E. Rossi (1995), "Determinants of Store-Level Price Elasticity," *Journal of Marketing Research*, 32 (February), 17–29.

54. Krishnamurthi, Lakshman and S. P. Raj (1991), "An Empirical Analysis of the Relationship Between Brand Loyalty and Consumer Price Elasticity," *Marketing Science*, 10 (Spring), 172–183.

55. Krishnamurthi, Lakshman and S. P. Raj (1991), "An Empirical Analysis of the Relationship Between Brand Loyalty and Consumer Price Elasticity," *Marketing Science*, 10 (Spring), 172–183.

56. Hoch, Stephen J., Byung-Do Kim, Alan L. Montgomery, and Peter E. Rossi (1995), "Determinants of Store-Level Price Elasticity," *Journal of Marketing Research*, 32 (February), 17–29.

57. Lichtenstein, Donald R., Nancy M. Ridgway, and Richard G. Netemeyer (1993), "Price Perceptions and Consumer Shopping Behavior: A Field Study," *Journal of Marketing Research*, 30 (May), 234–245.

58. Blattberg, Robert C. and Scott A. Neslin (1990), *Sales Promotion Concepts, Methods, and Strategies,* Englewood Cliffs, NJ: Prentice Hall.

59. McAlister, Leigh (1986), "The Impact of Price Promotions on a Brand's Market Share, Sales Pattern and Profitability," Marketing Science Institute Working Paper 86–110.

60. Blattberg, Robert C., Richard Briesch, and Edward J. Fox (1995), "How Promotions Work," *Marketing Science*, 14 (Number 3, Part 2 of 2), G122–G132.

61. Mulhern, Francis J. and Robert P. Leone (1990), "Retail Promotional Advertising: Do the Number of Deal Items and Size of Deal Discounts Affect Store Performance?" *Journal of Business Research*, 21, 179–194.

62. Blattberg, Robert C., Richard Briesch, and Edward J. Fox (1995), "How Promotions Work," *Marketing Science*, 14 (Number 3, Part 2 of 2), G122–G132.

63. Raju, Jagmohan (1992), "The Effect of Price Promotions on Variability in Product Category Sales," *Marketing Science,* 11 (Summer), 207–220.

64. Blattberg, Robert C. and Kenneth J. Wisniewski (1989), "Price-Induced Patterns of Competition," *Marketing Science*, 8 (Fall), 291–309.

65. Blattberg, Robert C. and Kenneth J. Wisniewski (1989), "Price-Induced Patterns of Competition," *Marketing Science*, 8 (Fall), 291–309.

66. Blattberg, Robert C., Richard Briesch, and Edward J. Fox (1995), "How Promotions Work," *Marketing Science*, 14 (Number 3, Part 2 of 2), G122–G132.

67. Lal, Rajiv (1990), "Price Promotions: Limiting Competitive Encroachment," *Marketing Science*, 9 (3), 247–262.

68. Bronnenberg, Bart J. and Luc Wathieu (1996), "Asymmetric Promotion Effects and Brand Positioning," University of Texas Working Paper, (June).

69. McAlister, Leigh and Michael J. Zenor (1992), "The Impact of Retailer Differences on Promotional Response: A Link Between Unusual Levels of Support and Unusual Levels of Response." University of Texas at Austin Working Paper.

70. Nelson, Philip (1970), "Information and Consumer Behavior," *Journal of Political Economy*, 78 (2), 311–29.

71. Etgar, Michael and Naresh K. Malhotra (1981), "Determinants of Price Dependency: Personal and Perceptual Factors," *Journal of Consumer Research*, 8 (September), 217–22.

72. Huber, Joel and John McCann (1982), "The Impact of Inferential Beliefs on Product Evaluations," *Journal of Marketing Research*, 19 (August), 324-33.

73. Kahn, Barbara E. and Therese A. Louie (1990), "Effects of Retraction of Price Promotions on Brand Choice Behavior for Variety-Seeking and Last-Purchase Loyal Consumers," *Journal of Marketing Research*, 27 (August), 279–89.

74. Davis, Scott, J. Jeffrey Inman, and Leigh McAlister (1992), "Promotion Has a Negative Effect on Brand Evaluations—Or Does it? Additional Disconfirming Evidence," *Journal of Marketing Research*, 29 (February), 143–148.

75. Neslin, Scott A. and Robert Shoemaker (1989), "An Alternative Explanation for Lower Repeat Rates After Promotional Purchases," *Journal of Marketing Research*, 26 (May), 205–13.

76. Davis, Scott, J. Jeffrey Inman, and Leigh McAlister (1992), "Promotion Has a Negative Effect on Brand Evaluations—Or Does it? Additional Disconfirming Evidence," *Journal of Marketing Research*, 29 (February), 143–148.

77. Neslin, Scott A., Caroline Henderson, and John Quech (1985), "Consumer Promotions and the Acceleration of Product Purchases," *Marketing Science*, 4 (2), 147–165.

78. Gupta, Sunil (1988), "Impact of Sales Promotions on When, What, and How Much to Buy," *Journal of Marketing Research*, 25 (November), 342–355.

79. Krishna, Aradhna, Imran S. Currim, and Robert W. Shoemaker (1991), "Consumer Perceptions of Promotional Activity," *Journal of Marketing*, 55 (April), 4–16.

80. Krishna, Aradhna, Imran S. Currim, and Robert W. Shoemaker (1991), "Consumer Perceptions of Promotional Activity," *Journal of Marketing*, 55 (April), 4–16.

81. Meyer, Robert J. and Joao Assuncao (1990), "The Optimality of Consumer Stockpiling Strategies," *Marketing Science*, 9 (Winter), 18–41.

82. Meyer, Robert J. and Joao Assuncao (1990), "The Optimality of Consumer Stockpiling Strategies," *Marketing Science*, 9 (Winter), 18–41.

83. Simonson, Itamar (1992), "The Influence of Anticipating Regret and Responsibility on Purchase Decisions," *Journal of Consumer Research*, 19 (June), 105–118.

84. Mittal, Banwari (1994), "Bridging the Gap Between Our Knowledge of 'Who' Uses Coupons and 'Why' Coupons are Used," Marketing Science Institute Working Paper #94–112, (August).

85. Narasimhan, Chakravarthi (1984), "A Price Discrimination Theory of Coupons," *Marketing Science*, 3 (Spring), 128–47.

86. Fader, Peter S. and Leonard M. Lodish (1990), "A Cross-Category Analysis of Category Structure and Promotional Activity for Grocery Products," *Journal of Marketing*, 54 (October), 52–65.

87. Bawa, Kapil and Robert W. Shoemaker (1987), "The Coupon-Prone Consumer: Some Findings Based on Purchase Behavior Across Product Classes," *Journal of Marketing*, 51 (October), 99–110.

88. Bowman, Russel (1980), *Couponing and Rebates: Profit on the Dotted Line*, New York: Lebhar-Friedman Books.

89. Inman, J. Jeffrey and Leigh McAlister (1994), "Do Coupon Expiration Dates Affect Consumer Behavior?" *Journal of Marketing Research*, 31 (August), 423–428.

90. "The Changing Nature of Sales and Product Supply," speech given by Steve David, Procter & Gamble, at "The Changing Landscape in Grocery Retailing: The Information Highway Reaches the Trading Post," MSI Conference, June 13–14, 1994.

91. Neslin, Scott A. (1990), "A Market Response Model for Coupon Promotions," *Marketing Science*, 9 (Spring), 125–145.

92. Raju, Jagmohan S., Sanjay K. Dhar, and Donald G. Morrison (1994), "The Effect of Package Coupons on Brand Choice," *Marketing Science*, 13 (Spring), 145–164.

93. Raju, Jagmohan S., Sanjay K. Dhar, and Donald G. Morrison (1994), "The Effect of Package Coupons on Brand Choice," *Marketing Science*, 13 (Spring), 145–164.

94. Valeriano, Lourdes Lee (1993), "Inquisitive Gadgets, *Wall Street Journal*, October 7, 1.

95. Spethmann, Betsy (1994), "Coupons Shed Low-Tech Image," *Brandweek*, October 24, 30–31.

96. Martin, Ellen James (1996), "Those Coupons Being Used a Furious Clip," *Philadelphia Inquirer*, January 10, C1, C4.

97. Dhar, Sanjay K. and Stephen J. Hoch (1996), "Price Discrimination Using In-Store Merchandising," *Journal of Marketing*, 60 (January), 17–30.

98. Dhar, Sanjay K. and Stephen J. Hoch (1996), "Price Discrimination Using In-Store Merchandising," *Journal of Marketing*, 60 (January), 17–30.

99. Dhar, Sanjay K. and Stephen J. Hoch (1996), "Price Discrimination Using In-Store Merchandising," *Journal of Marketing,* 60 (January), 17–30.

100. "The Changing Nature of Sales and Product Supply," speech given by Steve David, Procter & Gamble, at "The Changing Landscape in Grocery Retailing: The Information Highway Reaches the Trading Post," MSI Conference, June 13–14, 1994.

101. Mittal, Banwari (1994), "Bridging the Gap Between Our Knowledge of 'Who' Uses Coupons and 'Why' Coupons are Used," Marketing Science Institute Working Paper #94112, (August).

102. McKenna, Mary L. (1966), "The Influence of In-Store Advertising," in *On Knowing the Consumer*, Joseph Newman, Ed., New York: Wiley, 114–25.

103. Spiggle, Susan (1987), "Grocery Shopping Lists: What Do Consumers Write?" in *Advances in Consumer Research*, Vol. XIV, Melanie Wallendorf and Paul Anderson, Eds., Chicago, IL: Association for Consumer Research.

104. Fader, Peter S. and Leonard M. Lodish (1990), "A Cross-Category Analysis of Category Structure and Promotional Activity for Grocery Products," *Journal of Marketing*, 54 (October), 52–65.

105. Inman, J. Jeffrey, Leigh McAlister, and Wayne D. Hoyer (1990), "Promotion Signal: Proxy for a Price Cut?" *Journal of Consumer Research*, 17 (June), 74–81.

106. McCarthy, Michael (1993), "James Bond Hits the Supermarket: Stores Snoop on Shoppers' Habits to Boost Sales," *The Wall Street Journal: Marketplace*, (August 25), B1, B8.

107. Inman, J. Jeffrey, Leigh McAlister, and Wayne D. Hoyer (1990), "Promotion Signal: Proxy for a Price Cut?" *Journal of Consumer Research*, 17 (June), 74–81.

108. Inman, J. Jeffrey and Leigh McAlister (1993), "A Retailer Promotion Policy Model Considering Promotion Signal Sensitivity," *Marketing Science*, 12 (Fall), 339–356.

109. Blattberg, Robert C. and Scott A. Neslin (1990), *Sales Promotion Concepts, Methods, and Strategies,* Englewood Cliffs, NJ: Prentice Hall.
110. Neslin, Scott A., Caroline Henderson and John Quech (1985), "Consumer Promotions and the Acceleration of Product Purchases," *Marketing Science,* 4 (2), 147–165.
111. Kaul, Anil and Dick R. Wittink (1995), "Empirical Generalizations about the Impact of Advertising on Price Sensitivity and Price," *Marketing Science,* 14 (No. 3, Part 2 of 2), G151–G160.

Summary and Conclusions

In the years following World War II, packaged goods manufacturers developed truly innovative products, sold them to consumers through mass media, and delivered them to consumers through a fragmented and essentially undifferentiated collection of retail outlets.

In recent years, the mind-numbing over-proliferation of "new" product offerings (a "new," smaller size to disguise a price increase; a "new," lemon-scented version to increase the brand's space on the shelf)—more than 15,000 per year—has blurred distinctions among brands. Rather than a fierce single-brand loyalty that might have characterized consumers in the 1950s, multi-brand acceptability is much more typical for consumers today.

Research shows us that, in this environment, price plays a critical role in a consumer's decision among acceptable brands. A consumer spends less than 12 seconds in a category before making a choice. This consumer probably handles only one brand in one size during the decision process. And, although unlikely to know the exact price of the brand chosen, he or she probably does know its relative price. A widely used choice strategy aimed at selecting the lowest priced acceptable brand is choosing the satisfactory brand that the retailer has highlighted as being on promotion. The significant sales spike that brands experience when promoted provides evidence consistent with the widespread use of this strategy.

The logical conclusion of this reasoning is that manufacturers no longer control consumer choice through advertising. Control has shifted to retailers who powerfully influence consumer choice with their merchandising, pricing, and promotion.

To exploit this shift in control fully, a retailer must define a viable strategic position in the marketplace and roll that strategy down through its categories, assigning each category an appropriate role to play (e.g., profit generator, traffic generator, destination, fill-in). Merchandising, pricing, and promotion activities should support the strategic position and should be used in ways that are consistent with each category's role.

Research into the pricing component of a retailer's strategy suggests that neither high–low nor EDLP is clearly superior. The success of either pricing strategy depends on the quality and consistency of its execution. This is not the case, however, for manufacturers' pricing strategies.

Part One of this book focused on the system-wide costs and inefficiencies associated with high–low pricing from the manufacturer to the retailer. Procter & Gamble's ability to drive down their own costs and those of their retail and wholesale customers is testimony to the effectiveness of their value pricing strategy. The 1996 reduction in wholesale prices and promotional support for breakfast cereal brands is another example of the industry's move away from high–low pricing for manufacturers.[1]

The picture that emerges for the retailer includes a need to define and deploy a consumer-driven strategy. Based on priorities for 1995 and 1996 as reported by *Supermarket News*[2], retailers seem to be moving in the right direction. A desire to understand the consumer is evidenced by the fact that upgraded systems for capturing information about consumers' purchases was listed as a priority for 22 percent of the retailers in 1995 and 17 percent in 1996. Frequent shopper programs grew from being a priority for 11 percent of retailers in 1995 to being a priority for 18 percent of retailers in 1996. Category management was the most frequently named priority in both years (32% in 1995, 28% in 1996), signalling the serious focus of strategy. Sixty percent of the respondents said that they were beginning to implement category management and another 27 percent said that they were well on their way with implementation. While only 19 percent of the respondents rated their category management efforts highly successful, another 78 percent of the respondents rated their efforts moderately successful.

The picture that emerges for the manufacturer includes a need to refocus product development efforts on really new products, a need to protect and try to grow existing brand equity, and a need to develop a sales and distribution arm capable of matching company and brand strengths with opportunities created by a retailer's strategic positioning.

Taking the number of "new" products launched in a year as an inverse measure of the progress toward rationalizing the product development process, we see that the manufacturers are growing worse on this dimension. Rather than the typical 15,000 to 17,000 "new" products launched each year from 1990 through 1993, 1994 saw 21,986 "new" products and 1995 saw 20,808 "new" products.[3] Most of these products fail.

Taking the number of coupons issued in a year (an activity that soaks up a third of a typical marketing budget and only serves to draw price-sensitive consumers to the brand) as an inverse measure of protection given to existing brand equity, we see that the industry as a whole grew better on this dimension. According to NCH Promotional Services,[4] only 291.9 billion coupons were issued in 1995, the lowest number issued since 1991.

To get a sense of the degree to which manufacturers are developing a sales and distribution arm capable of matching company and brand strengths with opportunities created by a retailer's strategic position, we look at who controls the budget. To the extent that the budget is controlled from headquarters by brand managers, it is unlikely that the budget will be spent in ways that demonstrate a deep understanding of a specific retail account. Using this metric, we see that progress is being made. According to an A. C. Nielsen poll,[5] in 1991 brand managers had control of trade promotion budgets in 42 percent of the responding companies. By 1995 that percentage had dropped to 13 percent.

In sum, we see an industry in turmoil. Everything suggests that the turmoil will continue. Those players who base their strategic position on a deep understanding of the consumer, and those who are willing to make profound changes and then are willing to change again, will lead the industry into the next millennium.

Endnotes

1. Much, Marilyn (1996), "Behind Cereal Price Cuts: Wrath of Fickle Shoppers," *Investor's Business Daily* (June 25).
2. Millstein, Marc (1996), "The State of the Industry," *Supermarket News* (February 5), 4a–22a.
3. "New Products More Plentiful than New Ideas" (1996), *Supermarket Business* (March), 9.
4. Narisetti, Raju (1996), "P&G Ad Chief Plots Demise of the Coupon," *Wall Street Journal* (September 17), B1.
5. Tenser, James (1996), "A. C. Nielsen Trade Survey Shows Size Does Matter," *Brand Marketing*, (June 3), 6.

References

Aaker, David A. (1991), *Managing Brand Equity,* San Francisco: Free Press.

Aaker, David A. and Kevin Lane Keller (1990), "Consumer Evaluations of Brand Extensions," *Journal of Marketing,* 54 (January), 27–41.

ACTMEDIA (1992), "ACTMEDIA: The In-store Marketing Network," sales brochure, Norwalk, CT.

Adams, Douglas (1993), "What Suppliers Must Do," *Progressive Grocer* (September), 24–25.

Adams, Michael (1991), "The Udder Delights of Stew," *Successful Meetings,* 40 (March), 59–61.

"Ahold Buying Red Food" (1994), *Progressive Grocer* (April), 12.

Alba, Joseph W. and J. Wesley Hutchinson (1987), "Dimensions of Consumer Expertise," *Journal of Consumer Research,* 13 (March), 411–454.

Alba, Joseph W., J. Wesley Hutchinson, and John G. Lynch, Jr. (1991), "Memory and Decision-Making," in *Handbook of Consumer Research,* edited by Thomas S. Robertson and Harold H. Kassarjian, New York: Prentice Hall.

Alba, Joseph W., Susan M. Broniarczyk, Terence A. Shimp, and Joel E. Urbany (1994), "The Influence of Prior Beliefs, Frquency Cues, and Magnitude Cues on Consumers' Perceptions of Comparative Price Data," *Journal of Consumer Research* (September), 21, 219–235.

Allenby, Greg M. and James L. Ginter (1995), "The Effects of In-Store Displays and Feature Advertising on Consideration Sets," *International Journal of Research in Marketing,* 12, 67–80.

"A Master Class in Radical Change" (1993), *Fortune* (December 13), 82–84, 88, 90.

American Management Association (1994), *1994 AMA Survey on Downsizing and Assistance to Displaced Workers, AMA Research Report,* New York.

Andersen Consulting (1993), *Wholesale Food Distribution Today and Tomorrow,* NAWGA/IFDA Information Services, Falls Church, Virginia.

Andersen Consulting (1996), "Where to Look for Incremental Sales Gains: The Retail Problem of Out-of-Stock Merchandise," a study conducted for the Coca-Cola Retailing Research Council, (January 16).

Arnold, Stephen J., Tae H. Oum, and Douglas J. Tigert (1983), "Determinant Attributes in Retail Patronage: Seasonal, Temporal, Regional, and International Comparisons," *Journal of Marketing Research,* 20 (May), 149–157.

"A Stellar Performance" (1994), *Supermarket Business,* 49 (July), 89, 93.

Atlas, Riva (1994), "Food, Drink and Tobacco," *Forbes* (January 3), 152.

Baker, Julie, Michael Levy, and Dhruv Grwal (1992), "An Experimental Approach to Making Retail Store Environmental Decisions," *Journal of Retailing,* 68 (Winter), 445–460.

Baron, Robert A. (1990), "Environmentally Induced Positive Affect: Its Impact on Self-Efficacy, Task Performance, Negotiation and Conflict," *Journal of Applied Social Psychology,* 20 (March), 368–384.

Baron, Robert A. and Marna I. Bronfen (1994), "A Whiff of Reality: Empirical Evidence Concerning the Effects of Pleasant Fragrances on Work-Related Behavior," *Journal of Applied Social Psychology,* 24 (13), 1179–1203.

Barsalou, Lawrence (1983), "Ad Hoc Categories," *Memory and Cognition,* 11 (3), 211–227.

Bawa, Kapil and Robert W. Shoemaker (1987), "The Coupon-Prone Consumer: Some Findings Based on Purchase Behavior Across Product Classes," *Journal of Marketing,* 51 (October), 99–110.

Bawa, Kapil, Jane T. Landwehr, and Aradhna Krishna (1989), "Consumer Response to Retailers' Marketing Environments: An Analysis of Coffee Purchase Data," *Journal of Retailing,* 65 (Winter), 471–495.

Beckwith, Neil and Donald R. Lehmann (1975), "The Importance of Halo Effects in Multi-Attribute Models," *Journal of Marketing Research,* 12 (August), 265–275.

Belk, Russell W. (1975), "Situational Variables and Consumer Behavior," *Journal of Consumer Research,* 2 (December), 157–163.

Bellizzi, J. A., A. E. Crowley, and R. W. Hasty (1983), "The Effects of Color in Store Design," *Journal of Retailing,* 59, 21–45.

Bellizzi, Joseph A. and Robert E. Hite (1992), "Environmental Color, Consumer Feelings and Purchase Likelihood," *Psychology and Marketing,* 9 (September/October), 347–363.

Berkowitz, Harry (1993), "Marketers Assess Buying Power of Children," *The Philadelphia Inquirier,* September 8, C7.

Berman, Phyllis (1994), "We Don't Do an Exact Copy," *Forbes* (October 10), 79.

Bernhardt, Jim (1994), "The Decline of Consumer Package Goods Marketing As We Know It . . . and Its Implications for You," presentation at The University of Texas at Austin on February 23, 1994.

Bettman, James R. (1979), *An Information Processing Theory of Consumer Choice,* Reading, MA: Addison-Wesley.

Bettman, James R. and P. Kakkar (1977), "Effects of Information Presentation Format on Consumer Information Acquisition Strategies," *Journal of Consumer Research,* 3 (March), 233–240.

Biehal, Gabriel and Dipankar Chakravarti (1986), "Consumers' Use of Memory and External Information in Choice: Macro and Micro Perspective," *Journal of Consumer Research,* 12 (March), 382–405.

References

Biswas, Abhijit and Edward A. Blair, (1991), "Contextual Effects of Reference Prices in Retail Advertisements," *Journal of Marketing,* 55 (July), 1–12.

Biswas, Abhiji, Elizabeth J. Wilson, and Jane W. Licata (1993), "Reference Pricing Studies in Marketing: A Synthesis of Research Results," *Journal of Business Research,* 27 (July), 239–256.

Blattberg, Robert C. and Kenneth J. Wisniewski (1989), "Price-Induced Patterns of Competition," *Marketing Science,* 8 (Fall), 291–309.

Blattberg, Robert C. and Scott A. Neslin (1990), *Sales Promotion Concepts, Methods, and Strategies,* Englewood Cliffs, NJ: Prentice Hall.

Blattberg, Robert C., Richard Briesch, and Edward J. Fox (1995), "How Promotions Work," *Marketing Science,* 14 (Number 3, Part 2 of 2), G122–G132.

Borin, Norm and Paul Farris (1990), "An Empirical Comparison of Direct Product Profit and Existing Measures of SKU Productivity," *Journal of Retailing,* 66 (Fall), 297–314.

Bowman, Russel (1980), *Couponing and Rebates: Profit on the Dotted Line,* New York: Lebhar-Friedman Books.

Boyd, Malia (1994), "New Directions in Supermarkets," *Incentive* (November), 41–45.

"Brands Fight Back Against Private Labels," (1995), *Marketing News* (January 16), 8–9.

Broniarczyk, Susan and Leigh McAlister (1994), "Arranging Category Displays to be Congruent with Consumers' Mental Representations: The Effect of Choice on Perceptions of Variety Offered," paper presented at the Association for Consumer Research Annual Conference, Boston, MA, 1994.

Broniarczyk, Susan and Joseph W. Alba (1994), "The Importance of the Brand in Brand Extension," *Journal of Marketing Research,* 31 (May), 214–228.

Broniarczyk, Susan, Wayne Hoyer, and Leigh McAlister (1996), "Consumer's Perceptions of the Assortment Offered in a Grocery Category: The Influence of Number of items and Heuristics," University of Texas Working Paper (October).

Bronnenberg, Bart J. and Luc Wathier (1996), "Asymmetric Promotion Effects and Brand Positioning," *Marketing Science,* (forthcoming).

Brookes, Richard (1995), "Recent Changes in the Retailing of Fresh Produce: Strategic Implications for Fresh Produce Suppliers." *Journal of Business Research,* 32 (February), 149–161.

Burleson, G. L. (1979), "Retailer and Consumer Attitudes Toward Background Music," unpublished paper, Department of Business Administration, University of Texas at El Paso.

"Cadbury to Buy Out Dr. Pepper/Seven-Up" (1995), *Austin American Statesman* (January 23), A8.

"Change at the Check-Out" (1995), *The Economist* (March 4), 3–18.

Clark, Theodore H. (1995), "Procter & Gamble: Improving Consumer Value Through Process Redesign," Harvard Busines School Case 9-195-126, 4–6.

Consumer Reports (1993), "Survival Guide to the Supermarket," *Consumer Reports,* Vol. 58, No. 9 (September), 559–570.

Corfman, Kim P. and Barbara E. Kahn (1995), "The Influence of Member Heterogeneity on Dyad Judgment: Are Two Heads Better than One?" *Marketing Letters,* 6 (1), 23–32.

Cox, Keith K. (1970), "The Effect of Shelf Space Upon Sales of Branded Products," *Journal of Marketing Research,* 7 (February), 55–58.

Crowley, Ayn E. (1993), "The Two-Dimensional Impact of Color on Shopping," *Marketing Letters,* 4 (1), 59–69.

Curhan, Ronald C. (1982), "Deals, Time for a Reshuffle?" *Progressive Grocer* (January), 88–9, 92, 94, 96.

Currim, Imran, Robert J. Meyer, and Nhan T. Le (1988), "Disaggregate Tree-Structured Modeling of Consumer Choice," *Journal of Marketing Research,* 25 (August), 153–165.

David, Steve (1994), of the Procter & Gamble Company in a speech called, "The Changing Nature of Sales and Product Supply," at the MSI conference, Evergreen Conference Center and Resort, Atlanta, GA, June 13–14.

Davis, Scott, J. Jeffrey Inman, and Leigh McAlister (1992), "Promotion Has a Negative Effect on Brand Evaluations—Or Does it? Additional Disconfirming Evidence," *Journal of Marketing Research,* 29 (February), 143–148.

Della Bitta, Albert J. and Kent B. Monroe (1974), "The Influence of Adaptation Levels on Subjective Price Perceptions," in *Advances in Consumer Research,* Vol. 1, Scott Ward and Peter Wright, Eds., Urbana, IL: Association for Consumer Research, 359–369.

De Santa, Richard (1996), "Grabbing Share with Vise Grips," *Supermarket Business* (September), 17–18, 20, 24, 26, 28, 32, 34, 36, 38.

Deveny, Kathleen (1993), "What's in the Bag?" *Wall Street Journal,* October 26.

Dhar, Sanjay K. and Stephen J. Hoch (1996), "Price Discrimination Using In-Store Merchandising," *Journal of Marketing,* 60 (January), 17–30.

Dickson, Peter R. and Alan G. Sawyer (1990), "The Price Knowledge and Search of Supermarket Shoppers," *Journal of Marketing,* 54 (July), 42–53.

"Do Consumers Underestimate 9-Ending Prices?" (1995), *Stores* (Winter), RR10, RR11.

Donovan, Robert J. and John R. Rossiter (1982), "Store Atmosphere: An Environmental Psychology Approach," *Journal of Retailing,* 58 (Spring), 34–57.

Donovan, Robert J., John R. Rossiter, Gilian Marcoolyn, and Andrew Nesdale (1994), "Store Atmosphere and Purchasing Behavior," *Journal of Retailing,* 70 (3), 283–294.

"Don't Cry Over Spilt Cash," (1994), *Supermarket Business,* (February), 50–54.

"Don't Die Until You've Seen this Store!" (1994) *Supermarket Business* (January), 27–33.

References

Doyle, Peter and Ian Fenwick (1974–1975), "How Store Image Affects Shopping Habits in Grocery Chains," *Journal of Retailing,* 50 (Winter), 39–52.

Dreze, Xavier (1994), "Loss Leaders: Store Traffic and Cherry Picking," Doctoral Dissertation, University of Chicago.

Dreze, Xavier, Stephen J. Hoch, and Mary E. Purk (1994), "Shelf Management and Space Elasticity," *Journal of Retailing,* 70 (4), 301–326.

Duff, Mike (1989), "A Moveable Feast," *Supermarket Business* (July), 9A–12A.

Dworin, Diana (1994), "Cold Warriors," *Austin American Statesman* (September 4), E1.

Dwyer, Steve (1993), "C-Store Merchandising: For Candy Consumers, Seeing is Buying," *National Petroleum News* (September), 50–52.

"ECR and Partnering Go Hand in Hand" (1996), *Grocery Marketing* (May), 8.

Ehrlichmann, Howard and Jack N. Halpern (1988), "Affect and Memory: Effects of Plesant and Unpleasant Odors on Retrieval of Happy and Unhappy Memories," *Journal of Personality and Social Psychology,* 55 (5), 769–779.

Eisman, Regina (1993), "Giving Away the Goods," *Incentive* (May), 39–44.

"Electronics Wage Hidden War on Shoppers," (1993), *The Sunday Times* (London, England), (October 24), 9.

Emert, Carol (1996), "Wal-Mart Aim: To Increase Food Market Penetration," *Supermarket News* (June 17).

Etgar, Michael and Naresh K. Malhotra (1981), "Determinants of Price Dependency: Personal and Perceptual Factors," *Journal of Consumer Research,* 8 (September), 217–222.

Fader, Peter. S. and Leigh McAlister (1990), "An Elimination by Aspects Model of Consumer Response to Promotion Calibrated on UPC Scanner Data," *Journal of Marketing Research,* 28 (August), 322–332.

Fader, Peter S. and Leonard M. Lodish (1990), "A Cross-Category Analysis of Category Structure and Promotional Activity for Grocery Products," *Journal of Marketing,* 54 (October), 52–65.

Farquhar, Peter H. (1989), "Managing Brand Equity," *Marketing Research* (September), 24–33.

Fensholt, Carol (1994), "Unsalables, Does an Information Gap Do the Real Damage?" *Supermarket Business* (August), 25–34.

Folkes, Valerie (1988). "The Availability Heuristic and Perceived Risk," *Journal of Consumer Research,* 15 (June), 13–23.

Food Marketing Institute (1987), "Superstore Formats of the Future," *Progressive Grocer,* Food Marketing Institute, Washington, DC, December 1986, April 1987.

Food Marketing Institute (1992), *Alternative Store Formats: Competing in the Nineties,* Report #9-511, Washington, DC (January).

"For Customer Data, It's In the Cards; Using Check Cashing Cards to Determine Customer Base," (1988), *Supermarket News* 38, (May 9), 74.

Frederick, Joanne (1995), "Supercenters: The Threat du Jour," *Grocery Marketing* (March), 14–17.

Gabor, Andre and Clive W. J. Granger (1966), "Price as an Indicator of Quality: Report on an Enquiry," *Economica,* 46 (February), 43–70.

Garry, Michael (1993), "Making It on Supermarket Row," *Progressive Grocer* (December), 65–68.

Garry, Michael (1994), "A&P Strikes Back: Tough Times for A&P," *Progressive Grocer* (February), 32–34.

Garry, Michael (1996), "HEB: The Tech Leader," *Progressive Grocer* (May), 63–64, 66, 68.

General Mills (1980), "A Summary Report on U.S. Consumers' Knowledge, Attitudes and Practices About Nutrition," prepared by Maracom Research Corp., published by General Mills, Inc., Minneapolis, MN.

George, Michael, Anthony Freeling, and David Court (1994), "Reinventing the Marketing Organization," *The McKinsey Quarterly,* No. 4, 43–62.

Glazer, Rashi, Barbara E. Kahn, and William L. Moore (1991), "The Influence of External Constraints on Brand Choice: The Lone-Alternative Effect," *Journal of Consumer Research,* 18 (June), 119–127.

Glemet, Francois and Rafael Mira (1993), "The Brand Leader's Dilemma," *The McKinsey Quarterly,* No. 2, 3–15.

"Grocers Say Best Place to Influence Consumers is in the Store" (1993), *Marketing News* (August 30), 7.

Gupta, Sunil (1988), "Impact of Sales Promotions on When, What, and How Much to Buy," *Journal of Marketing Research,* 25 (November), 342–355.

Gutner, Toddi (1994), "Food Distributors," *Forbes* (January 3), 148–150.

Hammer, Michael and James Champy (1993), *Reengineering the Corporation,* New York: HarperCollins.

Hardie, Bruce G. S., Eric J. Johnson, and Peter S. Fader (1993), "Modeling Loss Aversion and Reference Dependence Effects on Brand Choice," *Marketing Science,* 12 (4), 378–394.

Hartley, Robert F. (1986), *Marketing Mistakes,* 3rd Edition, New York: Wiley.

Hauser, John R. and Birger Wernerfelt (1990), "An Evaluation Cost Model of Consideration Sets," *Journal of Consumer Research,* 16 (March), 393–408.

Heinbockel, John E. and Israel M. Ganot (1995), "Quarterly Supermarket Statistical," *Goldman Sachs: U.S. Research, Retailing: Food and Drug,* December 15.

Helson, Harry (1964), *Adaptation-Level Theory,* New York: Harper & Row.

Herndon, Neil (1994), "Wal-Mart Goes to Hong Kong, Looks at China," *Marketing News* (November 21), 2.

Hess, James D. and Eitan Gerstner (1987), "Loss Leader Pricing and Rain Check Policy," *Marketing Science,* 6 (Fall), 358–374.

Heyman, C. David (1989), *A Woman Named Jackie,* New York: Lyle Stuart.

References

Hoch, Stephen J. (1988). "Who Do We Know: Predicting the Interests and Opinions of the American Consumer," *Journal of Consumer Research* 15 (December), 315–324.

Hoch, Stephen J. (1996), "How Should National Brands Think about Private Labels?" *Sloan Management Review,* 37 (Winter), 89–102.

Hoch, Stephen J., Byung-Do Kim, Alan L. Montgomery, and Peter E. Rossi (1995), "Determinants of Store-Level Price Elasticity," *Journal of Marketing Research,* 32 (February), 17–29.

Hoch, Stephen J. and Shumeet Banerji (1993), "When Do Private Labels Succeed?" *Sloan Management Review* (Summer), 57–67.

Hoch, Stephen, Xavier Dreze, and Mary E. Purk (1994), "EDLP, Hi-Lo, and Margin Arithmetic," *Journal of Marketing,* 58 (October), 16–27.

Hogarth, Robin M. (1987), *Judgment and Choice,* 2nd Edition, New York: Wiley.

Hortman, Sandra McCurley, Arthur W. Allaway, J. Barry Mason, and John Rasp (1990), "Multisegment Analysis of Supermarket Patronage," *Journal of Business Research,* 21 (November), 209–223.

"How Consumers Evaluate Private Label Brand Quality" (1995), *Stores* (Winter), RR1, RR2.

Hoyer, Wayne D. (1984), "An Examination of Consumer Decision Making for a Common Repeat Purchase Product," *Journal of Consumer Research,* 11 (December), 822–829.

Huber, Joel and Christopher P. Puto (1983), "Market Boundaries and Product Choice: Illustrating Attraction and Substitution Effects," *Journal of Consumer Research,* 10 (June), 31–44.

Huber, Joel and John McCann (1982), "The Impact of Inferential Beliefs on Product Evaluations," *Journal of Marketing Research,* 19 (August), 324–333.

Huber, Joel, John W. Payne, and Christopher P. Puto (1982), "Adding Asymmetrically Dominated Alternatives: Violations of Regularity and the Similarity Hypothesis," *Journal of Consumer Research,* 9 (June), 90–98.

Huffman, Cynthia and Michael J. Houston (1993), "Goal-Oriented Experiences and the Development of Knowledge," *Journal of Consumer Research,* 20 (September), 190–207.

Husson, Mark and Erika Gritman Long (1994), *Private Label: Cornerstone of the New Supermarket Brand Architecture,* JP Morgan Securities, Inc., Equity Research, New York (January 31).

Information Resources, Inc. (1993), *Managing Your Business in an EDLP Environment,* Chicago: IRI.

Ingram, Bob (1994), "At Minyard, 'Big D' Stands for Diversity," *Supermarket Business* (May), 41–48.

Inman, J. Jeffrey and Leigh McAlister (1993), "A Retailer Promotion Policy Model Considering Promotion Signal Sensitivity," *Marketing Science,* 12 (Fall), 339–356.

Inman, J. Jeffrey and Leigh McAlister (1994), "Do Coupon Expiration Dates Affect Consumer Behavior?" *Journal of Marketing Research,* 31 (August), 423–428.

Inman, J. Jeffrey, Leigh McAlister, and Wayne D. Hoyer (1990), "Promotion Signal: Proxy for a Price Cut?" *Journal of Consumer Research,* 17 (June), 74–81.

Ippolito, Pauline and Alan D. Mathios (1990), "Information, Advertising, and Health Choices: A Study of the Cereal Market," *Rand Journal of Economics,* 21 (Autumn), 459–480.

Isenberg, Daniel J. (1981), "Some Effects of Time-Pressure on Vertical Structure and Decision Making in Small Groups," *Organizational Behavior and Human Performance,* 27 (February), 119–134.

"Is Mainstream But a Dream?" (1994), *Supermarket Business* (February), 67–68.

Iyer, Easwar S. (1989), "Unplanned Purchasing: Knowledge of Shopping Environment and Time Pressure," *Journal of Retailing,* 65 (Spring), 40–57.

Jacoby, Jacob (1984), "Perspectives on Information Overload," *Journal of Consumer Research,* 10 (March), 432–435.

Jacoby, Jacob, Carol A. Kohn, and Donald E. Speller (1973), "Time Spent Acquiring Information as a Function of Information Load and Organization," *Proceedings of the American Psychological Association's 81st Annual Convention,"* Washington, DC, 8, 813–814.

Jager, Durk I., President & COO, Procter & Gamble (1996), "Focusing on the Consumer: The Operative Word in Efficient Consumer Response," keynote address, Grocery Products Manufacturers Council (April 10), Toronto.

Jager, Durk I., President & COO, Procter & Gamble (1996), "General Session-Opening Remarks," presentation to Joint Industry ECR Conference, Chicago Hilton & Towers (March 21).

Johnson, Bradley (1993), "Supermarkets Take Position," *Advertising Age,* 64 (May 10), S-1, S-4.

Johnson, Eric J. and J. Edward Russo (1984), "Product Familiarity and Learning New Information," *Journal of Consumer Research,* 11 (June), 542–549.

Kahn, Barbara E. (1995), "Consumer Variety-Seeking Among Goods and Services," *Journal of Retailing and Consumer Services,* 2 (3), 139–148.

Kahn, Barbara E. and Alice M. Isen (1993), "The Influence of Positive Affect on Variety-Seeking Among Safe, Enjoyable Products," *Journal of Consumer Research,* 20 (September), 257–270.

Kahn, Barbara E. and David C. Schmittlein (1989), "Shopping Trip Behavior: An Empirical Investigation," *Marketing Letters,* 1 (1), 55–69.

Kahn, Barbara E. and David C. Schmittlein (1992), "The Relationship Between Purchases Made on Promotion and Shopping Trip Behavior," *Journal of Retailing,* 68 (3), 294–315.

References

Kahn, Barbara E. and Donald R. Lehmann (1991), "Modeling Choice Among Assortments," *Journal of Retailing,* 67 (Fall), 274–299.

Kahn, Barbara E. and Therese A. Louie (1990), "Effects of Retraction of Price Promotions on Brand Choice Behavior for Variety-Seeking and Last-Purchase Loyal Consumers," *Journal of Marketing Research,* 27 (August), 279–89.

Kahn, Barbara E., William L. Moore, and Rashi Glazer (1987), "Experiments in Constrained Choice," *Journal of Consumer Research,* 14 (June), 96–113.

Kalwani, Manohar U. and Chi Kin Yim (1992), "Consumer Price and Promotion Expectations: An Experimental Study," *Journal of Marketing Research,* 29 (February), 90–100.

Kalwani, Manohar U., Chi Kin Yim, Heikki J. Rinne, and Yoshi Sugita (1990), "A Price Expectations Model of Customer Brand Choice," *Journal of Marketing Research,* 27 (August), 251–262.

Kalyanaram, Gurumurthy and John D. C. Little (1994), "An Empirical Analysis of Latitude of Price Acceptance in Consumer Package Goods," *Journal of Consumer Research,* 21 (December), 408–418.

Kalyanaram, Gurumurthy and Russell S. Winer (1995), "Empirical Generalizations from Reference Price Research," *Marketing Science,* 14 (No. 3, Part 2 of 2), G161–G169.

Kardon, Brian E. (1992), "Consumer Schizophrenia: Extremism in the Marketplace," *Planning Review,* 20 (July/August), 18–22.

Kaul, Anil and Dick R. Wittink (1995), "Empirical Generalizations about the Impact of Advertising on Price Sensitivity and Price," *Marketing Science,* 14 (No. 3, Part 2 of 2), G151–G160.

Keehner, Kami (1994), "Strategeries," (sic) *Dairy Field* (May), 23–26.

Keeney, R. L. and Howard Raiffa (1976), *Decisions with Multiple Objectives: Preferences and Value Tradeoffs,* New York: Wiley.

Keller, Kevin Lane (1991), "Conceptualizing, Measuring and Managing Customer-Based Brand Equity," Marketing Science Institute Working Paper #91-123, October 1991.

"Kimberly-Clark to Sell Some Parts of Scott" (1995), *Supermarket News* (December 25), 39.

Kim, Peter (1993), "Restore Brand Equity!" *Directors and Boards,* (Summer), 21–29.

Klepacki, Laura (1993), "P&G Commits Its Heavy Guns," *Supermarket News* (April 12), 10.

"Kmart to Close 110 Stores, Cutting 6,000 Jobs" (1994), *Austin American Statesman* (September 9), D1, D2.

Knasko, Susan (1989), "Ambient Odor and Shopping Behavior," *Chemical Senses,* 14 (94), 718.

Kollat, David T. and R. P. Willet (1967), "Customer Impulse Purchasing Behavior," *Journal of Marketing Research,* 4, 21–31.

Kollat, David T. and R. P. Willet (1969), "Is Impulse Purchasing Really a Useful Concept for Marketing Decisions?" *Journal of Marketing,* 33 (January), 79–83.

Kotler, Philip (1973–1974), "Atmospherics as a Marketing Tool," *Journal of Retailing,* 49 (Winter), 48–64.

Krishna, Aradhna, Imran S. Currim, and Robert W. Shoemaker (1991), "Consumer Perceptions of Promotional Activity," *Journal of Marketing,* 55 (April), 4–16.

Krishnamurthi, Lakshman and S. P. Raj (1991), "An Empirical Analysis of the Relationship Between Brand Loyalty and Consumer Price Elasticity," *Marketing Science,* 10 (Spring), 172–183.

Krishnamurthi, Lakshman, T. Mazumdar, and S. P. Raj (1992), "Asymmetric Response to Price in Consumer Choice and Purchase Quantity Decisions," *Journal of Consumer Research,* 19 (December), 387–400.

Krum, Franklin (1994), "Quantum Leap," *Progressive Grocer* (January), 41–43.

Kumar, V. and Robert P. Leone (1988), "Measuring the Effect of Retail Store Promotion on Brand and Store Substitution," *Journal of Marketing Research,* 25 (May), 178–185.

Kurt Salmon Associates (1993), *Efficient Consumer Response: Enhancing Consumer Value in the Grocery Industry,* Food Marketing Institute Report #9-526, Washington, DC (January).

Lal, Rajiv (1990), "Price Promotions: Limiting Competitive Encroachment," *Marketing Science,* 9 (3), 247–262.

Lal, Rajiv and Carmen Matutes (1994), "Retail Pricing and Advertising Strategies," *Journal of Business,* 67 (3), 345–371.

Langford, Nancy and Stephen A. Greyser (1994), "P&G and Everyday Low Prices," Harvard Business School Case 9-593-108 (July 25).

Leavitt, Harold J. and Thomas L. Whisler (1958), "Management in the 1980's," Harvard Business Review (November–December), 41–48.

Lehmann, Donald R. and Yigang Pan (1994), "Context Effects, New Brand Entry, and Consideration Sets," *Journal of Marketing Research,* 21 (August), 364–374.

Lesly, Elizabeth (1994), "The Carving of Elsie, Slice by Slice," *Business Week* (January 17), 29.

Levin, Irwin P. and Gary J. Gaeth (1988), "How Consumers are Affected by the Framing of Attribute Information Before and After Consuming the Product," *Journal of Consumer Research,* 15 (December), 374–378.

Levin, Irwin P., Richard D. Johnson, Craig P. Russo, and Patricia J. Deldin (1985), "Framing Effects in Judgment Tasks with Varying Amounts of Information," *Organizational Behavior and Human Decision Processes,* 36 (December), 362–377.

References

Lichtenstein, Donald R., Nancy M. Ridgway, and Richard G. Netemeyer (1993), "Price Perceptions and Consumer Shopping Behavior: A Field Study," *Journal of Marketing Research,* 30 (May), 234–245.

Lichtenstein, Donald R. and William O. Bearden (1989), "Contextual Influences on Perceptions of Merchant-Supplied Reference Prices," *Journal of Consumer Research,* 16 (June), 55–66.

Lichtenstein, Sarah, Paul Slovic, Baruch Fischhoff, Mark Layman, and Barbara Combs (1978), "Judged Frequency of Lethal Events," *Journal of Experimental Psychology: Human Learning and Memory,* 4 (November), 551–578.

Linsen, M. A. (1975), "Like Our Music Today, Ms. Shopper?" *Progressive Grocer,* 56 (October), 156.

Litwak, David (1993), "Standing the Test of Time," *Supermarket Business,* 48 (May), 87–95.

Litwak, David (1996), "What Price Sales Glory," *Supermarket Business* (July), 25, 27, 29, 31, 33, 35.

Litwak, David and Nancy Maline (1993), "Who Said HBC Wasn't Perishable?" *Supermarket News* (May), 137–144.

Loken, Barbara and Deborah Roedder John (1993), "Diluting Brands Beliefs: When Do Brand Extensions Have a Negative Impact?" *Journal of Marketing,* 57 (July), 71–84.

Loken, Barbara, Ivan Ross, and Ronald L. Hinkle (1986), "Consumer 'Confusion' of Origin and Brand Similarity Perceptions," *Journal of Public Policy and Marketing,* 5, 195–211.

Loro, Laura (1994), "Doing What Comes Naturally," *Advertising Age,* 65 (August 8), 22.

Loro, Laura (1994), "H-E-B, Wegmans Freshen Up Stale Image of Grocery," *Advertising Age,* 65 (May 2), S-15.

Lowe, Kimberly (1995), "Rating Progress Through Category Management," *Grocery Marketing* (May), 22–25.

Lowe, Kimberly (1995), "Retailers Offered a Full Plate of Category Management," *Grocery Marketing* (June), 14–17.

Lynch, John G. Jr., and Thomas K. Srull (1982), "Memory and Attentional Factors in Consumer Choice: Concepts and Research Methods," *Journal of Consumer Research,* 9 (June), 18–37.

Maholtra, Naresh K. (1982), "Information Load and Consumer Decision Making," *Journal of Consumer Research,* 9 (March), 419–430.

Mandel, Jr., Stephen F. (1990), "Implications of Declining Cost Structures in Mass Merchandise Retailing," speech given to Second Annual Seminar for International Investors in Retailing (April 5), Goldman Sachs Research.

Mandel, Jr., Stephen F. (1991), "A Competitive Challenge: How Supermarkets Can Get Into the Productivity Loop," *Andersen Consulting International Trends in Retailing,* Vol. 8, No. 1 (Spring).

"Manufacturers Rate Retailers" (1995), *Supermarket Business* (October).

Marter, Marilynn (1994), "Measure for Measure?" *Philadelphia Inquirer* (April 6), F1, F5.

Martin, Ellen James (1996), "Those Coupons Being Used at a Furious Clip," *Philadelphia Inquirer,* January 10, C1, C4.

Mathews, Ryan (1993), "Relearning the 'ABC' of Business," *Grocery Marketing* (August), 5–6, 8, 10, 12, 20.

Mathews, Ryan (1993), "'Rudimentary' ABC Efforts Yield Big Results for Spartan," *Grocery Marketing* (August), 12.

Mathews, Ryan (1994), "Is the Damage Done?" *Progressive Grocer* (June), 35.

Mathews, Ryan (1994), "Street Smart," *Progressive Grocer* (August), 56–57.

Mathews, Ryan (1995), "In the Trenches," *Progressive Grocer* (March), 30–36.

Mathews, Ryan (1996), "Partnerships and Progress," *Progressive Grocer* (June) 30–32.

Mayhew, Glenn E. and Russell S. Winer (1992), "An Empirical Analysis of Internal and External Reference Prices Using Scanner Data," *Journal of Consumer Research,* 19 (June), 62–70.

Mazumdar, Tridib and Kent B. Monroe (1990), "The Effects of Buyers' Intentions to Learn Price Information on Price Encoding," *Journal of Retailing,* 66 (1), 15–32.

McAlister, Leigh (1986), "The Impact of Price Promotions on a Brand's Market Share, Sales Pattern and Profitability," Marketing Science Institute Working Paper 86–110.

McAlister, Leigh and Edgar A. Pessemier (1982), "Variety-Seeking Behavior: An Interdisciplinary Review," *Journal of Consumer Research,* 9 (December), 311–322.

McAlister, Leigh and Michael J. Zenor (1992), "The Impact of Retailer Differences on Promotional Response: A Link Between Unusual Levels of Support and Unusual Levels of Response," University of Texas at Austin Working Paper.

McCarthy, Michael (1993), "James Bond Hits the Supermarket: Stores Snoop on Shoppers' Habits to Boost Sales," *The Wall Street Journal: Marketplace,* (August 25), B1, B8.

McElnea, Jeffrey (1994), "Rising Power of Retail Trade is Good News for Brand Marketers," *Brandweek,* (April 4), 16.

McFarlan, Warren F. (1994), "Organizational Transformation," *Proceedings of the Food Marketing Institute's Midwinter Executive Conference,* January 16–19, 52–58.

McKenna, Mary L. (1966), "The Influence of In-Store Advertising," in *On Knowing the Consumer,* Joseph Newman, Ed., New York: Wiley, 114–125.

McNair, Bill (1994), "My Brand—Your Brand: Co-existence and Collaboration in the Dairy Case," a Nielsen presentation at the International Dairy/Deli/Bakery Association, June 7.

References

Mehrabian, A. and J. A. Russell (1974), *An Approach to Environmental Psychology,* Cambridge, MA: MIT Press.

Mendelson, Seth (1994), "A Conflict of Interest," *Supermarket Business* (May), 143–144.

Menon, Satya and Barbara E. Kahn (1995), "The Impact of External Context on Variety-Seeking in Product Choices," *Journal of Consumer Research,* 22 (December), 285–295.

Meyer, Robert J. and Joao Assuncao (1990), "The Optimality of Consumer Stockpiling Strategies," *Marketing Science,* 9 (Winter), 18–41.

Miller, Cyndee (1993), "U.S., European Shoppers Seem Pleased with their Supermarkets," *Marketing News* (June 21), 1.

Millman, R. E. (1982), "Using Background Music to Affect the Behavior of Supermarket Shoppers," *Journal of Marketing,* 46 (3), 86–91.

Mitchell, Deborah, Barbara E. Kahn, and Susan Knasko (1995), "There is Something in the Air: The Effects of Congruent or Incongruent Ambient Odor on Consumer Decision Making," *Journal of Consumer Research,* 22 (September), 229–238.

Mittal, Banwari (1994), "Bridging the Gap Between Our Knowledge of 'Who' Uses Coupons and 'Why' Coupons are Used," Marketing Science Institute Working Paper #94-112, (August).

Mogelonsky, Marcia (1994), "Please Don't Pick the Cherries: How Supermarketers Use Electronic Price Scanning to Build Store Loyalty," *Marketing Tools,* (September/October), 10–13.

Monroe, Kent (1973), "Buyers' Subjective Perceptions of Price," *Journal of Marketing Research,* 8 (November), 70–80.

Monroe, Kent B. and Susan M. Petroshius (1981), "Perceptions of Price: An Update of the Evidence," in *Perceptions in Consumer Behavior,* Harold H. Kassarjian and Thomas S. Robertson, Eds., 3rd Edition, Glenview, IL: Scott Foresman and Company, 43–55.

Morgenson, Gretchen (1991), "The Trend is Not their Friend," *Forbes* (September 16), 115–119.

Morgenson, Gretchen (1996), "Denial in Battle Creek," *Forbes* (October 7), 44–46.

Morgenson, Gretchen (1996), "Too Much of a Good Thing?" *Forbes* (June 3), 115–119.

Morris, Kathleen (1993), "No-Name Power," *Financial World* (March 16), 32.

Morton, Jerry (1993), "ESL: (Electronic Shelf Label Systems): Up and Running," *Progressive Grocer* (December), 23–24.

Much, Marilyn (1996), "Behind Cereal Price Cuts: Wrath of Fickle Shoppers," *Investor's Business Daily* (June 25).

Mueller, William (1991), "Who Reads the Label?" *American Demographics* (January), 36–40.

Mulhern, Francis J. and Robert P. Leone (1990), "Retail Promotional Advertising: Do the Number of Deal Items and the Size of Deal Discounts Affect Store Performance?" *Journal of Business Research,* 21 (November), 179–194.

Mulhern, Francis J. and Robert P. Leone (1991), "Implicit Price Bundling of Retail Products: A Multi-product Approach to Maximizing Store Profitability," *Journal of Marketing* (October), 63–76.

Nagle, Thomas T. (1987), *The Strategy and Tactics of Pricing,* Englewood Cliffs, NJ: Prentice-Hall.

Narasimhan, Chakravarti (1984), "A Price Discrimination Theory of Coupons," *Marketing Science,* 3 (Spring), 128–147.

Narasimhan, Chakravarti (1990), "Managerial Perspectives on Trade and Consumer Promotions," *Marketing Letters,* 1 (3), 239–252.

Nedungadi, Prakash (1990), "Recall and Consumer Consideration Sets: Influencing Choice Without Altering Brand Evaluations," *Journal of Consumer Research,* 17 (December), 263–276.

Nedungadi, Prakash and J. Wesley Hutchinson (1985), "The Prototypicality of Brands: Relationships with Brand Awareness, Preference and Usage," in *Advances in Consumer Research,* Vol. 12, Elizabeth C. Hirschman and Morris B. Holbrook, Eds., Provo, UT: Association for Consumer Research, 498–503.

Nelson, Philip (1970), "Information and Consumer Behavior," *Journal of Political Economy,* 78 (2), 311–329.

Neslin, Scott A. (1990), "A Market Response Model for Coupon Promotions," *Marketing Science,* 9 (Spring), 125–145.

Neslin, Scott A. and Robert Shoemaker (1989), "An Alternative Explanation for Lower Repeat Rates After Promotional Purchases," *Journal of Marketing Research,* 26 (May), 205–213.

Neslin, Scott A., Caroline Henderson, and John Quelch (1985), "Consumer Promotions and the Acceleration of Product Purchases," *Marketing Science,* 4 (2), 147–165.

Nichol, Dave (1993), "Hell is Truth Seen Too Late," keynote address to the Private Label Manufacturing Conference, Miami, Florida (March).

Nystrom, Harry, Jans Tamsons, and Robert Thams (1975), "An Experiment in Price Generalization and Discrimination," *Journal of Marketing Research,* 12 (May), 177–181.

O'Connor, Michael J. (1991), "What Every CEO Should Know About New Merchandising Technology," *Supermarket Business* (May), 63–70.

Oster, Patrick with Gabrielle Saveri and John Templeman (1993), "Procter & Gamble Hits Back: Its Dramatic Overhaul Takes Aim at High Costs-and Low-Price Rivals," *Business Week* (July 19), 20–22.

Pare, Terence P. (1993), "A New Tool for Managing Costs," *Fortune* (June 14), 124.

References

Park, C. Whan (1994), "Strategic Implication of Branding Decision," presented at the 1994 AMA Doctoral Consortium at Santa Clara University, August.

Park, C. Whan, Easwar S. Iyer, and Daniel C. Smith (1989), "The Effects of Situational Factors on In-Store Grocery Behavior: The Role of Store Environment and Time Available for Shopping," *Journal of Consumer Research,* 15 (March), 422–433.

Partch, Ken (1991), "'Partnering': A Win-Win Proposition of the Latest Hula Hoop in Marketing?" *Supermarket Business* (May), 29–31, 34, 165–166.

Partch, Ken (1993), "It's the Customer, Stupid," *Supermarket Business* (June), 23–36.

Partch, Ken (1994), "Category Management Drumbeat," *Supermarket Business* (April), 26–28.

Payne, John (1976), "Task Complexity and Contingent Processing in Decision-Making: An Information Search and Protocol Analysis," *Organizational Behavior and Human Performance,* 16 (August), 366–387.

Payne, John, James R. Bettman, and Eric J. Johnson (1993), *The Adaptive Decision Maker,* New York: Cambridge University Press.

"P&G Plans to Restructure Its Logistics and Pricing" (1994), *Supermarket News* (June 27), 1, 49.

Pritchett, Lou (1995), *Stop Paddling & Start Rocking the Boat,* New York: HarperBusiness.

"Procter's Gamble" (1992), *The Economist* (July 25), 61–62.

Putler, D. (1992), "Incorporating Reference Price Effects into a Theory of Consumer Choice," *Marketing Science,* 11 (Summer), 287–309.

Radice, Carol (1996), "A View from the Street," *Progressive Grocer* (May), 235–236, 238, 240.

Raftery, Dan (1993), "Trim the Deadwood," *Progressive Grocer,* (September), p. 42–43.

Rajecki, D. W., J. A. Dame, K. J. Creek, P. J. Barrickman, C. A. Reid, and D. C. Appleby (1993), "Gender Casting in Television Toy Advertisements: Distributions, Message Content Analysis, and Evaluations," *Journal of Consumer Psychology,* 2, 307–327.

Rajendra, K. N. and Gerald J. Tellis (1994), "Contextual and Temporal Components of Reference Price," *Journal of Marketing,* 58 (January), 22–34.

Raju, Jagmohan (1992), "The Effect of Price Promotions on Variability in Product Category Sales," *Marketing Science,* 11 (Summer), 207–220.

Raju, Jagmohan S., Raj Sethuraman, and Sanjay K. Dhar (1995), "The Introduction and Performance of Store Brands," *Management Science,* 41 (June), 957–973.

Raju, Jagmohan S., Sanjay K. Dhar, and Donald G. Morrison (1994), "The Effect of Package Coupons on Brand Choice," *Marketing Science,* 13 (Spring), 145–164.

Raju, P. S. (1980), "Optimum Stimulation Level: Its Relationship to Personality, Demographics, and Exploratory Behavior," *Journal of Consumer Research,* 7 (December), 272–282.

Raphel, Murray and Neil Raphel (1994), "Everybody Sells!" *Progressive Grocer,* 73 (May), 21–22.

Raphel, Murray and Neil Raphel (1996), "What the 'I' in IGA Stands For," *Progressive Grocer* (June), 21–22.

Rapoport, Carla (1994), "Nestle's Brand Building Machine," *Fortune* (September 19), 147–148, 150, 154, 156.

"Retailer Reactions to Competitive Price Changes," (1994), *Retailing Review,* University of Florida, Center for Retailing Education and Research, (Fall), RR3-RR5, (based on a summary of an article by Peter R. Dickson and Joel E. Urbany from the *Journal of Retailing*).

"Rethinking the Service Counter," (1994), *Supermarket Business* (April), 65–66.

Reyes, Robert M., William C. Thompson, and Gordon H. Bower (1980), "Judgmental Biases Resulting from Differing Availabilities of Arguments," *Journal of Personality and Social Psychology,* 39 (July), 2–12.

Richardson, Paul S., Alan S. Dick, and Arun K. Jain (1994), "Extrinsic and Intrinsic Cue Effects on Perceptions of Store Quality," *Journal of Marketing,* 58 (4), 28–36.

Rigney, Peter (1994), "How Do You Promote Private Label?" *Progressive Grocer* (August), 162.

Rook, Dennis W. (1987), "The Buying Impulse," *Journal of Consumer Research,* 14 (September), 189–199.

Rook, Dennis W. (1990), "Is 'Impulse Buying' (Yet) a Useful Marketing Concept?" Working Paper, Northwestern University (May).

Russo, J. E. (1977), "The Value of Unit Price Information," *Journal of Marketing Research,* 14, 193–201.

Russo, J. Edward, Richard Staelin, Catherine A. Nolan, Gary J. Russell, and Barbara L. Metcalf (1986), "Nutrition Information in the Supermarket," *Journal of Consumer Research,* 13 (June), 48–70.

"Sales Manual/Top Performers: What's Hot," (1994), *Progressive Grocer* (July), 69–82.

Saporito, Bill (1994), "Behind the Tumult at P&G," *Fortune* (March 7), 75–76, 78, 81–82.

Saxton, Lisa (1994), "Private Label Gains Ground," *Supermarket News* (November 13), 45–46.

Schifrin, Matthew (1994), "Last Legs?" *Forbes* (September 12), 150–154, 158.

Schiller, Zachary (1993), "Procter & Gamble Hits Back," *Business Week* (July 19), 21.

Schiller, Zachary and Wendy Zellner (1992), "Clout! More and More, Retail Giants Rule the Marketplace," *Business Week* (December 21), 66–69, 72–73.

References

Schiller, Zachary, Greg Burns, and Karen Lowry Miller (1996), "Make It Simple," *Business Week* (September 9), 96–99, 102, 104.

Schindler, Robert M. and Alan R. Wiman (1989), "Effect of Odd Pricing on Price Recall," *Journal of Business Research,* 19, (November), 165–177.

Sellers, Patricia (1993), "Brands: It's Thrive or Die," *Fortune* (August 23), 52.

Shankar, Venktesh and Lakshman Krishnamurthi (1996), "Relating Price Sensitivity to Retailer Promotional Variables and Pricing Policy," *Journal of Retailing,* 72 (3), Fall, 249–272.

Shermach, Kelly (1995), "Study: Most Shoppers Notice P-O-P Material," *Marketing News,* (January 2), 27.

Shocker, Allan D., Moshe Ben-Akiva, Bruno Boccara, and Prakash Nedungadi (1991), "Consideration Set Influences on Customer Decision-Making and Choice: Issues, Models, and Suggestions," *Marketing Letters,* 2 (August), 181–198.

"Shoot Out at the Check-Out" (1993), *The Economist* (June 5), 69.

Shore, Andrew and Gary Giblen (1992), "Household Products and Cosmetics: Everyday Low (or "value") Pricing: An Idea Whose Time Has Come," *Paine Webber* (October 13).

Shore, Andrew and Margaret Lenahan (1993), "Cosmetic and Household Products: When the Sun Comes Up Tomorrow, You Had Better Be Running," *Paine Webber* (October 11).

Simmons, Tim (1994), "If They Stay, They'll Pay," *Supermarket Business,* February, 103–107.

Simon, Herbert A. (1955), "A Behavioral Model of Rational Choice," *Quarterly Journal of Economics,* 69, 99–118.

Simonson, Itamar (1989), "Choice Based on Reasons: The Case of Attraction and Compromise Effects," *Journal of Consumer Research,* 16 (September), 158–174.

Simonson, Itamar (1990), "The Effect of Purchase Quantity and Timing on Variety-Seeking Behavior," *Journal of Marketing Research,* 27 (2), 150–162.

Simonson, Itamar (1992), "The Influence of Anticipating Regret and Responsibility on Purchase Decisions," *Journal of Consumer Research,* 19 (June), 105–118.

Simonson, Itamar (1993), "Get Closer to Your Customers by Understanding How They Make Choices," *California Management Review* (Summer), 68–83.

Simonson, Itamar (1994), "Shoppers' Easily Influenced Choices," *New York Times* (November 6), 11.

Simonson, Itamar and Amos Tversky (1992), "Choice in Context: Tradeoff Contrast and Extremeness Aversion," *Journal of Marketing Research,* 29 (August), 281–295.

Simonson, Itamar and Russell S. Winer (1992), "The Influence of Purchase Quantity and Display Format on Consumer Preference for Variety," *Journal of Consumer Research,* 19 (June), 133–138.

Sirvanci, Mete B. (1993), "An Empirical Study of Price Thresholds and Price Sensitivity," *Journal of Applied Business Research,* 9 (2), 43–49.

Smith, Kerry E. (1993), "No Brand Too Small," *PROMO/Progressive Grocer,* Special Report (December), 4–5.

Smith, Patricia Cane and Ross Curnow (1966), "Arousal Hypotheses and the Effects of Music on Purchasing Behavior," *Journal of Applied Psychology,* 50 (3), 255–256.

Snyder, Glenn (1994), "Category Switching Expands GM/HBC's Role," *Progressive Grocer* (April), 27–38.

Sommer, Robert and Susan Aitkens (1982), "Mental Mapping of Two Supermarkets," *Journal of Consumer Research,* 9 (September), 211–215.

Spethmann, Betsy (1994), "Borden's Milkman Wants You to Drop that Snapple and Buy Diary," *Brandweek* (November 7), 30–31.

Spethmann, Betsy (1994), "Coupons Shed Low-Tech Image," *Brandweek* (October 24), 30–31.

Spethmann, Betsy and Karen Benezra (1994), "Co-Brand or be Damned," *BrandWeek* (November 21), 21–24.

Spiggle, Susan (1987), "Grocery Shopping Lists: What Do Consumers Write?" in *Advances in Consumer Research,* Vol. 14, Melanie Wallendorf and Paul F. Anderson, Eds., Provo, UT: Association for Consumer Research, 241–245.

Staten, Vince (1993), *Can You Trust a Tomato in January?* New York: Simon and Schuster.

"State of the Industry" (1995), *Chain Store Age Executive* (August), 3A–7A.

Stern, Aimee L. (1985), "New Payoff from Old Brand Names," *Dun's Business Month,* 26 (April), 42–44.

Stern, Hawkins (1962), "The Significance of Impulse Buying Today," *Journal of Marketing* (April), 59–62.

Stewart, Thomas A. (1993), "Welcome to the Revolution," *Fortune* (December 13), 66–8, 70, 72, 76–7.

Stiven, Kristine (1989), "Future Store? It's . . . Black-and-White for Format Leader, A&P's James Wood," *Advertising Age* (May 8), S-17, S-18.

"Store-Brand Sales Reported Rising in Supermarkets" (1996), *Supermarket Business* (July), 9.

Strauss, Gary (1993), "Company Makes Big Cuts to Stay Fit," *USA Today* (July 16).

"Supermarket Nonfoods Business: Minding Your Magazines," (1994), *Supermarket Business* (December), 61–66.

"Supermarket Nonfoods Business: The Home" (1994), *Supermarket Business* (October), 91–94.

"Supermarket Profits Slip" (1994), *Food Distribution Magazine,* Vol. 35, No. 1 (January), 11.

Swinyard, William R. (1993), "The Effects of Mood, Involvement and Quality of Store Experience on Shopping Intentions," *Journal of Consumer Research,* 20 (September), 271–280.

References

Tauber, Edward M. (1981), "Brand Franchise Extension: New Product Benefits from Existing Brand Names," *Business Horizons,* 24 (2), 36–41.

Taylor, Shelley E. (1987). "The Availability Bias in Social Perception and Interaction," in Daniel Kahneman, Paul Slovic, and Amos Tversky, Eds., *Judgment under Uncertainty: Heuristics and Biases,* NY: Cambridge University Press, 190–200.

Teerling, A. Nixdorf, R. R, and Koster, E. P. (1992), "The Effects of Ambient Odours on Shopping Behaviour," from the Abstracts of the 10th Congress of ECRO, August 23–28, Munich Germany, p. 155.

Teinowitz, Ira and Jennifer Lawrence (1993), "Brand Proliferation Attacked," *Advertising Age* (May 10), 1, 49.

Tenser, James (1995), "Realigned Kraft Planning 300 Dedicated Teams," *Brand Marketing* (January 16), 1, 4.

Tenser, James (1996), "Polls Concur: Spending is Flowing to the Trade," *Brand Marketing* (June 3), 1, 4.

Thaler, Richard (1985), "Mental Accounting and Consumer Choice," *Marketing Science,* 4 (Summer), 199–214.

"The Marsh Super Study," *Progressive Grocer* Special Report (December 1992), 66–67.

Thomas, Art and Ron Gardland, (1993), "Supermarket Shopping Lists," *International Journal of Retail & Distribution Management,* 21 (2), 8–14.

"To End a Trend" (1994), *Supermarket Business* (September), 155–159.

Tordjman, Andre (1988), "A Review of the United States Food Retailing Industry," *International Journal of Retailing,* 3 (4), 55–69.

Tully, Shawn (1993), "The Real Key to Creating Wealth," *Fortune* (September 20), 38–50.

Turcsik, Richard (1995) "General Mills Shuffle Is Called a Good Move," *Supermarket News* (June 5), 27–8.

"Turning Traffic Into Transactions," (1994), a study funded by the American Greetings Research Council with the Cooperation of Food Marketing Institute.

Tversky, Amos (1972), "Elimination by Aspects: A Theory of Choice," *Psychological Review,* 79, 281–299.

Tversky, Amos and Daniel Kahneman (1973), "Availability: A Heuristic for Judging Frequency and Probability," *Cognitive Psychology,* 5 (2), 207–232.

Tversky, Amos and Daniel Kahneman (1974), "Judgment under Uncertainty: Heuristics and Biases," *Science* 185, 1124–1131.

Tversky, Amos and Itamar Simonson (1993), "Context-Dependent Preferences," *Management Science,* 39 (10, 1179–1189.

Urbany, Joel E., William O. Bearden, and Dan C. Weilbaker (1988), "The Effect of Plausible and Exaggerated Reference Prices on Consumer Perceptions and Price Search," *Journal of Consumer Research,* 15 (June), 95–110.

Valeriano, Lourdes Lee (1993), "Inquisitive Gadgets," *Wall Street Journal* (October 7), 1.

"Vendors Pushed Record Slew of Not-So-New Items" (1994), *Supermarket Business* (March), 13.

Von Bergen, Jane M. (1994), "Updating the Shopping List," *The Philadelphia Inquirer* (September 20), C1, C2.

"Vons Cuts Prices" (1994), *Progressive Grocer* (March), 12.

Wallace, David J. (1989), "Convenience Stores Push Fast-Lane Pace," *Advertising Age* (May 8), S-16, S-17.

"Wal-Mart Delays Plans for Mexico" (1995), *Austin American Statesman* (January 25), C3.

"Wal-Mart's 99-Quarter Earnings Growth Streak Ending" (1996), *Investor's Business Daily* (January 18).

Walters, Donna K. H. (1993), "Big Guys Rule Toy Industry Playground," *Austin American Statesman* (September 7).

Walters, Rockney G. and Scott B. MacKenzie (1988), "A Structural Equations Analysis of the Impact of Price Promotions on Store Performance," *Journal of Marketing Research,* 55 (April), 17–28.

Ware, Jeff and Gerald L. Patrick (1984), "Gelson's Supermarkets: Effects of MUZAK Music on the Purchasing Behavior of Supermarket Shoppers," MUZAK Research Report.

Warm, J. S., W. N. Dember, and R. Parasuraman (1991), "Effects of Olfactory Stimulation on Performance and Stress in a Visual Sustained Attention Task," *Journal of the Society of Cosmetic Chemists,* 12, 1–12.

Wehling, Robert L. (1996), "The Future of Brands: Getting Brands In Shape Today to Win the Loyalty of Tomorrow's Consumers," remarks by Robert L. Wehling, senior vice president of advertising, Procter & Gamble, at The Fisher School's Cullman Symposium, Ohio State University, April 25, 1996.

Weinstein, Steve (1992), "Will Procter's Gamble Work?" *Progressive Grocer* (July), 36–38.

Weller, Ed (1992), "Sampling Sells," *Progressive Grocer,* October, 121.

Wells, Melanie and David Henry (1995), "Kimberly-Clark Deal Seeks to Unseat P&G," *USA Today* (July 18).

Wernerfelt, Birger (1995), "A Rational Reconstruction of the Compromise Effect: Using Market Data to Infer Utilities," *Journal of Consumer Research,* 21 (March), 627–633

Whalen, Bernie (1995), "Retail Customer Service: Marketing's Last Frontier," *Marketing News* (March 15), 16, 18.

Willard Bishop Consulting Ltd. (1993), *Variety or Duplication: A Process to Know Where You Stand,* Food Marketing Institute Report, Washington, DC.

Winer, Russell S. (1986), "A Reference Price Model of Brand Choice for Frequently Purchased Products," *Journal of Consumer Research,* 13 (September), 250–256.